We the People

THE CITIZEN & THE CONSTITUTION

LEVEL 2

Center for Civic Education

5115 Douglas Fir Road, Suite J
Calabasas, CA 91302
www.civiced.org
818.591.9321

We the People: The Citizen & the Constitution
Level 2

Directed by the
Center for Civic Education

Cover: *The Continentals* by Frank Blackwell Mayer,
Prints & Photographs Division, Library of Congress,
PGA-Mayer-Continentals (C size) [P&P]

© 2017 Center for Civic Education
First Print Edition 1988
Second Print Edition 2007
Enhanced Ebook Edition 2015
Third Print Edition 2017
19 18 17 01 02 03

ISBN-10: 0-89818-220-4

ISBN-13: 978-0-89818-220-0

About We the People: The Citizen and the Constitution

We the People: The Citizen and the Constitution, was developed in 1987 and adopted by the Commission on the Bicentennial of the U.S. Constitution, chaired by Chief Justice Warren E. Burger, as the principal education program of the federal Constitution's bicentennial. The success of the program at the Bicentennial Commission led to Congress continuing the program through the U.S. Department of Education from 1993 to 2011 as an authorized program of the Elementary and Secondary Education Act.

The foundation of the We the People program is the classroom curriculum. It complements the regular school curriculum by providing upper elementary, middle, and high school students with an innovative course of instruction on the history and principles of U.S. constitutional democracy.

The We the People program's culminating activity is a simulated congressional hearing in which students "testify" before a panel of judges acting as members of Congress. Students demonstrate their knowledge and understanding of constitutional principles and have opportunities to evaluate, take, and defend positions on relevant historical and contemporary issues. Teachers may engage their students in a noncompetitive simulated congressional hearing or a competitive hearing at some levels in certain states.

The We the People National Invitational Competition

Middle school classes qualify to attend the National Invitational competition by participating in a simulated congressional hearing at the school, district, or state levels. The National Invitational competition takes the form of simulated congressional hearings. Classes have the opportunity to compete or showcase at the event. The format provides students an excellent opportunity to demonstrate their knowledge and understanding of constitutional principles while providing the judges with an excellent means of assessing students' knowledge and application to historical and current constitutional issues. While in Washington, D.C., students will have the opportunity to tour our nation's capital and meet with members of Congress and other important dignitaries. For more information on the We the People National Invitational competition, visit http://civiced.org/programs/wtp.

National Advisory Committee

Acknowledgments

The following staff and consultants contributed to the development of the third edition of this textbook:

Principal Writers
Charles N. Quigley
Maria Gallo
John Hale

Additional Contributors
Gregory Bernstein
Margaret Branson
Alissa Irion-Groth
Robert Leming
Mark Molli

Director of Publishing and Digital Content
Mark Gage

Design
Natalia Naduris-Weissman

Proofreading
Katie Hale
Jade Danner Masterson

Director of Information Technology
Greg Synnott

Administrative Assistance
Janel Huber
Tony Milianni
Valerie Milianni
Sierra Swanson

The following staff and consultants contributed to the development of the text upon which the third edition is based:

Principal Writers
Charles N. Quigley
Ken Rodriguez

Contributing Writer
Charles F. Bahmueller

Illustrator
Richard Stein

Warren E. Burger (1907–1995)

Chief Justice of the United States, 1969–1986

**Chair, Commission on the Bicentennial of the
United States Constitution**

*In 1987 Chief Justice of the U.S. Supreme Court Warren E. Burger was
the chairman of the Commission on the Bicentennial of the United States
Constitution. He wrote these words, which were included in the first edition
of this textbook.*

The years 1987 to 1991 marked the 200th anniversary of the writing,
ratification, and implementation of the basic documents of American
democracy, the Constitution and the Bill of Rights. Our Constitution has
stood the tests and stresses of time, wars, and change. Although it is not
perfect, as Benjamin Franklin and many others recognized, it has lasted
because it was carefully crafted by men who understood the importance
of a system of government sufficiently strong to meet the challenges of the
day, yet sufficiently flexible to accommodate and adapt to new political,
economic, and social conditions.

Many Americans have but a slight understanding of the Constitution, the
Bill of Rights, and the later amendments to which we pledge our allegiance.
The lessons in this book are designed to give you, the next generation of
American citizens, an understanding of the background, creation, and
subsequent history of the unique system of government brought into being by
our Constitution. At the same time, it will help you understand the principles
and ideals that underlie and give meaning to the Constitution, a system of
government by those governed.

Contents

Contents

Introduction

Most history books tell the story of people and events of the past. This book is a history of ideas. It explains the most important ideas of our Constitution and how they were developed. It also highlights the people and events that were important in the history of these ideas.

The Constitution of the United States was created as a plan for the new government of our country. It was written in Philadelphia in 1787, more than 215 years ago. We study the Constitution and its history to understand our government and how it is supposed to work. Knowing our past will help us understand the rights and responsibilities that we have today.

In this book, you will discover what the people who wrote our Constitution thought the purposes of government should be. They believed government should protect our lives, liberty, and property. They also believed government should promote the common good. You will also learn why they thought it was necessary to limit the powers of government.

You will learn about some of the things that have happened to the Constitution since it was written in 1787. You will study ways in which it has changed and how these changes came about. You will also learn about ways the Constitution has stayed the same.

This book will help you develop a good understanding of the Constitution and our system of government. It will also help you understand more about how our government affects your life, and how you can influence your government.

What Were the Founders' Basic Ideas about Government?

What Were the Founders' Basic Ideas about Government?

UNIT PURPOSE

In the spring and summer of 1787, fifty-five men met in Philadelphia. These men knew a great deal about government. They wrote our Constitution. They and many other Americans gained their knowledge by reading and discussing books about history and political philosophy. Political philosophy is the study of basic ideas of government.

Americans also knew about government from their own experience. Many of the men who met in Philadelphia had been leaders in the American colonies when they were ruled by Great Britain. Many were leaders in the new state governments formed after the American Revolution.

The men who wrote the Constitution used their knowledge and experience to create the best kind of government they could. An understanding of their knowledge and experience will give you some insight into why they created the kind of government we have today. It will also help you discover and appreciate the most important ideas in our Constitution.

KEY CONCEPTS

- checks and balances
- civic virtue
- common good
- consent of the governed
- constitution
- constitutional government
- natural rights
- purpose of government
- republican government
- separation of powers
- social contract

LESSON

1

What Were the British Colonies in America Like in the 1770s?

LESSON PURPOSE

People living in Britain's American colonies in the 1770s were in many ways quite different from the people living in Europe. The colonists brought British laws and customs to America, but they were developing their own way of life as well.

LESSON OBJECTIVES

When you finish this lesson, you should be able to

❑ explain how the average person in the American colonies lived in the 1770s, and

❑ explain how life in the colonies influenced people's ideas about good government.

TERMS TO UNDERSTAND

- authority
- Founders
- government
- institution
- indentured servant
- self-sufficient
- subject

Why was the rigid class system of England harder to maintain in the American colonies?

Why study the British colonies in North America?

We begin our study of the U.S. Constitution by looking back in history. The period is the 1770s. By that time, there had been European colonies established in North America for more than 150 years. Nations that had set up colonies in America included France, Great Britain, the Netherlands, and Spain.

Our study will focus on the British colonies. It was these thirteen colonies that would become the United States of America.

By the 1770s, the British colonies along the eastern coast of North America were well established. The British colonists were subjects of Great Britain. Being a **subject** in this case means being under the rule of a monarch. In 1770, King George III was the ruler of Great Britain. Our nation did not yet exist.

Learning about how the people lived in the British colonies can help us understand why they developed their ideas about government. When we talk about **government**, we mean the people and **institutions** with **authority** to make and enforce the laws and manage disputes about laws. People living in the 1770s in the British colonies held certain beliefs about good government that still affect our lives today.

How did American Indians live before the Europeans came?

The Europeans were newcomers to North America. Hundreds of different groups of Native American people had inhabited the continent for thousands of years. Along the eastern seacoast, where the British colonists settled, the native Indian people lived in well-organized tribes. They are known as the Eastern Woodland tribes. They lived by fishing, hunting, gathering wild plants, and tending small crops of corn.

The Eastern tribes maintained loose political ties among themselves. In some cases, entire tribes formed leagues so that they could come together to discuss common problems. The best known league was the Iroquois League. The Iroquois League was made up of five tribes that lived in what today is the state of New York.

Why do you think Native Americans were not initially considered to be American citizens?

Where did the British colonists settle?

The British colonies in America occupied a large area of land. The colonies stretched twelve hundred miles along the coast of the Atlantic Ocean and ran two hundred miles inland. Between the settled area and the Mississippi River lay a vast, forested country. Few Europeans explored beyond the area of settlement. The nations of Europe were small in area compared to America. Great Britain was only slightly larger than the colony of New York.

Although the land was expansive, there were few people living on it. In 1790, the population of the colonies was almost 4 million, compared with more than 300 million people living in the United States today.

How did people in the colonies earn a living?

Boston, New York, and Philadelphia were the largest cities in the colonies. Each had a population of more than 25,000 people. Most people in cities or towns earned their living by working in professions, trades, crafts, or small factories.

Most colonists did not live in cities. They lived in small communities or villages or on farms. Ninety percent of the colonists were farmers. Farm size varied from the small 30-acre plot of the poorest New England farmers to giant Southern plantations with thousands of acres. A typical farm was between 90 and 160 acres. Not all colonists were independent farmers. Some were hired laborers or craftspeople working on the larger farms.

Outside the cities and small communities, people in the colonies lived as far as ten miles from their nearest neighbor. As a result, they had to develop the knowledge and skills to provide for themselves in order to survive.

The people became self-sufficient. **Self-sufficient** means that people had to provide for their own needs. Not only did the colonists grow their own food, they also wove cloth to make their own clothing. They made their own medicines, built their own homes and barns, and made their furniture and tools. Colonists took the surplus produce from their farms and traded it for goods they could not make.

Although families worked independently, they traded among their neighbors and helped each other. Neighbors got together to build houses and barns. People rarely traveled more than fifty miles from their homes.

A farm family frequently included a hired laborer or an indentured servant. **Indentured servants** were men and women who sold their labor in exchange for the cost of the trip from Europe to the colonies. Farm families often relied on the labor of slaves, especially in the South.

The typical colonial family in the 1770s worked hard and had the highest standard of

How did most colonists earn a living?

How do you think the diversity of people in America contributed to the character of the country?

living in the world. The land was fertile and crops grew well. As a result, the colonists had diets rich in protein and tended to be healthier than people in Europe.

The colonists were also better educated than most Europeans. In fact, a greater percentage of people in the colonies were able to read and write than in any European nation. The most popular publications, other than the Bible, were newspapers. Four times as many newspapers were published in the colonies than in France.

While most colonists lived fairly well, this was not true of everyone. One-fifth of the population was held in slavery. The slaves were people who were brought as laborers to the colonies from different regions of Africa. Slavery was permitted in all the colonies, North and South. Slavery continued to be practiced until 1865.

How were the people living in the colonies different from one another?

Most colonists were descended from British or Irish settlers. Therefore, most people in the colonies spoke English. Some colonists did not come from English-speaking countries, however. Settlers also came from France, Germany, the Netherlands, Spain, Sweden, and other countries. All brought with them their own customs and ideas about government and rights.

The colonists also held different religious beliefs. There were many different groups of Protestants; there were also Catholics and Jews. Compared to most European nations of the time, the population of the colonies was diverse.

How did this colonial farmer compare life in America with life in Great Britain?

In the 1700s a French colonist who settled in New York wrote a book containing a series of letters from a fictional Pennsylvania farmer to his friend in Great Britain. J. Hector St. John was the pen name St. Jean de Crèvecoeur used for his book. The letters describe Crèvecoeur's views about life in America. Some sections of these letters follow. Read them and answer the questions at the end of the selection.

Behold, Sir, a humble American Planter... addressing you from the farther side of the Atlantic....

[The English traveler to America] is arrived on a new continent; a modern society... different from what he had hitherto seen. It is not composed, as in Europe, of great lords who possess everything and of a herd of people who have nothing. Here are no aristocratical families, no courts, no kings.... The rich and the poor are not so far removed from each other as they are in Europe. Some few towns excepted, we are all tillers of the earth.... [Here we are] united by the silken bands of mild government, all respecting the laws, without dreading their power, because they are equitable [fair].

[Here the traveler] views not the hostile castle, and the haughty mansion, contrasted with the clay-built hut and miserable cabin, where cattle and men help to keep each other warm, and dwell in meanness [humility], smoke, and indigence [poverty].... The meanest [most humble] of our log-houses is a dry and comfortable habitation.

Lawyer or merchant are the fairest titles our towns afford.... We have no princes, for whom we toil, starve, and bleed: we are the most perfect society now existing in the world. Here man is free; as he ought to be....

Can a wretch...call England or any other kingdom his country? A country that had no bread for him, whose fields procured him no harvest, who met with nothing but the frowns of the rich, the severity of the laws, with jails and punishments; who owned not a single foot of the extensive surface of the planet? No! urged by a variety of motives here they came. Everything has tended to regenerate them; new laws, a new mode of living, a new social system....

Formerly they were not numbered in any civil lists of their country, except in those of the poor; here they rank as citizens.

What do you think?

1 What was it that Crèvecoeur liked about life in the colonies?

2 What rights did he enjoy?

3 Given what you know of Crèvecoeur's experiences, explain why he would or would not favor laws that

- guarantee each individual the right to own property,

- limit an individual's right to buy and sell goods to anyone he or she chooses, and

- give people certain rights because they are wealthy or from a certain family background or group.

4 How might people in Great Britain have reacted to Crèvecoeur's comparisons of life in America and life in Europe? Explain.

What does this picture tell you about the right to vote in colonial America?

Why were class differences not important in the colonies?

The colonies were not divided into a few rich people and a large mass of poor people as in most of Europe. In the colonies, there was no royalty and no titled nobility.

The difference between wealthy and poor people was less important in colonial society. A poor person could become wealthy by using knowledge, skills, and opportunities. In many cases, a man who was not part of the wealthy class could be elected to a government position.

Whose opportunities were limited?

Not all people shared the same opportunities to gain wealth or to become leaders. Usually, only adult white males who owned property could vote. In most colonies, a person had to own fifty acres of land to be qualified to vote. But land was easily available. Therefore, more people in the colonies had the right to vote than in any other country at that time.

Native Americans, African Americans, white men without property, and women were typically not allowed to vote or hold office.

Women usually were not allowed to own property. Under the law, married couples were considered one person and the husband controlled the property.

What rights did the colonists value?

Since most colonists were self-sufficient, they valued their freedom highly. The people in the colonies thought that their society was superior to the corrupt societies of Europe. Colonists considered themselves to be virtuous, hardworking, simple people.

John Adams, one of our nation's Founders, once said that "revolution was in the hearts and minds of the people long before Lexington and Concord." What does this statement mean?

As subjects of Great Britain, the colonists enjoyed the rights included in the British constitution. You will learn about these rights in Lesson 6. Many colonial governments also protected the rights of the colonists. For example, the Massachusetts Body of Liberties of 1641 included the right to trial by jury, free elections, and the right of free men to own property. The state of Pennsylvania guaranteed freedom of belief or conscience.

In the years before the American Revolution, the colonists were very sensitive to any attempts by the British government to limit their rights. After the Revolution, Americans were concerned with protecting the rights they had just fought for.

Who were the Founders?

Throughout this text, we refer to a group of people as the **Founders**. The Founders were the political leaders of the colonies. They had developed their own ideas about what might be the best kind of government. These ideas were formed from their own experiences and their studies of governments of the past. The Founders led the fight to free the American colonies from British rule. The Founders helped create the state governments, and their ideas influenced the writing of the Constitution. Some of the Founders' names you might recognize include John and Abigail Adams, Benjamin Franklin, Patrick Henry, Thomas Jefferson, Mercy Otis Warren, and George Washington.

Reviewing and Using the Lesson

1 In what ways were people's lives in the British colonies of the 1770s different from those of people living in Europe?

2 Suppose you were a member of a typical colonial family in the 1770s. What might be the similarities and differences between your life then and your life today?

3 What diversity of people and ideas existed in the British colonies in the 1770s?

4 What difference did gender, race, and wealth make to people in colonial society?

5 What rights did the colonists value?

6 Who were the Founders?

Activities

1 Go to your library or search the Internet. Find information about what life in the colonies was like for one of the following groups:

- Children and adolescents

- Indentured servants

- Native Americans

- People held in slavery

- Women

2 The British colonies in America are generally divided into three regions: the New England Colonies, the Middle Colonies, and the Southern Colonies. Learn more about what life was like in each region. Write a brief summary for your class.

3 On an outline map of the United States, mark the British, French, and Spanish colonies with different colors. What states are these colonies now?

Why Do We Need Government?

LESSON PURPOSE

Our form of government is based on a set of ideas. These ideas establish what the purpose of government should be and what kind of government is best. This lesson introduces you to some of the basic ideas that were of great importance to the Founders. In this lesson you will learn about the idea of natural rights.

LESSON OBJECTIVES

When you finish this lesson, you should be able to

❑ explain what the Founders believed to be the natural rights of human beings,

❑ explain why the Founders believed that the people need a government, and

❑ explain how people create governments.

TERMS TO UNDERSTAND

- consent
- natural rights
- purpose of government
- social contract
- state of nature

How did the ideas of John Locke influence the Founders?

The Founders were students of history and philosophy. They studied books, read newspapers, and listened to sermons in church. The Founders discussed and exchanged ideas with each other and with other people.

One philosopher whose writings influenced the thinking of the Founders was John Locke. John Locke was a well-known English philosopher. He lived from 1632 to 1704. Locke published a book called *Two Treatises of Government* in 1689. In that book Locke explained his ideas about **natural rights**. Locke's book was widely read and discussed in the American colonies. Many of the Founders' ideas about government were based on Locke's philosophy.

John Locke arrived at his ideas by imagining what life might be like if people were living in a **state of nature**. By this, Locke did not mean necessarily people living in the wilderness. Locke simply saw a state of nature as a condition in which no governments or laws existed at all.

What might life be like in a state of nature?

It is now your turn to be a philosopher like John Locke. First, imagine that you and all the students in your school are living in a state of nature. You have plenty of food and other resources to maintain life and to live well. But there is no government and there are no laws or rules that you have to follow. There is no one to tell you what to do and no one to protect you.

What did John Locke mean by a "state of nature"?

With your partner or group, discuss the questions in the following exercise about your rights in a state of nature. Be prepared to share your ideas with your class. Finally, compare your ideas with those of John Locke—after you read the section "What were Locke's ideas about natural rights?"

Critical Thinking Exercise

Thinking like a political philosopher

1. What might life be like in a state of nature?

   - What might be some advantages and disadvantages of living in a state of nature?

   - What rights, if any, might you expect to have in a state of nature?

   - What might people who are stronger or smarter than others try to do? Why?

   - What might people who are weaker or less skilled than others try to do? Why?

   - What might life be like for everyone living in a state of nature?

   - Would anyone have the right to govern you? Would you have the right to govern anyone else? Why?

   - What are some things the people could do to protect their lives, liberty, or property?

2. What ideas about government might you develop from thinking about life in a state of nature?

By imagining life in a state of nature, Locke was able to answer some important questions like these. Before seeing Locke's answers, develop your own so you can compare them with Locke's.

- What is human nature? For example, are all people mainly interested in their own welfare, or do they tend to care for the good of others?

- What should be the main purpose of government?

- How do people who run government get the right to govern?

- What kinds of government should people support and obey?

- What kinds of government should people resist?

How did the Founders use Locke's ideas?

The Founders discussed and debated John Locke's answers to the questions you have just answered. Locke's ideas were used in the Declaration of Independence to explain why Americans were opposed to British rule in the colonies. After winning the Revolutionary War, the Founders used most of the same ideas to write their state constitutions. The ideas of natural rights philosophy also are important to the kind of government that we have today.

What were Locke's ideas about natural rights?

John Locke believed that through reasoning, we can determine what rights people would have in a state of nature.

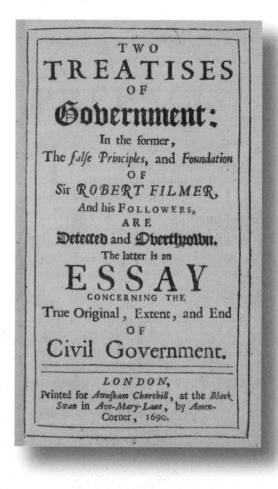

What were Locke's ideas about natural rights?

Locke reasoned that in a state of nature, all people seek to have the following rights:

- **Life** People want to survive. People want to be as safe as possible from threats to their lives.

- **Liberty** People want to be as free as possible. People want to be able to make their own decisions and to live as they please.

- **Property** People want to own the things that are necessary to survive, such as food, houses, tools, or land. People want the freedom to work and to gain economic benefits.

Locke said that the rights to life, liberty, and property are **natural rights**. These rights are a part of the law of nature. This means that all people have the rights to life, liberty, and property just because they are human beings.

The Founders believed that such rights as those to life, liberty, and property are not man-made. Instead, they believed these rights are based on the laws of nature, which were made by God. The Declaration of Independence, for example, speaks of "the Laws of Nature and of Nature's God." It says that people are "endowed by their Creator" with certain basic rights and that no one may take away these rights.

Why do you think it helps to determine what our natural rights are by imagining life in a state of nature?

What did John Locke say might happen in a state of nature?

1 Locke believed that most people are reasonable and good. Most people respect the rights of others because their conscience tells them that they have a duty to do so. But people are also driven by self-interest. A few humans are not so reasonable and good. Sometimes people who are stronger or more skilled abuse those who are weaker or less skilled.

2 Locke believed that in a state of nature, people protect their natural rights by using their own strength and skill. People who are weaker or less skilled would find it very hard to protect their rights. Instead, weaker people would try to protect their rights by joining together against the strong.

3 Locke believed that in a state of nature, no one's life, liberty, or property would be safe. People would feel insecure. In a state of nature, there are no governments or laws to protect life, liberty, or property. This is why people agreed to form governments. According to Locke, governments do not exist until people create them.

4 Locke believed that in a state of nature, no one would have the right to govern you, and you would not have the right to govern anyone else. According to Locke, there is only one way that people get the right to govern anyone else: the people to be governed must give their consent. **Consent** means to approve of something or allow something to take place. If the people have not given their consent to create a government, there is no legitimate government. In other words, the power of legitimate government comes from the consent of the people.

How might individuals protect their natural rights in a state of nature?

Why do people agree to form a social contract?

Although people agreed that certain natural rights existed, they worried about how those rights could be protected. In a state of nature, people might feel free to do anything they want to do. Their rights would not be protected, however, and that would make them feel insecure.

For John Locke and other natural rights philosophers, the great problem was to find a way to protect each person's natural rights so that everyone could enjoy them and live in peace with one another. Locke said that the best way to solve this problem is for each individual to agree with others to create and live under a government and give that government the power to make and enforce laws. Locke called this kind of agreement a **social contract**.

As in all contracts, to get something, you must give up something. In a social contract, everyone promises to give up the absolute right to do anything she or he wants to do.

Absolute means without any limits. In return, everyone receives the security that can be provided by a government. Each person consents to obey the limits placed upon her or him by the laws created by the government. Everyone gains the security of knowing that their rights to life, liberty, and property are protected.

Government, then, is the better alternative to a state of nature, which would be imperfect because some people might not respect the rights of others. According to Locke, the main **purpose of government** is to protect those natural rights that the individual cannot effectively protect in a state of nature.

In a later lesson, you will study the Declaration of Independence. You will see how the Founders included all the ideas that you have studied in this lesson. You will also learn to examine questions about what kind of government the people should support and obey and what kind they should resist.

What do you think?

Most people would agree that there are certain rights all people should have. For example, you probably agree that everyone has the right to be protected from robbers and murderers. You probably also agree that a person's right to vote should be protected. Most people in the United States share the belief that everyone should have these rights.

Work with a partner or in a group of three students. Together answer the questions that follow. Be prepared to share your ideas with the class.

❶ List five rights that you think all people in our nation should have. Why do you think that it is important that all people should have these rights?

❷ Which of the rights on your list seem to be the most important? Arrange the rights you listed in the order of their importance. Explain why you ranked the rights on your list in this order.

❸ What might you do to ensure that these rights are protected?

In a state of nature, how might one's life, liberty, or property be protected?

Reviewing and Using the Lesson

1. What are natural rights? How do people get their natural rights?

2. What might life be like for people living in a state of nature? Explain.

3. Where does government get its right to govern, according to the natural rights philosophy?

4. What is a social contract?

5. What is the main purpose of government, according to John Locke?

6. You learned about social contracts. Most passengers aboard the Mayflower signed the Mayflower Compact in 1620, before the ship landed in Plymouth. Read the Mayflower Compact below. Write a brief essay explaining how the Mayflower Compact is an example of a social contract.

   Having undertaken, for the glory of God, and advancement of the Christian Faith and Honour of our King and Country, a Voyage to plant the First Colony in the Northern Parts of Virginia, do by these presents solemnly and mutually in the presence of God and of one another, Covenant and Combine ourselves together into a Civil Body Politic, for our better ordering and preservation and furtherance of the ends aforesaid; and by virtue hereof, to enact, constitute, and frame such just and equal Laws, Ordinances, Acts, Constitutions, and Offices, from time to time, as shall be thought most meet and convenient for the general good of the Colony, unto which we promise all due submission and obedience.

Activities

1. Draw a cartoon that illustrates what life might be like in a state of nature. Use your cartoon to illustrate why we need government.

2. Read *Lord of the Flies* by William Golding. It is a novel about what happened when a group of young boys found themselves in a situation where there were no laws and no government. Share the story with your class. Does this story support Locke's ideas? If so, which ones?

3. Write a short story that tells how the rights to life, liberty, and property apply to you and your family. Share your story with the class.

What Is Republican Government?

LESSON PURPOSE

This lesson introduces the ideas of republican government, the common good, and civic virtue. These were ideas the Founders learned from studying the government of the ancient Roman Republic. You will learn how these ideas shaped the Founders' thinking about the kind of government they believed to be best.

LESSON OBJECTIVE

When you finish this lesson you should be able to explain the ideas of republican government, the common good, and civic virtue.

TERMS TO UNDERSTAND

- aristocrats
- civic virtue
- common good
- delegate
- direct democracy
- faction
- representative
- representative democracy
- republic
- republican government

What did the Founders learn about government from the Roman Republic?

What did the Founders learn about government from the Romans?

Two thousand years before our own nation began, there was a **republic** that greatly influenced the ideas of the Founders. A republic is a country that has a government in which power is held by the people who elect representatives. Those representatives manage the government for the people, for the sake of the common good.

The government that fascinated the Founders was the Roman Republic, which lasted nearly 500 years, from 509 BC to 27 BC. The capital of the Roman Republic was Rome, located in what today is Italy.

The Founders read what historians and the Romans themselves wrote about the people and government of the Roman Republic. The Founders learned that during the Republic, the Roman people governed themselves without a king. In the Roman Republic, both the common people and the **aristocrats**, or wealthy upper class, shared the power to govern.

The Founders called the government of Rome a republican government. **Republican government** is a type of government in which the

- citizens have the power to govern,

- citizens **delegate** or entrust their power to leaders they elect to represent them and to serve their interests, and

- citizens and their representatives work cooperatively to promote the common good rather than their own interests. The term **common good**, or common welfare, means that which is good for the community as a whole.

What advantages did the Founders see in republican government?

The Founders thought a republican form of government was the best form of government they could create for themselves. They thought that they would have some of the same benefits that the ancient Romans had enjoyed. These are some of the benefits the Founders saw in republican government:

- **Representatives are elected to serve the common good.** A representative is a person elected to act and speak for others. The main purpose of republican government is to serve the common good. Representatives should not make laws to serve the interests of one person or one group. The representatives make laws that serve the entire community.

- **Having representatives make the laws is more efficient.** To make good and fair laws, you have to understand every problem well. But most people do not have the time to

What are the advantages of a republican government in a large and diverse society?

learn about every problem. Representatives can create laws faster and better because it becomes their responsibility to do so.

- **The people have a say in their government.** By delegating power to their representatives, the people do not give up their voice in government. The people still have to decide who will represent them. The people have to communicate their ideas and the actions they want taken to their representatives.

How did James Madison define the difference between direct democracy and republican government?

- **The representatives are responsible to the people.** The people hold their representatives responsible for making good and fair laws. If the representatives do not make good and fair laws, the people can vote them out of office and select new leaders to represent them.

What were the disadvantages of republican government?

The Founders worried about whether republican government would work in the colonies. The Founders saw that republican government as practiced in the Roman Republic had a few disadvantages. These are some of the possible disadvantages:

- Republican government works best in small communities. In small communities, the people know and care for each other and the common good. The colonies, on the other hand, occupied a large territory.

- The people in a republic have to be very much alike. There cannot be a high degree of diversity. The people cannot be very different in their wealth, moral beliefs, or ways of life. In the colonies, however, the people had many different religious beliefs and ways of life.

- People in a large and diverse republic would naturally divide into **factions**, or interest groups. Such interest groups might work against other groups or the people as a whole, rather than work for the common good.

How did the Founders adapt the idea of republican government?

James Madison was one of the most important Founders. We often call him "the Father of the Constitution" because he played such an important role in creating our Constitution. Madison adapted the idea of republican government to the reality of American life.

Madison defined the difference between a direct democracy and republican government in the following ways:

- In a **direct democracy**, the people themselves control government. The people create the laws they need. Direct democracy works best in small communities. As communities grow larger, it becomes difficult for people to make the decisions that are needed for the good of all.

- In a republican government, the people's representatives make the laws and run government. This makes it possible for those in government to administer a much larger area.

Madison believed that America could and should have a republican form of government. Laws would be made and administered by representatives elected by the people. Madison said that members of government should be elected by a large number of the people rather than by a small number or a favored group. Such a government was a democracy in the sense that it received its right to govern from the people as a whole. This kind of government is now called a representative democracy. In a **representative democracy**, the people choose leaders to make and administer laws for their country.

How did Madison adapt the ideas of republican government to the colonies?

Madison also believed that you could organize government in a way that might help avoid the abuse of power by any one person or faction. You will study these ideas in the next lesson.

What do you think?

1 What were some of the characteristics of the American colonies that required adaptations of the ideas of republican government to make it work well in America?

2 How did Madison think it was possible to organize a government so no one person or self-interested group could control and abuse its powers. What evidence is there that supports or fails to support his idea?

Why should citizens promote the common good?

The idea of **civic virtue** was one of the most important parts of the classical republican philosophy. It was the idea that citizens should put aside their own self-interests in favor of the common good of their communities and countries. The Founders had read about the famous Roman leader Cincinnatus who they believed was a model of civic virtue.

In the year 460 BC, Rome was in great danger. An army from the east was burning and plundering the countryside. The enemy surrounded the defending Roman army on all sides. The leaders of the government of Rome decided to ask Cincinnatus, a skilled military leader, to help them during this crisis. The government leaders sent messengers asking Cincinnatus to serve as dictator of the country for as long as the crisis might last.

Cincinnatus was a hard-working farmer with only four acres of land. When the messengers found him, he was quietly plowing the fields. Because he loved his country, he left his plow to go to Rome to lead the army. In a battle that lasted two days, his army defeated the enemy and saved the country. In gratitude, the people of Rome honored and praised Cincinnatus. But when the crisis was over, Cincinnatus did not try to remain as dictator of his country. He did not want continued power. Instead, he returned to his home and his life as a farmer and a citizen.

By returning to his home, Cincinnatus showed that he valued being a good citizen of Rome more than he valued fame and personal power. He respected the government of Rome. He did not want to use his popularity to take power away from the representatives elected by the citizens.

What do you think?

1. What is the common good as represented in this story? What are the self-interests represented in the story? Do you agree with the actions taken by Cincinnatus? Why or why not?

2. Describe a person you know or a leader in our nation who you think has civic virtue. Give reasons for your opinion based on the person's life.

3. Explain some situations where you think you should put the common good above your own interests.

4. Explain some situations in which you might not want to put the common good above your own interests.

5. Explain some situations in which people might disagree about what is best for the common good. What should be done when there are such disagreements? Why?

Why is civic virtue necessary for republican government to work well?

The Founders thought that republican government was possible in Rome only because of the high degree of civic virtue of Roman citizens. Civic virtue meant that both citizens and their leaders set aside their private interests and personal concerns for the common good.

In the Roman Republic, the responsibilities or duties of citizens were emphasized as more important than their personal rights. When a conflict between one's personal rights and interests and the common good arose, citizens were expected to set aside their interests in favor of the common good.

The Founders thought that civic virtue was important to make a government work well. Citizens need to participate in their government to promote the common good. Citizens were expected to be well informed and to participate in community affairs.

Citizens did have political rights, such as the right to vote, to express their opinions about government, and to serve in public office. But there were often limits on other rights, such as privacy or freedom of conscience or religion.

Madison understood the importance of civic virtue to good government. In this way, he was like the other Founders. Madison also accepted John Locke's view of human nature. He believed that people often act in their self-interest. He thought that the pursuit of self-interest could in its own way further the common good. For example, a statesman's desire for fame and the admiration of others could lead him or her to practice civic virtue. He also believed that the common good could be served by individuals pursuing their economic self-interest. Each would contribute to the general prosperity, which served the common good.

Madison also realized that as people pursue their own interests, they sometimes act against the interests of the common good. He knew that civic virtue alone could not be relied upon to ensure a good government that promoted the common good. Madison wanted to create a government that would fit human nature as it is, not as one might wish it to be.

Do you think that a statesman's desire for fame and admiration can lead him or her to pursue the public or common good? Why or why not?

What do you think?

Work with two or three other students to develop answers to the following questions.

Why do you think so many government buildings in Washington, D.C., are designed to look like Greek or Roman buildings?

❶ Do you think you can rely upon the civic virtue of most citizens to promote the common good? Why or why not?

❷ Do you think you can rely upon the civic virtue of most people elected to serve in government to promote the common good? Why or why not?

❸ Do you think that if people all pursue their self-interest, the common good will be promoted? Why or why not?

❹ Do you think that if people all pursue their economic self-interest the country will be more prosperous and the common good will be promoted? Why or why not?

❺ Why do you suppose Madison thought you could not rely upon civic virtue alone to be sure government would promote the common good?

❻ If you cannot rely upon civic virtue alone to ensure that government promotes the common good, what can you rely upon?

How did the colonists teach the values of republican government?

People living in the American colonies were taught the value of civic virtue and other values of republican government in many ways. Parents taught these values to their children. Teachers taught them in school. Clergy taught them in sermons and writings. Leading citizens of the country were expected to set good examples. The values of republican government were a part of the customs and traditions of the people.

The ideas and values of the Roman Republic were promoted throughout the American colonies in the stories that people read. Public buildings designed to resemble the buildings of ancient Rome also reminded people of the ideas and values of the Roman Republic.

The Founders thought it was important to teach and promote civic virtue among citizens. They believed that the Roman Republic had failed in the end because its citizens lost their civic virtue. They had promoted their own interests at the expense of the common good.

By the time of the American Revolution, the Founders had come to believe strongly in the ideals of republican government. They thought that Great Britain was violating these ideals. They claimed the British government was guilty of serving selfish interests at the expense of the common good. It had violated those rights that good government was supposed to protect.

After the Revolution, the Founders were able to establish their own government. They tried to make sure this government would not violate the people's rights. An essential step, they thought, was to create a constitutional government. You will learn what a constitution and constitutional government are in the next lesson.

Reviewing and Using the Lesson

① What is republican government? What are the advantages and disadvantages of republican government?

② What is the meaning of the term *common good*?

③ What is the difference between direct democracy and representative democracy?

④ What is civic virtue? Why is it important that citizens and their representatives have civic virtue?

⑤ How were the values of republican government promoted in the colonies? Why were these values promoted?

⑥ In this lesson you learned about the values taught in colonial communities. The following excerpts are from the *Blue-Back Speller*, a popular school text of the late 1700s. What values do the lessons stress?

Lesson 6 I will not walk with bad men; that I may not be cast off with them. I will love the law, and keep it. I will walk with the just, and do good.

Lesson 12 Be a good child; mind your book; love your school and strive to learn. Tell no tales; call no ill names; you must not lie, nor swear, nor cheat, nor steal. Play not with bad boys; use no ill words at play, spend your time well, live in peace, and shun all strife.   This is the way to make good men of you, and save your soul from pain and woe.

Lesson 15 As for those boys and girls that mind not their books, and love not church and school, but play with such as tell tales, tell lies, curse, swear, and steal, they will come to some bad end, and must be whipped till they mend their ways.

Activities

① His fellow Americans often referred to George Washington as "our Cincinnatus." Find stories and works of art that illustrate the life of George Washington as a model of civic virtue. Share what you learn with your class.

② Many government buildings in Washington, D.C., and many state capitols across the country look like Greek or Roman buildings. Find photographs of government buildings. Compare them with drawings or photographs of ancient Greek or Roman buildings. Explain how this architectural style in our country symbolizes the influences of ancient Greece and Rome on the Founders.

③ Look through different issues of your local newspaper. Find articles that concern the common good in your community. Share the articles with your class.

What Is Constitutional Government?

LESSON PURPOSE

This lesson introduces the ideas of a constitution and constitutional government. It also introduces the idea that a constitution is a higher law.

LESSON OBJECTIVES

When you finish this lesson, you should be able to

❑ explain the ideas of a constitution, constitutional government, and higher law, and

❑ explain some of the important differences between constitutional governments and autocratic or dictatorial governments.

TERMS TO UNDERSTAND

- autocratic or dictatorial government
- constitution
- constitutional government
- higher law
- limits
- monarchy
- private domain

What is a constitution?

A **constitution** is a legal framework for government. A constitution tells how a government is organized and run. Every nation has a constitution. Both good and bad governments have constitutions.

Most constitutions are in writing. The United States and Russia are two examples of countries with written constitutions. Some constitutions contain both written and unwritten parts. The British constitution is the best-known example of this kind of constitution because it is based on both written laws and unwritten customs. It also is possible to have a constitution that is not in writing at all. Many societies in history had constitutions based on unwritten customs and traditions.

You can learn about a government and its citizens by studying a nation's constitution. Here are some of the questions a constitution usually answers:

What might be some advantages of a written constitution?

Questions about Government

- What are the purposes of government?
- What is the organization of government? What parts does it have? What does each part do?
- How is government supposed to go about doing its business? For example, how does the government make its laws?
- How are people selected to serve in government?

Questions about Citizens

- Who is a citizen?
- Are citizens supposed to have control over their government? If so, how is this control supposed to work?
- What rights and responsibilities, if any, are the citizens supposed to have?

What is a constitutional government?

Having a constitution does not mean that a nation has a **constitutional government**. A constitutional government means that there are **limits** on the powers of the person or group running the government. The word "limits," as used here, means things that government may not do or actions that it may not take.

Our Constitution limits the power of government. The limits are written into the Constitution. For example, the courts cannot force a person to be a witness against himself. The courts cannot deny a person accused of a crime the right to an attorney.

In some nations, the power of government is not limited. It is possible for the constitution of a nation to provide for the unlimited use of power. In other cases, the constitution of a

What are the advantages of constitutional government?

nation might say that the power of government should be limited. But it might neglect to say how those limits are to be enforced.

Suppose the constitution of a nation does not limit the powers of its government. On the other hand, suppose it limits the power, but those limits are not enforced. In either case, the government is not a constitutional government. We call a government of unlimited power an **autocratic or dictatorial government**.

What is a higher law?

In a constitutional government, the constitution must effectively limit the use of power. The constitution is a higher law. A **higher law** is a set of laws that establish and limit the power of government. All the people, including government leaders, must obey the higher law of the land. The people running the government must do what the constitution says. The constitution describes ways to

ensure that people in government obey the limits on their power.

In a constitutional government, the constitution has the following five important characteristics:

Why should a constitution be considered a higher law?

What rights does the U.S. Constitution protect?

1 It lists the basic rights of citizens to life, liberty, and property.

2 It establishes the responsibility of government to protect those rights.

3 It places limits on how the people in government may use their powers. Here are some examples of how our Constitution limits the powers of government:

- **Citizens' rights** People in government cannot unfairly deprive a person of the right to freedom of speech.

- **How resources are distributed** People in government cannot take a person's property without paying the person a fair price for it.

- **How conflicts are handled** People in government must give all persons accused of a crime a fair trial.

4 It establishes the principle of a **private domain**. A private domain is that part of a person's life that is not the business of government.

5 It can only be changed with the widespread consent of citizens and according to certain set procedures.

What do you think?

1 What are the most important differences between a constitutional government and an autocratic or dictatorial government?

2 How might the existence of a private domain in a country promote individual freedom?

3 What parts of your life do you think should not be the business of government? Why?

4 Which characteristics of a constitutional government do you think are most important? Why?

When, if ever, should someone obey a law higher than the laws of their government?

The Tragedy of Antigone

The following story has been summarized and adapted from the Greek play *Antigone* written in 442 BC by Sophocles. In the play, Antigone disobeys her uncle, Creon, the ruler of Thebes. The government of Thebes was a monarchy. A **monarchy** is a form of government in which political power is held by a single ruler, such as a king or queen. The king ruled the city; he made and enforced the laws, and he decided on punishments for people who violated his laws. The story raises questions about limits on the power of government.

Thebes was an important city in ancient Greece. Antigone lived there with her sister, Ismene, her two brothers, Polyneices and Eteocles, and their uncle Creon.

The citizens of Thebes had chosen Eteocles, the younger brother, to be their king. Polyneices believed that since he was older, it was his right to rule the land. The two brothers quarreled and Eteocles banished Polyneices from the city.

Polyneices left Thebes and gathered a large army to fight his brother for the throne. It was a long and bitter civil war; many people died and much property was destroyed. Finally, Polyneices and Eteocles killed each other.

The people of Thebes immediately elected Creon to be their next king. Creon decreed that Eteocles was to receive a hero's funeral for defending the city. But Polyneices was to rot on the battlefield. Any person who tried to bury Polyneices would be put to death. "These are my laws!" Creon declared. "Only by these laws can our city be safe and prosper. Only by obedience to these laws can we avoid civil war and ruin."

The citizens of Thebes debated the wisdom of Creon's law. On one side, many people were opposed to it. These people believed it was the duty of the living to bury the dead. According to this belief, unburied souls were doomed to wander alone throughout eternity. This group of people complained that Creon's law violated their rights without a good reason for doing so.

Other citizens supported Creon. They believed that Creon's law was justified because the city had suffered from rebels and lawbreakers. It was the king's duty to decide what to do with people who violated the law. They felt that the fate of Polyneices could serve as an example to those who did not respect the laws of the king.

Antigone believed that the laws of the gods were higher laws than the laws of any ruler. So Antigone decided to bury the body of her brother. "I will never be false to my brother," she said. Antigone attempted to convince Ismene to help her.

"Are you not going too far, exceeding the limits, when you do what the king has forbidden?" Ismene asked Antigone. "I do not wish to dishonor our brother, but I have no strength to defy the king. If we defy Creon's law, we will find ourselves alone against the powers of the king and we will perish! Since we must obey Creon's law, we can ask the gods for forgiveness," Ismene said.

"Obey the law if you must, Ismene. I will not urge you further to join me," Antigone replied.

Later that day, a guard suddenly burst into the garden where Creon was resting. The guard brought the news that Polyneices had been buried. Creon angrily gave orders to find the guilty person. The guard returned with Antigone in custody.

"Tell me, did you not know that there is a law forbidding what you did? Why did you disobey it?" Creon asked. "You are my niece, how can this be?"

"I knew the law," Antigone answered. "If I had allowed my brother to lie unburied, that would have disturbed me deeply. Your law is not part of eternal justice. I disobeyed your law. I am not sorry for what I did," Antigone said to Creon.

"This brother of yours was attacking his own country," Creon replied. "The gods require no such loyalty to evildoers. It is my duty to produce order and peace in this land. If I do not act, the citizens of Thebes will think me weak. The public order, the state itself will be in jeopardy. It is the laws of the state that hold this city together. If those who break the law go unpunished, we will be a lawless city. Even the innocent will suffer. You have thrown away your future happiness, Antigone," Creon said. "You make it impossible for me to avoid putting you to death. Guards, take this woman and lock her away!"

As the guards escorted Antigone from the garden, she turned to Creon and said, "You further violate the rights of the people by passing sentence upon me without a fair and public hearing."

Critical Thinking Exercise

Higher law and governmental power

As you were able to observe in the story, there were no laws that set reasonable limits on the power of the king. But the king had a Council of Advisers, as in some other cities of ancient Greece. The role of the council was to investigate problems and advise the king on what he might do to solve them.

Let us imagine that Antigone has asked the Council of Advisers to investigate the unlimited power of the king. Further, imagine that Creon has agreed to permit the council to study the issue and make recommendations. The Council of Advisers will conduct a hearing and then decide what recommendations, if any, to give the king.

Suppose that Creon, Antigone, and Ismene each will have an opportunity to present arguments favoring their positions to the council. Work with two or three other students to prepare arguments for each of these persons.

Then, after considering the arguments you have prepared for each position, write and justify the decision you would make if you were a member of the Council of Advisers.

As an alternative, divide into groups representing each of the following positions and create arguments for them. Then each group should present its position before the Council of Advisers, which should consider them and render a decision on the issue.

1. **Creon** Prepare arguments against any limits on the power of the king. Base your arguments on what you read about Creon in the story. In your presentation, be sure to explain the reasons why you believe the power of the king should remain as is.

2. **Antigone** Prepare arguments in favor of limiting the power of the king. Base your arguments on what you read about Antigone in the story. In your presentation, propose specific limits on the king's power that you would like the council to recommend to Creon.

3. **Ismene** Prepare arguments that represent Ismene's point of view. Present specific reasons why you hold this opinion.

4. **Member of the Council of Advisers** Consider the arguments you have created for each position, and write and justify your decision on the issue.

Reviewing and Using the Lesson

1 What is a constitution? What can you learn about a nation's government by studying its constitution?

2 Explain the differences between a constitutional government and an autocratic or dictatorial government.

3 What are the characteristics that define a constitution as a "higher law"?

4 Identify two areas of private life in which you think government should not interfere. Explain why you think government should not intrude in these areas.

Activities

1 In the history of the world, there have been governments that ignored the limits on their power. Conduct research on one of these governments and give examples of how it violated the natural rights of the people.

2 Read the play *Antigone*. Research how the play was rewritten during World War II to inspire resistance to Nazi rule. Write a short report on your findings and share it with your class.

3 Draw a cartoon for your class bulletin board that illustrates the difference between a constitutional government and a dictatorial government.

How Can We Organize Government to Prevent the Abuse of Power?

LESSON PURPOSE

Constitutional governments are designed to protect the people from abuses of government power. In this lesson you learn how people might organize government to make the abuse of power less likely.

LESSON OBJECTIVES

When you finish this lesson, you should be able to

❑ explain the ideas of separation of powers and checks and balances,

❑ explain the Founders' reasons for creating a system that limits governmental power, and

❑ list some powers of the three branches of government.

TERMS TO UNDERSTAND

- bill
- checks and balances
- executive branch
- judicial branch
- legislative branch
- separation of powers

Do you agree with Benjamin Franklin that the love of power and money have a powerful influence over people? Why or why not?

Why did the Founders fear the abuse of power?

The Founders knew that throughout history, many governments had used their power unfairly. This is why they created the system of limits on power described in this lesson. To understand their thinking, read the quotations below.

What do you think?

1 What view of human nature is expressed in each of the quotations?

2 What view of human nature did Alexander Hamilton, Benjamin Franklin, and George Mason share?

3 Do you agree or disagree with these views of human nature? Why or why not?

4 If you do agree with these views of human nature, how would you organize our government to protect your rights?

Alexander Hamilton

"Give all power to the many, they will oppress the few. Give all power to the few, they will oppress the many."

Benjamin Franklin

"There are two passions which have a Powerful influence on the affairs of men. These are ambition and avarice [greed]; the love of power and the love of money."

George Mason

"From the nature of man, we may be sure that those who have power in their hands ... will always, when they can ... increase it."

Why did the Founders think the power of government should be limited by a written constitution?

How might people organize a government to prevent the abuse of power?

Constitutional governments are organized to prevent one person or group from getting enough power to dominate the government. When they wrote the U.S. Constitution, the Framers used the following ways to do this.

- **Separate the powers of government.** They divided the powers of government among different branches, or parts.

Doing so prevents any one person or group from having all the power.

- **Balance the powers among the branches of government.** They divided the powers of government in such a way that no one branch controls the other branches. Give each branch methods to check the use of power by the other branches.

How does separation of powers work?

A study of constitutional governments shows that they are often divided into three different groups, or branches. The power of government is not given to any one branch. Instead, some of the power is given to each branch. This is called **separation of powers**. For example, we divide our government into the following three branches:

- The **legislative branch** has the power to make laws.

- The **executive branch** has the power to carry out and enforce laws.

- The **judicial branch** has the power to manage conflicts about the meaning, application, and enforcement of laws.

Why are the powers of government separated and balanced?

How can the House of Representatives and the Senate check each other's power?

How does a system of checks and balances work?

The phrase **checks and balances** means that the powers of the different branches of government are balanced. No one branch has so much power that it can completely dominate the others. Although each branch of government has its own special powers, the powers are checked because some powers are shared with the other branches.

According to our Constitution, Congress is the legislative branch. It has the power to make laws. The power of Congress is divided between two houses, the House of Representatives and the Senate. Each house can check the power of the other by refusing to pass a law proposed by the other house.

In addition, our Constitution gives the executive and judicial branches ways to check and control the power of Congress to make laws. For example,

- A **bill** is a proposed law. When Congress passes a bill, the president must sign it before it can become law. The president has the right to refuse to sign a bill.

If this happens, the bill cannot become a law unless Congress votes again and passes the bill by a two-thirds majority of both houses.

- The U.S. Supreme Court can check the power of Congress. The Court can declare a law to be in violation of the Constitution and, therefore, invalid.

There are similar ways to check the powers of the president and U.S. Supreme Court. You will learn more about the system of checks and balances in a later lesson.

This system of separation of powers and checks and balances helps ensure that government power is limited. Because constitutional governments are organized in complicated ways, getting things done may take time. Although it might seem strange, this is often considered an advantage. Many people think that these complications make it more likely that when government does finally make a decision, it will have been well thought out.

Reviewing and Using the Lesson

1 How does a system of separation of powers work?

2 What are the three branches of our government and what power does each hold?

3 How does a system of checks and balances work? Give some examples.

4 The separation and sharing of powers means that government usually cannot reach decisions quickly. Why might this be an advantage? Why might it be a disadvantage?

Activities

1 Read Articles I, II, and III of the U.S. Constitution. Then, examine the constitution of your state. Create two charts that illustrate the process of checks and balances, one for your state government and one for the U.S. government. Share your charts with the class.

2 Find news articles that illustrate our system of separation of powers and checks and balances. Use the articles to create a bulletin board for your classroom.

What Shaped the Founders' Thinking about Government?

UNIT
2

What Shaped the Founders' Thinking about Government?

UNIT PURPOSE

In the last unit, you learned some important ideas and questions concerning government. You studied natural rights philosophy, republicanism, and constitutionalism. These were the ideas that influenced the Founders of our nation and helped shape their views about government.

In this unit, you will learn more about the Founders. You will read about the experiences that shaped their thinking about government. You will study their values and the things they believed were important. You will also learn why they thought a new constitution was necessary.

KEY CONCEPTS

- Articles of Confederation
- inalienable rights
- popular sovereignty
- rule of law

How Did Constitutional Government Develop in Great Britain?

LESSON PURPOSE

Constitutional government developed in Great Britain over a period of many centuries. In this lesson, you learn how the monarchy came to share power with the nobles. You will study some documents that limited the power of the British government. This study will help you better understand our ideas about limited government.

LESSON OBJECTIVES

When you finish this lesson, you should be able to

❑ describe the struggles for power between the English monarch and Parliament,

❑ explain how these struggles led to a system of separated powers and representative government, and

❑ describe some of the important constitutional documents in British history that influenced the writing of our constitution.

TERMS TO UNDERSTAND

- common law
- English Bill of Rights
- feudalism
- Magna Carta
- Parliament
- Petition of Right
- rights of Englishmen
- rule of law
- subject

Why did the American colonists have the rights of Englishmen?

At the time of the American Revolution, Great Britain was composed of the Kingdom of England (including Wales) and the Kingdom of Scotland. The term **rights of Englishmen** was developed over centuries in the Kingdom of England before it merged with Scotland and became Great Britain. They were certain basic rights that all subjects of the English king or queen were believed to have. They included

- the right to a trial by jury,

- security from unlawful entry into one's home, and

- no taxation without consent.

Before the American colonies became independent, the colonists were **subjects** of the British monarchy. That is to say that they were under the rule of the monarchy. As subjects of the king or queen, the colonists enjoyed the rights of Englishmen. All subjects of the king or queen had these rights. The colonists knew and understood their rights as Englishmen.

The colonists' experiences with British government greatly influenced what they thought about limited government. For our study, it is important to understand these rights and how they developed over time. It is also important to know that the constitution of Great Britain is not a single written document. Instead, it is made up of long-established practices known as common law and laws passed by Parliament. **Common law** is based on custom and the decisions of law courts. **Parliament** is the legislative body of British government.

What were some important rights of Englishmen?

What was the feudal system?

Until 1066, each region of England had its own ruler. William the Conqueror from France invaded England in that year and became king of all the regions.

William the Conqueror brought a system for governing called feudalism. **Feudalism** was a system of social, economic, and political organization. The system was based on the control of land.

Under feudalism, the people in England belonged to one of three social groups.

❶ **Royalty** This was the king and queen and their families. Government by a king or queen is a monarchy.

❷ **Nobility** This group included the "lords" and "ladies" who held titles such as earl, duke, duchess, and baron. The noblemen worked for the monarchy and made it possible for the king or queen to control England.

❸ **Common people** These were the rest of the people. This group included the knights, or soldiers of the king, merchants, and peasants. The peasants were also known as serfs. They farmed the land and were not free to leave the area in which they worked.

All public land in England belonged to the monarch, but it was too much land for one person to rule. So, the monarch gave some responsibility for governing the kingdom to the nobility. Under the feudal system, the nobles controlled parts of the land, as well as the people who lived there. In exchange, the nobles pledged to be loyal to the king and to go to war for him.

The nobles further divided the land into smaller areas. A nobleman assigned control of the land and people living on it to men called vassals. The vassals in turn owed the nobleman loyalty and military service.

For the system to work, it depended on a series of agreements or contracts. There had to be contracts between the monarch and the nobles. There also had to be contracts between the nobles and vassals. Each contract included rights and responsibilities that the parties owed to one another. Thus, feudalism introduced the idea of government based on a contract. Those in power pledged to respect the rights of the people who gave them loyalty.

The feudal system was important to the development of constitutional government. It was during this period that the monarchs started to share power with the nobles.

What problems, if any, might arise from dividing society into social groups?

Why is the Magna Carta an important document?

Under the feudal system, it became a custom or tradition for the royalty to share some of its power with the nobility. As a result, the nobles became used to having certain rights and powers. When King John tried to take back some of these rights, the nobles rebelled.

The nobles were powerful enough to force King John to sign an agreement with them in the year 1215. This agreement is the **Magna Carta**, or Great Charter. The Magna Carta was a major step in the growth of English constitutional government. The Magna Carta was perhaps the most important early example of a written statement of law limiting the power of a ruler. The Magna Carta contains two important ideas that influenced the Founders.

1 Government is based on a contract between the ruler and people to be ruled. Government by contract also includes the idea that if either side breaks the contract, that contract is no longer valid.

How did the Magna Carta limit the power of the king?

What is the relationship between the Magna Carta and constitutional government?

2 Both government and the governed must obey the law. This is called the **rule of law**. The law limits the powers of government. The king could not take away the property of a noble without following agreed-upon procedures and rules. The Magna Carta expresses the idea of limited government by requiring the king to govern according to established rules of law.

The Magna Carta was a contract between the king and the nobility. Most of the people of England were not a part of this agreement. But the Magna Carta is an early step leading to the idea that government should be based on a contract that includes all the people.

Government by contract means that both sides of the agreement are responsible for fulfilling its terms. The Magna Carta states that the king cannot deprive the nobility of their rights. The nobility, in return, must support and obey the king and the laws.

Although the Magna Carta was written in 1215, its influence can be seen in the U.S. Constitution and Bill of Rights adopted in 1789 and 1791—hundreds of years later.

Critical Thinking Exercise

Examining the Magna Carta

Each of the rights below was a right of Englishmen listed in the Magna Carta. Read the rights and respond to the questions that follow them for each right.

- For a trivial [minor] offence, a free man shall be fined only in proportion to the degree of his offence, and for a serious offence correspondingly.

- No free man shall be taken, or imprisoned ... exiled, or in any way harmed ... save by the lawful judgment of his peers or by the law of the land.

- No constable [officer] or other bailiff [sheriff] of ours shall take the corn [grain] or other chattels [personal property] of anyone except ... he gives money for them.

- To none will we sell, to none deny or delay, right of justice.

1 What is the meaning of this statement?

2 What right does the statement guarantee?

3 Why is this right important?

4 Explain how this right limits the power of government.

5 Where in the Constitution or Bill of Rights can you find this right?

How do the rights of Englishmen limit the power of government?

Why was the creation of Parliament important?

Important changes in the English government caused the establishment of other basic principles of government in addition to those in the Magna Carta. These principles are the separation of powers and representative government.

What events contributed to the shift of power from the monarchy to Parliament?

In 1258, the nobles forced the king to create an advisory council. This council was called Parliament. Parliament is the legislative branch of the English government. It was made up of two houses that represented the most powerful groups in the kingdom: the House of Lords and the House of Commons. The House of Lords represented the nobles. The House of Commons represented people who owned large amounts of land but were not nobles.

Gradually during the next centuries the role of Parliament grew. Its members were no longer simply advising the monarch—they were representing the interests of their regions. For hundreds of years after the creation of Parliament, the royalty, nobility, and commons had struggled for power. No one group was able to be completely in control for long.

Then in 1628, the king tried to pressure the people for money without the consent of Parliament. He also required the people to house soldiers in their homes. As a result, Parliament forced him to agree to the **Petition of Right** of 1628. The Petition stated that the king could only raise taxes with the consent of Parliament. It also no longer allowed the king to house soldiers in the homes of the people. The Petition of Right strengthened the idea that English subjects had certain rights that government could not violate.

The struggle between the monarch and Parliament became so intense during the seventeenth century that a series of civil wars broke out. The nobles finally won, and in 1649 Parliament ordered the execution of the king. By 1688, the balance of power had shifted in favor of Parliament.

What limitations were placed upon the power of the monarchy by the Petition of Right?

What was the English Bill of Rights?

In 1689, Parliament passed the **English Bill of Rights**. This law gave certain rights to Parliament that further limited the powers of the monarch. It said, among other things, that elections to Parliament must be free and that the people have the right to petition the king. It also said that the monarchy was no longer allowed to

- collect taxes without the consent of Parliament,

- interfere with the right to free speech and debate in Parliament,

- maintain an army in peacetime,

- prevent Protestants from having arms for their defense,

- require excessive bail or administer cruel punishment for those accused or convicted of crimes, and

- declare that laws made by Parliament should not be obeyed.

By the end of the 1600s, the British government was much more limited in what it could do. This was at the same time that the British were establishing colonies in North America. So, the colonists brought these ideas about good government with them to the new world.

Reviewing and Using the Lesson

1. Explain how the feudal system promoted the idea that government is a contract between government and the governed.

2. Explain the importance of each of these documents:

   • Magna Carta

   • Petition of Right

   • English Bill of Rights

3. Explain how the struggles between the monarchy and the nobility led to limited government in Great Britain.

Activities

1. Learn more about the social, economic, and political aspects of feudalism. Find information in your library or on the Internet. Create a diagram that illustrates how the system worked.

2. Create a script for a talk show for an imaginary television station. The host of the program can interview some of the historical figures who lived during the time mentioned in this lesson, such as William the Conqueror, King John, noblemen, vassals, and commoners.

3. Imagine that you are a member of the nobility living in England in the 1200s. Write a letter to the editor or draw an editorial cartoon illustrating the importance of the rights listed in the Magna Carta.

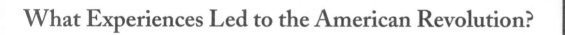

What Experiences Led to the American Revolution?

LESSON PURPOSE

This lesson explains how British ideas about government were put to use in the colonies. The lesson also describes why the colonists came to feel that the British government threatened their rights.

LESSON OBJECTIVES

When you finish this lesson, you should be able to

❑ explain how constitutional government developed in the colonies, and

❑ explain why the colonists decided to fight for their independence.

TERMS TO UNDERSTAND

- charter
- committees of correspondence
- Daughters of Liberty
- First Continental Congress
- Second Continental Congress
- Sons of Liberty
- writs of assistance

This is the royal charter for the state of Delaware. What is a charter? Why did the colonists need one?

Which ideas did the colonists in America use to create their governments?

To establish a British colony, one generally needed to have a charter from the king. A **charter** is a legal document. In colonial times, a charter granted land to a person or a company along with the right to start a colony on that land.

Most colonial charters said little about what kind of government a colony should have. As a result, the settlers had to develop their own form of government. Each of the thirteen colonies had a government of its own.

In creating their own governments, the colonists tried to do two things. They tried to protect themselves from abuse of power by the British government. They also tried to protect themselves from abuse of power by their colonial governments. To achieve these goals, the colonists used the basic ideas of constitutional government. All colonial governments were based on the following ideas:

How did the colonists try to protect themselves from the abuse of power by the British government and their own colonial governments?

1. **Natural rights** Colonial governments were based on the idea that the purpose of government is to protect the people's natural rights to life, liberty, and property.

2. **Representative government** The colonists elected representatives to their colonial legislatures. The first elected legislature was in Virginia in 1619.

3. **Rule of law** The colonists created a government of laws. The people who made and enforced the laws did not have unlimited power and they, too, had to obey the laws. The colonial governments recognized the idea of higher law. This meant that colonial governments could not pass laws that violated the British constitution.

4. **Separation of powers** The powers of the colonial governments were divided among three branches.

   - A governor headed the executive branch. The governor carried out and enforced the law. In most colonies, the king or the owner of the colony appointed the governor.

   - The legislative branch made the laws. Most colonies had legislatures with two houses.

   - The judicial branch was made up of judges or magistrates. The governor usually appointed the judges. The judges were responsible for handling conflicts about the laws. The judges presided at the trials of people accused of a crime. The judges also made sure that colonial laws did not violate the British constitution.

5. **Checks and balances** In many colonies, the branches of government shared power, but one branch could check the use of power by another branch. For example, the governors could not collect taxes without the consent of the legislature.

What do you think?

1. What differences, if any, were there between the colonial governments and our state and national governments today?

2. Were the colonial governments "constitutional governments"? Why or why not?

Why did the British government tighten control over the colonies?

For much of the colonial period, Great Britain paid little attention to the colonies. Britain had become a world power and was often busy fighting wars in Europe. The government in Britain did not have much time to devote to the colonies. In addition, the colonies were a long distance away. Communication between the colonies and Britain was slow because news had to travel by ship.

News of events in the colonies reached Britain months later. Orders from the

What does this picture illustrate about British control over the American colonies for most of the colonial period?

government to the colonies took months to arrive.

During the years of British neglect, the colonists became used to ruling themselves. Further, the colonists had been able to ignore many of the laws made by Parliament.

By the mid-1700s, however, the British began to show a new interest in the colonies. In 1763, Britain won a long and costly war against France. The cost of the conflict left the British with a large national debt. Parliament saw the colonies as a source of much-needed money. They felt that the colonies should pay their portion of the cost of the war since, among other reasons, the British army had protected colonists on the western frontier from Native American tribes who were helping the French. To reduce the national debt, Parliament raised taxes in both Britain and the colonies. The British government also began to tighten trade regulations between the colonies and other nations.

These are some examples of British laws that affected the colonies:

- **Proclamation of 1763** The law banned settlement in certain western lands. Its purpose was to reduce tensions between the colonists and Native Americans. The British army could then withdraw from the frontier and, thus, save the government money.

- **Sugar Act of 1764** The purpose of the law was to stop the smuggling of goods into and out of the colonies. It gave the British navy greater power to search colonial ships. Naval officers used **writs of assistance**, or search warrants, that allowed them to board colonial ships. The law also required products such as tobacco, sugar, and timber to be shipped directly from the colonies to Britain. The law set taxes on cloth, sugar, coffee, and wine coming into the colonies.

- **Stamp Act, 1765** The law imposed a tax on every legal document, newspaper, pamphlet, and deck of cards coming into the colonies.

What events led the British government to tighten its control over the colonies? Were the British justified? Why or why not?

- **Quartering Act, 1765** The British government moved the army from the western lands into the cities. The law required colonists who were innkeepers or public officials to house and feed the British soldiers.

- **Declaratory Act, 1766** The law stated that Parliament had the right to pass laws for the colonies in "all cases whatsoever." Its purpose was to remind the colonists that the authority of the king and Parliament was superior to colonial governments.

- **Tea Act, 1773** The law gave the East India Company the sole right to sell tea to the colonies. The East India Company was a large and important corporation in Britain. The purpose of the law was to keep the company from going broke.

The colonists viewed the new laws differently than did the government in Great Britain. Many colonists came to believe that Parliament was threatening their rights. They believed that Britain was becoming oppressive.

The tax and trade laws meant that some colonists would lose money. More important, the laws went against the colonists' belief in representative government. The colonies had no right to elect representatives to Parliament. Therefore, the colonists claimed, Parliament had no right to tax the colonies.

What was the result of colonial resistance?

The colonists felt that tax laws should be passed only by their colonial legislatures. "No taxation without representation" became a rallying cry of the colonists.

To the British, the laws seemed reasonable. King George felt that the colonists were acting like ungrateful children. The well-being and safety of the colonies were due to the help they got from the British government. It was only fair that the colonists pay their share of the cost of government. The issue of representation made little sense to most British people. Parliament did not represent individuals. Nor did it represent areas of the country. Instead, Parliament represented the interests of the whole nation, no matter where British subjects lived.

What do you think?

1 Which positions did the British government take that you consider reasonable and fair? Why?

2 Which positions did the British government take that you consider unreasonable and unfair? Why?

3 Which positions did the colonists take that you consider reasonable and fair? Why?

4 Which positions did the colonists take that you consider unreasonable and unfair? Why?

5 Each of the following illustrates an event resulting from the enforcement of British laws in the colonies. Examine each situation. List the right or rights each person might claim the British government had violated. Then, explain why you think having each right is important.

A Elsbeth Merrill was baking bread and awaiting the return of her husband. An agent of the king arrived at her inn. The agent informed her that she must house and feed four British soldiers.

B Lemuel Adams had a warehouse full of goods near Boston Harbor. The king's magistrate issued a writ of assistance allowing British officials to search all homes, stores, and warehouses in Boston. The officials used the writ to search his business for evidence of smuggling.

C James Otis was a lawyer who represented people who were in prison. A judge denied prisoners a trial by a jury in their own community. Otis argued that this was illegal because it violated the British constitution. The judge denied his request and sent the prisoners to England for trial.

D William Bradford printed an article in his newspaper criticizing the deputy governor of his colony. The king appointed the deputy governor. Bradford wrote that the deputy governor was like a "large cocker spaniel about five foot five." He was arrested and his printing press was destroyed.

How did the colonists resist British control?

Between 1763 and 1775, tension was growing between the colonies and the British government. To protest against British actions the colonists organized town meetings and wrote angry letters to the newspapers. They also put together independent voluntary groups that organized other ways to resist the British.

The most significant of these groups were the **committees of correspondence**. Their mission was to make sure that each colony knew about events and opinions in the other colonies. Although the committees began as voluntary associations, their success led to their establishment by most of the colonial governments. The committees raised the spirits of the people and united them against the British. Eventually all the colonies were linked by committees of correspondence.

Two other important groups were the **Sons of Liberty** and the **Daughters of Liberty**. The Sons began in 1765 and quickly spread throughout the country. The Sons of Liberty organized resistance to the Stamp Act. Mobs of people attacked the homes of tax collectors. The Sons of Liberty burned effigies, or straw dummies, made to look like royal officials. They marched in the streets and sometimes committed violent acts.

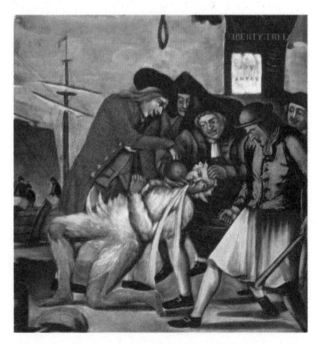

Why were the colonists so unhappy with British rule?

Women soon got together and formed the Daughters of Liberty. They helped to make the boycott of British trade effective. Instead of buying British goods, they began spinning their own yarn and making their own linen. After the British Parliament passed the Tea Act of 1773, many women gave up drinking tea.

Both the Sons and Daughters of Liberty continued with acts of resistance until the start of the Revolutionary War. There were two well-known events that resulted in violence.

- **The Boston Massacre, 1770** British troops opened fire on a crowd of protesters outside the customs house in Boston. Five people died as a result. The tragedy convinced many colonists that the British government would use military force to make them obey the laws.

- **The Boston Tea Party, 1773** The colonists attempted to prevent the unloading of a cargo of tea that had arrived in Boston Harbor. The protesters ripped open 342 chests and dumped the tea into the harbor. The British responded by closing the harbor to all trade.

By the fall of 1774, these events had led many colonists to decide that it was time to take united action. The committees of correspondence called for representatives from all the colonies to meet in a general congress once a year. They were to deliberate on the general interests of all the colonies.

This call laid the foundation for the Continental Congress. The **First Continental Congress** met in Philadelphia. Twelve of the thirteen colonies sent representatives. It was the start of a unified American government. The purpose of the Congress was to decide on the best response to the actions of the British government. The members of Congress agreed to impose

What happened at the First Continental Congress?

their own ban on trade with Great Britain. Congress hoped that this move would force the British government to change its policies toward the colonies.

On April 19, 1775, fighting broke out between Great Britain and the American colonies. On that day, British troops marched to the towns of Lexington and Concord in Massachusetts. The army was supposed to capture hidden guns and supplies by surprise, but a system of signals warned the Americans. The Americans fired on the British and forced them back to Boston. That was the beginning of the Revolutionary War.

A few weeks later, representatives of the colonies met in Philadelphia for the **Second Continental Congress**. The delegates to the Congress decided to resist the British. Congress organized the Continental Army and called upon the colonies to send troops. The delegates selected George Washington to lead the army. A year later, Congress asked a committee to draft a document explaining why the colonists felt it was necessary to free themselves from British rule. This document is known as the Declaration of Independence.

Reviewing and Using the Lesson

1. Why was it necessary for the colonists to create their own colonial governments?

2. What ideas of constitutional government did the colonists use in creating their governments?

3. Why did the British begin to tighten control over the colonies after 1763?

4. What tax and trade laws did Parliament pass? What was the purpose of these laws? What effects did the laws have on the colonists?

5. Why did the colonists feel that the laws passed by Parliament violated their rights?

6. Why did the British believe that the tax and trade laws were fair?

Activities

1. Many people and groups played important roles in the Revolutionary War. Choose one of the organizations listed below to research. Share what you learn with your class.
   - Committees of Correspondence
   - Daughters of Liberty
   - Sons of Liberty

2. Research the life of Thomas Paine using the school library or the Internet. Write a review of his pamphlet, *Common Sense*. Explain the importance of Thomas Paine's writing to the Revolutionary War.

3. Imagine that you were living in the colonies in the 1770s. Write a speech arguing why the laws passed by Parliament violated your rights. Then, imagine that you were a Member of Parliament. Write a speech arguing why these laws were necessary. Present your speeches to the class.

4. Create a timeline of the important events discussed in this lesson. Illustrate your timeline with drawings.

5. Draw two cartoons, one showing how the colonists felt about the Boston Tea Party and the other showing the same event from a British point of view.

What Basic Ideas about Government Are in the Declaration of Independence?

LESSON PURPOSE

One of the most important documents in American history is the Declaration of Independence. It summarizes the colonists' basic ideas about government. The Declaration lists the colonies' complaints against the British government. The Declaration also explains the reasons why the colonies decided to declare their independence from Great Britain.

LESSON OBJECTIVE

When you finish this lesson, you should be able to explain the main ideas that are in the Declaration of Independence.

TERMS TO UNDERSTAND

- abolish
- Loyalists
- natural law
- Patriots
- self-evident
- Tories
- unalienable rights

Why was the Declaration of Independence written?

On June 7, 1776, the Continental Congress called for the colonies to declare independence from Great Britain. The Congress had to inform the British and the world that the colonies were now free and independent states. The Congress wanted to be sure that the reasons for its actions were clear.

A committee to draft the Declaration of Independence was quickly appointed. Members of the committee were Benjamin Franklin, John Adams, Roger Sherman, Robert Livingston, and a young Virginian named Thomas Jefferson. Jefferson was a man of many talents. He was a statesman, diplomat, author, architect, and scientist. He was a member of the Continental Congress during the Revolutionary War. Jefferson was a quiet, shy man, not known as a great speaker. He worked well in small groups and was an excellent writer. The committee chose Jefferson to write the first draft of the Declaration of Independence.

Jefferson spent many days writing. He discussed the draft with other members of the committee. They suggested changes and Jefferson made the revisions. When the committee finished its work, they sent the document to Congress.

On July 4, 1776, the members of Congress passed the Declaration of Independence.

Why do you think Congress appointed a committee to draft the Declaration of Independence?

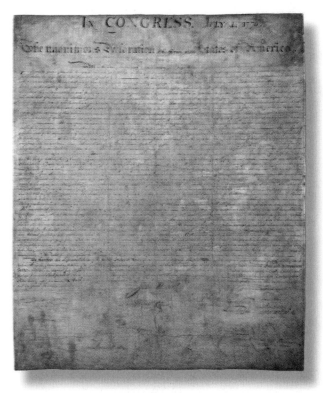

Why do you think the Founders wanted a written Declaration of Independence?

How is the Declaration of Independence organized?

The Declaration is not a very long document. It is easy to understand when you see how it is organized. The Declaration has four important parts.

- **Ideals** The Declaration sets forth the Founders' beliefs about the purposes of government. It explains how government is created. It is one of the best statements of the ideals of our nation.

- **Arguments** The Declaration gives the reasons why the colonies thought they were justified in breaking away from Great Britain.

- **Complaints** The Declaration includes a list of complaints against the British king. The items on the list are there to show

how the British government violated the rights of the colonists.

- **Conclusion** In the end, the Declaration states that the bond between Great Britain and the colonies is dissolved. It states "that these United Colonies are, and of Right ought to be, Free and Independent States."

What principles of government does the Declaration include?

The Declaration of Independence sets forth some of the most important ideals of our nation. The Declaration states that "all men are created equal" and that they all have certain basic rights. These are the rights to life, liberty, and the pursuit of happiness.

The second paragraph of the Declaration of Independence is included below. It contains some of the most fundamental principles and values of natural rights philosophy underlying the American political system.

*We hold these Truths to be **self-evident** [easy for anyone to see], that all Men are created equal, that they are endowed [given] by their Creator [God] with certain **unalienable Rights** [rights that cannot be taken away], that among these are Life, Liberty, and the Pursuit of Happiness—That to secure these Rights, Governments are instituted [established] among Men, deriving [receiving] their just Powers from the Consent [agreement] of the Governed, that whenever any Form of Government becomes destructive of these Ends [purposes], it is the Right of the People to alter or to abolish [overthrow or put an end to] it, and to institute new Government.*

Critical Thinking Exercise

Examining ideas from natural rights philosophy in the Declaration of Independence

It is worth looking carefully at each phrase in the above paragraph from the Declaration. and trying to interpret and reflect upon its meaning. Work with two or three other students to read the phrases below and respond to the questions related to them.

1 *We hold these Truths to be self-evident* [easy for anyone to see] ...

List three things that you think are so obviously true that you don't need to explain *why* they are true.

2 *all Men are created equal ...*

Since it is obvious that all people are not equal in many ways, such as height, weight, skills, and abilities, in what way do you think the Declaration is saying they are equal? Do you agree? Why?

3 *all men ... are endowed by their Creator* [God] *with certain unalienable Rights* [rights that cannot be taken away],

What rights, if any, do you think cannot be taken away from people? Explain your reasoning.

4 *that among these* [rights] *are Life, Liberty, and the Pursuit of Happiness ...*

Explain what you think is meant by the right to life, the right to liberty, and the right to the pursuit of happiness.

5 *to secure these Rights, Governments are instituted* [established] *among Men,*

Explain what you think this means about why governments are created and what their purposes should be.

6 *Governments ... deriving* [receiving] *their just Powers from the Consent* [agreement] *of the Governed ...*

Why do you suppose this says that governments derive their "just Powers" from the consent of the governed?

7 *whenever any Form of Government becomes destructive of these Ends* [purposes], *it is the Right of the People to alter or to abolish* [overthrow or put an end to] *it, and to institute new Government.*

Under what conditions, if any, do you think people would be justified in changing or overthrowing their government?

What ideas from John Locke did Jefferson include in the Declaration of Independence?

What reasons does the Declaration give for independence?

The Declaration was a justification for the American Revolution. Jefferson used the ideas of natural rights philosophy in this argument. The main points of the argument are listed below. See if you can identify its relationship to natural rights philosophy.

1 The rights of the people are based on **natural law**. This means that there is an unchanging set of laws that govern human relations. Natural law is a higher law than law made by man. The Founders believed that natural law came from God. No constitution or government may violate the natural law. The only purpose of government is to protect the people's natural rights.

2 If a government violates the natural law, the people have the right to change or **abolish**—put an end to—that government and form a new one.

3 An agreement existed between the colonists and the king. The colonists consented to be governed by the king so long as he protected their rights to life, liberty, and property.

4 No agreement existed between the colonists and Parliament. Therefore, Parliament had no right to govern the colonies or to tax them. This was especially true, argued the colonists, since they did not have the right to send representatives to Parliament.

5 The king violated his agreement with the colonists. The king acted, along with Parliament, to deprive the colonists of their rights. Therefore, the colonists had the right to withdraw their consent to be governed by the king. The colonists were free to establish their own government.

According to natural rights philosophy, what do the people have a right to do when the government breaks its contract with them?

What complaints against the king does the Declaration include?

The Declaration contains a long list of complaints against the British king. For example, the Declaration accuses the king of

- refusing to approve laws necessary for the public good,

- seeking to destroy the colonial legislatures,

- obstructing justice by refusing to give certain powers to the colonial courts,

- keeping standing armies in time of peace,

- requiring the quartering or housing of British soldiers,

- imposing taxes without the consent of the people to be taxed,

- cutting off trade between the colonies and all parts of the world, and

- in some cases, denying the colonists the right to trial by jury.

What do you think?

Examine the text of the Declaration of Independence and select three complaints against the king or select three from the above list. Then complete the following steps.

- Rewrite the complaint in your own words.

- Explain the basis of the colonists' complaint.

- Explain what ideas about government are implied by each complaint.

Why do you suppose the writers of the Declaration focused their objections on King George III instead of on Parliament?

Why did some colonists want to remain British subjects?

To rebel against the British government was a serious matter. After all, generations of colonists had been loyal to Great Britain. It is understandable, then, that some people did not support the Revolution.

The colonists were almost evenly divided into those who supported the Revolution, those who did not, and the undecided. The people who remained loyal to the king were called **Loyalists** or **Tories**. They held deep feelings of loyalty to the home country.

Many Loyalists were large landowners, wealthy merchants, or officials of the king. The Loyalists did not like British taxes or other limits on their freedom any more than the Patriots did. But they did not think that

This drawing shows Loyalists in Virginia being forced to sign a document or risk being tarred and feathered. What rights of the Loyalists, if any, were violated by the Patriots?

breaking away from Britain was the answer to these problems.

Some colonial families split apart when the Revolution began. Family members chose sides. Those who supported the Revolution were called **Patriots**. Those who remained loyal to Britain were known as Loyalists. For example, Benjamin Franklin was a Patriot. His son was a Loyalist.

Many Loyalists joined the British army and fought for the king. Some Loyalists moved back to Great Britain while others went to Canada or the West Indies. Those Loyalists who remained in the colonies had a hard time. Sometimes their property was taken from them. Sometimes they were humiliated or put in jail. Even so, the Loyalists as a group suffered less than dissenters in other revolutions.

Critical Thinking Exercise

Patriots and Loyalists

Both the Patriots and the Loyalists held strong opinions about the Revolution. Patriots and Loyalists came from all sections of American life. Native Americans were forced to choose sides in the struggle. African Americans were Loyalists as well as Patriots.

Complete the following exercise to help understand both sides of the issue. If you are studying as a part of a class, you should divide into groups and debate both sides of the issue.

Supporter of the Revolution: A Patriot—
You are a member of the Second Continental Congress. Write a letter to your family or the editor of a colonial newspaper defending the actions of the Congress.

Supporter of the British: A Loyalist—
You are a colonial official, a sheriff, or a British soldier in the colonies. Write a letter to the editor of a colonial newspaper explaining why the British actions were justified.

Reviewing and Using the Lesson

1. What were the reasons for writing the Declaration of Independence?

2. What are the four parts of the Declaration of Independence?

3. What arguments does the Declaration make in support of the colonies' independence?

4. What complaints did the colonists have against the king of Great Britain?

5. What is the purpose of government as described in the Declaration of Independence?

6. What does the Declaration say people have the right to do if a government does not protect their rights?

7. What do the following phrases from the Declaration mean?

   • "all men are created equal"

   • "consent of the governed"

   • "self-evident"

   • "unalienable rights"

Activities

1. Rewrite the first two paragraphs of the Declaration of Independence in contemporary language. Share your revision with the class.

2. Read a novel about the Revolutionary War, such as *April Morning*, *Johnny Tremain*, *Cast Two Shadows*, or *My Brother Sam Is Dead*. Select a character from the story. Explain his or her opinions about the Revolutionary War.

3. Play the online game *The Road to Revolution* or another online game about the American Revolution: http://www.pbs.org/ktca/liberty/road.html.

What Happened during the American Revolution?
How Did the Government Function?

LESSON PURPOSE

In this lesson, you will learn what happened during the American Revolutionary War with Britain. You will also learn about the significance of the war for the rest of the world. You will learn about the difficulties of the colonists during the war and the role played by diplomacy.

LESSON OBJECTIVES

When you finish this lesson, you should be able to

❑ explain the course of the war and how the colonial armies overcame extreme difficulties, and

❑ explain some problems of government that Congress had to deal with during the war.

TERMS TO UNDERSTAND

- Battle of Saratoga
- diplomacy
- Quebec Campaign
- "The shot heard 'round the world"
- treason
- Treaty of Paris
- Yorktown Surrender

Where did the phrase "the shot heard 'round the world" come from? What does it mean?

How did the Revolutionary War begin, and what was its significance?

The night before fighting broke out, Paul Revere made his famous midnight ride. He warned members of the citizen militia, called Minutemen, to get ready to fight. They gathered in Lexington and Concord in Massachusetts. The role of the citizen militia reminds us that citizens are sometimes called upon to perform service to their nation. Calling upon the citizen militia as Revere did also gives us insight into why the Founders added the Second Amendment to the Constitution. The amendment says that "a well-regulated militia being necessary to the security of a free State, the right of the people to keep and bear Arms shall not be infringed."

The Revolutionary War, which lasted for six long years, ended in victory for the former American colonists. You learned in Lesson 7 that the first shots were fired on April 19, 1775. That morning, skirmishes between American colonists and British soldiers broke out. The gunfire that opened the fighting later became known as **"the shot heard 'round the world."** People said this because news of the American rebellion and its demand for independence spread all over the world. Many nations eventually made the same demand of their own colonial rulers. The American Revolution changed world history. Achieving independence, however, was far more difficult than declaring it. Success often seemed impossible, but the Americans did not give up.

What did the Second Continental Congress do to direct the Revolution?

On July 4, 1776, Congress issued its formal Declaration of Independence, making a complete break from Britain. There was no turning back. The Continental Congress endured great difficulties in trying to govern during the Revolution. There were many arguments among the delegates to Congress. Because it did not have a legal charter for its existence, Congress could not force the former colonies, now independent states, to pay the costs of fighting the British. So, soldiers often went unpaid, unfed, and without uniforms.

To finance military expenses, Congress decided to issue paper money. But the paper was not backed by any precious metal. Therefore, it could not hold a steady, reliable value. Paper money did not solve the problem of lack of funds, which remained for the whole war.

Congress tried to remedy the lack of a legal basis for its existence. In November 1777, Congress passed the Articles of Confederation. It was the country's first constitution. But the states took their time in agreeing to the new frame of government. It was not until March 1, 1781, when the fighting was nearly over, that the Articles took effect. Even then, the Articles did not solve the problems of the new national government. You will learn more about the Articles of Confederation in Lesson 11.

What problems were faced by the Continental Congress?

What did the battles of Trenton and Princeton do for American morale?

How successful were the Americans at the beginning of the Revolutionary War?

At the beginning of the war, the Americans were not successful. They invaded Canada in the **Quebec Campaign** of 1775–76, but failed. Then in August 1776, in the Battle of Long Island, near New York City, the British defeated George Washington. But he managed to save most of his troops from capture. This occurred only two months after independence was declared.

The military situation was bleak. Washington understood how grave matters were. He tried to rally the former colonists, about a third of whom were against independence and another third were neutral, to the cause of fighting for independence by making daring raids on British positions. Near the end of December, he crossed the ice-choked Delaware River and won small battles at Trenton and Princeton, New Jersey. But prospects for the American cause were poor. The troops needed food, their pay, and equipment.

In 1777, Washington lost more encounters with the British in Pennsylvania at Germantown and Brandywine Creek. In the same year, the British tried to strangle the Revolution by cutting the colonies in two. They took control of the Hudson River, which ran through New York. But the British failed. Instead, the Americans scored a victory in the **Battle of Saratoga**. Arms and supplies secretly sent by the French government through a private arms merchant arrived in time to help the Americans. This may have been the Revolution's most important campaign. The British plan had been defeated.

What was the importance of the Battle of Saratoga?

No one could see the importance of Saratoga until much later. In the meantime, conditions for the American army became desperate. Soldiers suffered terribly from lack of food and shelter during the winter of 1777–78 at their quarters in Valley Forge, Pennsylvania. But American spirits did not give out. Martha Washington joined her husband, sharing the hardships of a cold and bleak winter. She did what she could to assist the troops. She organized a campaign for supplies that the soldiers desperately needed. She was aided in her efforts by Benjamin Franklin's daughter, Sarah Franklin Bache. Together, they collected 2,200 shirts and 400 pairs of stockings for the freezing men.

During this winter in Valley Forge, Baron von Steuben, a German volunteer, gave important assistance by training the cold, ragged, half-starved soldiers. He raised their morale and helped make them into an effective fighting force. Some troops deserted, but others endured the terrible cold and hunger. The young French aristocrat and military commander, the Marquis de Lafayette, who was devoted to the American cause for independence, also spent the winter at Valley Forge. When spring arrived, the American forces, though in tatters, had endured.

How did Martha Washington contribute to the success of the Revolutionary War?

Why was Benjamin Franklin successful in his diplomatic mission to France?

What part did diplomacy play in the outcome of the war?

Events happening elsewhere, however, eventually turned the tide in the Americans' favor. Perhaps the most important event of 1778 occurred across the Atlantic in France. Congress had sent Silas Deane to France in 1776. He was successful in gaining arms and supplies as well as the services of competent military officers.

Later, however, Congress sent Benjamin Franklin to Paris, the capital of France, to seek aid. Franklin's fame as a writer and scientist preceded him. The French, who were sworn enemies of the British, admired him. For his part, Franklin showed great skill in diplomacy. **Diplomacy** is the practice of carrying on formal relationships with governments of other countries. The official representatives of countries meet and discuss issues important to their governments. They work together in a peaceful manner to find solutions to common problems.

In 1778, aided by the American victory at Saratoga, Franklin secured formal treaties between France and the United States. The new alliance ensured the assistance of the French army and navy.

Making the most of his enormous popularity among the French, Franklin asked for loan after loan and was never refused. Franklin was not above hinting that the colonists might make peace with Britain, France's enemy, if the Americans did not receive what they needed. In the end, French loans and soldiers and, especially, France's navy were critical were critical for the final victory in 1781.

What happened in the South during the war?

Little fighting took place in the Middle Atlantic region after Saratoga. In 1778–79, fighting shifted to the western frontier area, now Indiana, and to the South. Military campaigns took place in North and South Carolina and in Georgia, where Savannah fell to the British.

In South Carolina, Charleston had resisted two British attacks. But in 1780 it, too, fell to the British.

Things were not going well with the American army in other parts of the former colonies. In 1780, the Americans had to endure the **treason**—the betrayal of one's country—of General Benedict Arnold when he defected to the British. Complaints about the inefficient government of Congress were voiced. Congress did not have the authority to raise money for the war from taxes. The government could only beg for funds from the states, but received little. Conditions regarding food, clothing, and pay were so poor that in January 1781, some of the soldiers could stand it no longer, so they rebelled.

In the South, where most of the fighting was now taking place, there were great hardships. One example is that of Eliza Lucas Pinckney. She was a plantation owner famous for growing new crops to avoid dependence on cotton. When war broke out, Pinckney decided not to follow her economic interests. Believing in the ideas of political liberty, she supported the Revolution. But she paid dearly for her views. The British took over her mansion, burned her crops, and killed her farm animals. By the end of the war, she was economically ruined.

What was one consequence of the inability of Congress to tax the states?

This scene depicts the surrender of Lord Cornwallis at Yorktown on October 17, 1781. What events led the British to surrender?

How did the Revolutionary War turn in the Americans' favor and come to an end?

By the early 1780s, military matters in the South turned for the better. In 1780, American forces had defeated the British at King's Mountain, South Carolina. In the following year, American commanders forced the British army under Lord Cornwallis to leave the Carolinas and retreat to Virginia. Cornwallis soon found his armies trapped on the Yorktown Peninsula. With the French navy blocking the way, the British were unable to retreat by water.

Lafayette led American troops in containing the British on land. To the north, combined American–French forces marched south from New York to Virginia. On October 17–19, 1781, seeing that their position was hopeless, the British forces under Lord Cornwallis finally **surrendered at Yorktown**. The fighting was over. Two years later, in 1783, a formal peace treaty, known as the **Treaty of Paris**, was signed. A **treaty** is an official agreement between two or more countries. American independence was formally recognized.

Reviewing and Using the Lesson

1. What was the significance of the Revolutionary War for the world?

2. How did the American army stay together during the worst times of the early part of the Revolutionary War?

3. What problems did the Second Continental Congress have during the war, and how did Congress deal with them?

4. How did the Congress attempt to provide a legal basis for its authority?

5. What role did diplomacy play in the war?

6. How important was the assistance of France in the American victory?

7. What military campaigns led up to the end of Revolutionary War?

Activities

Listed below are examples of those who played significant roles in the American Revolution during the years leading to the outbreak of fighting and during the Revolutionary War. They did so through political, diplomatic, or military leadership, or through other means. Look up at least one person in each group and find out who they were and why they are famous.

These are some **American colonists** who participated in significant ways in the Revolutionary War:

Abigail Adams	Patrick Henry	Molly Pitcher
John Adams	Agrippa Hull	Paul Revere
Samuel Adams	Thomas Jefferson	Deborah Simpson
Crispus Attucks	Henry Knox	Haym Solomon
Benjamin Franklin	George Mason	Mercy Otis Warren
Horatio Gates	Robert Morris	George Washington
Nathaniel Greene	Thomas Paine	Martha Washington
John Hancock	Eliza Lucas Pinckney	"Mad" Anthony Wayne

These are some **foreign supporters** who participated in significant ways in the Revolutionary War:

John Paul Jones (English)   Thaddeus Kosciuszko (Polish)

Marquis de Lafayette (French)   Baron Friedrich von Steuben (German)

How Did the States Govern Themselves after the Revolution?

LESSON PURPOSE

Shortly after the start of the Revolutionary War in 1775, many of the new states began to write their constitutions. In this lesson you will learn about these new state constitutions. You will explore the basic ideas on which the new governments were founded.

LESSON OBJECTIVES

When you finish this lesson, you should be able to

❑ describe the basic ideas on which the new state governments were founded, and

❑ explain the major differences between the Massachusetts constitution and the constitutions of the other states.

TERMS TO UNDERSTAND

- legislative supremacy
- petition
- popular sovereignty
- veto

What were the basic ideas about government in the state constitutions?

After the Declaration of Independence, British government in the colonies came to an end. The colonies were free and independent states. Each state would have to create a new government.

The people wanted state governments that would protect their basic rights and promote the common good. When they began to write their state constitutions, they used the ideas they had learned from political philosophy. They also used what they had learned from their own experience with colonial and British government.

The ideas they included in the state constitutions were not new. Most of the ideas had been used in the governments of the colonies. The Founders tried to design their new governments with the best ideas from the past. Their experiences with these state governments would help them design the Constitution in 1787.

These are the basic ideas that the Founders included in their state constitutions.

1 **Natural rights and higher law** The purpose of government is to protect the rights of citizens to life, liberty, and property. Each state constitution was a higher law that everyone had to obey.

2 **Social contract** Each state made it clear that it believed government is formed as a social contract. The people agreed to form a government to protect their natural rights.

3 **Popular sovereignty** The term *sovereign* means to have the highest authority or power. **Popular sovereignty** means that the people are the highest authority. All

John Hancock was a governor of Massachusetts and a signer of the Declaration of Independence. In what ways did state constitutions limit the power of the governor?

the states adopted the idea that the people are the source of the authority of government. The people delegate their authority to government. Government gets its right to govern from the people.

4 **Representation** Each state considered it very important that the legislature be made up of elected representatives of the people. In most states, the right to vote was limited to white men who owned property. About seventy percent of the white men in America owned enough property to be able to vote. In contrast, only about ten percent were eligible to vote in Great Britain.

5 **Separation of powers** All the states used some form of separation of powers. They divided government into legislative, executive, and judicial branches.

6 **Checks and balances** Although the states favored a strong legislature, the constitutions did provide for some checks. Most of the checks were within the legislatures themselves. Most legislatures had two houses. Each house could check the power

of the other. The people also could check the power of the legislatures. The voters could elect new representatives to both houses if they did not like the way the government was working.

7 **Legislative supremacy** The majority of the states set up governments in which most of the power was given to the legislature. This system of government is known as **legislative supremacy**. The Founders believed that because the people elected the legislature, it was the most democratic branch of government. They were afraid of giving too much power to the executive branch. They remembered how the royal governors and the king had abused their power. So most of the state governors were given very limited power.

Despite checks on the power of the legislative branch, the legislature had far greater power than the other two branches of government. Legislative supremacy led to some serious problems in most states.

- State governments did not protect the property rights of some citizens. In these states, factions—groups of people who seek to promote their own interests—gained control of the legislature. The factions were accused of making laws that benefited themselves rather than the common good. They passed laws that canceled debts and they created paper money. These laws benefited the people who owed money and hurt those who had loaned it to them.

- The state legislatures passed laws that taxed and controlled their citizens far more than the British had done. The level of taxes during the 1780s was ten to twenty times what it had been before the Revolution.

- Many new state laws were passed which interfered with the private lives of the citizens. Laws were passed telling people what they should eat, drink, wear, and believe.

Why do you think most states required people to own property in order to be eligible to vote?

What was important about the Massachusetts constitution?

Massachusetts was the last state to write its constitution. The citizens adopted the state constitution in 1780. The people there had learned some important lessons from the experiences of the other states. They used this knowledge in creating their state government.

Most of the other states used the idea of legislative supremacy to protect people's rights. The Massachusetts constitution, however, distributed power more evenly among the branches of government. The governor had more power and was more independent of the legislature. This was possible because the people elected the governor directly. The people expected the governor to protect their interests.

Here is how some of the powers of the governor of Massachusetts were balanced in relation to the legislature.

- The governor received a fixed salary. His salary could not be changed by the legislature.

- The governor could **veto**—refuse to sign—proposed laws put forth by the legislature. A two-thirds vote of the legislature was needed to override his veto.

- The governor could appoint officials in the executive branch. He could also appoint judges in the judicial branch.

The Massachusetts constitution also divided the people into voting groups based on their wealth. They expected that government would then more accurately represent the interests of the groups that elected them.

- Only people with a large amount of property could vote for both the governor and the legislature.

- People with slightly less property could vote for both the upper and lower houses of the legislature.

- People with the minimum amount of property could only vote for the lower house of the legislature.

The experience of writing state constitutions was a useful one to the Founders. Americans were learning what type of government worked best. The differences between the Massachusetts constitution and those that were written earlier were a result of these experiences.

Did the Massachusetts constitution contradict the idea of popular sovereignty? Why or why not?

What do you think?

The illustrations below portray the difference between how power was distributed in the Massachusetts constitution and those of the other states. Answer the questions that follow.

1 How was power distributed in most states?

2 How did early state constitutions reflect Americans' fear of centralized political authority?

3 Which branch of government do you think is most responsive to the will of the people? Should that branch have more power than the other branches? Why or why not?

4 What might be the strengths and weaknesses of the way the Massachusetts state constitution distributed the right to vote for the lower and upper houses of its legislature and the leader of its executive branch?

What were the state declarations of rights?

The states did not depend solely on a system of separation of powers to protect people's rights. The first part of most state constitutions was a declaration of rights, or bill of rights. This section of the constitution listed the basic rights of citizens.

Listing the rights of the people first showed that citizens had certain basic rights that existed before the creation of the government. No constitution or government could take away these rights. Although the declarations of rights were different from state to state, they were all based on the idea that people have certain basic rights that must be protected.

How are the Virginia Declaration of Rights and the Bill of Rights similar? How are they different?

What important ideas are in the Virginia Declaration of Rights?

Virginia was the first state to adopt a bill of rights. George Mason wrote most of the Virginia Declaration of Rights. Mason later was opposed to the U.S. Constitution because it did not include a bill of rights. In writing Virginia's bill of rights, Mason relied on the writing of John Locke and the ideas of republican government.

The Virginia Declaration of Rights stated that

- all power comes from and is kept by the people,

- all men are by nature equally free and independent; they have certain basic rights that no social contract can take away, and

- government is created for the common good, protection, and safety of the people; if a government does not serve these purposes, the people have an inalienable right to alter or abolish it.

The Virginia Declaration of Rights also listed many of the rights that we enjoy today. These include the right to

- trial by jury,

- protection against forced self-incrimination,

- protection against cruel and unusual punishment,

- freedom of the press, and

- free exercise of religious beliefs.

Which of the freedoms protected by the states' bills of rights does this painting illustrate?

What rights were protected in the other states?

Most states adopted bills of rights like Virginia's. Some states' declarations also included the idea that civic virtue was essential to preserving freedom.

The states' bills of rights were different in the rights they chose to include or leave out. Most included such political guarantees as

- the right to vote by men who met certain property qualifications,

- free and frequent elections,

- freedom of speech and the press,

- the right to **petition** (make a formal request of) government, and

- no taxation without representation.

All the states' bills of rights included rights for people accused of a crime. These included the right to have

- an attorney,

- a jury trial,

- protection from illegal searches and seizure,

- protection against forced self-incrimination,

- protection from excessive bail and fines, and

- protection against cruel and unusual punishment.

Most of the states' bills of rights expressed a fear of standing armies. The bills of rights condemned standing armies in times of peace and the quartering of soldiers in civilian homes. Many bills of rights included the right of citizens to bear arms. The Vermont bill of rights was the first to outlaw the practice of slavery.

Reviewing and Using the Lesson

1. What basic ideas about good government were included in the state constitutions?

2. Why did Americans believe that the legislature was the most democratic branch of government?

3. Why did some Americans distrust the executive and judicial branches of government?

4. How did the Massachusetts constitution differ from the constitutions of other states? Why was this important?

5. What was the Virginia Declaration of Rights? What rights of citizens did it include?

6. What rights did the state constitutions protect?

Activities

1. These are a few examples of the rights listed in the Maryland constitution of 1776. Examine each and write a brief explanation of what the right means and why it is important.

   • That every man hath a right to petition the Legislature, for the redress of grievances, in a peaceable and orderly manner.

   • That no ... tax ... ought to be set ... without consent of the Legislature.

   • That no freeman ought to be taken, or imprisoned ... or deprived of his life, liberty, or property, but by the judgment of his peers, or by the law of the land.

   • That the liberty of the press ought to be inviolably preserved.

2. Create a news interview set in 1780. Interview your classmates acting as representatives of the states of Massachusetts and Virginia. During the interview, the representatives should discuss the differences between their state constitutions and why they are important.

3. Find a copy of your state's constitution. What are some of the rights that your state constitution protects? How does your state constitution compare with the Virginia Declaration of Rights?

LESSON
11

How Did the Articles of Confederation Organize the First National Government?

LESSON PURPOSE

Our first government, the Continental Congress, drew up a constitution stating its powers. This constitution was called the Articles of Confederation. In this lesson, you will learn about some of the problems the Founders faced in creating our first national government. You will learn about the successes of the first national government. You also will learn about the weaknesses of government under the Articles and why some people believed that a new constitution was necessary.

LESSON OBJECTIVES

When you finish this lesson, you should be able to

❑ explain how the Articles organized the national government, and

❑ explain how the problems with the Articles caused the Founders to write a new constitution.

TERMS TO UNDERSTAND

- Articles of Confederation
- national government
- Northwest Ordinance
- Shays' Rebellion

What are the Articles of Confederation?

Once the war against Great Britain had started, each state was like a separate nation. Each state had its own constitution and government. To the people, their state was their country.

The Founders believed that a **national government** was needed to unify the states and to conduct the war. A national government could also control trade and manage conflicts among the states. The states also needed to be united in how they related with the rest of the world.

On June 7, 1776, Richard Henry Lee introduced two proposals to the Second Continental Congress. In one, Lee proposed independence from Great Britain. In the other, Lee proposed a national government to unify the states. Both resolutions were adopted.

Our nation's first constitution was the **Articles of Confederation**. The Articles created our first national government. Congress adopted the Articles in 1777. Final approval by the states occurred in 1781, and then the Articles came into effect.

What was our nation's first constitution?

What problems did the Founders face in writing the Articles of Confederation?

It was not easy to write and agree upon a constitution for the United States. The Founders had to deal with a number of difficult questions. What type of national government should they create? How much power should they give it?

The first problem the Founders faced was the people's fear of a strong national government. Americans believed that the British government had deprived people of their rights. They thought this was likely to happen with any national government that was both powerful and far away from the people. Citizens were convinced that government should be close to the people. That way the people could control their government and make certain that it did not violate their rights.

The second problem the Founders faced was the fear that some states would have more power in a national government than other states. The leaders in each state wanted to make sure that a national government would not threaten their state's interests. As a result, the most important issue was how states would vote in Congress. Would each

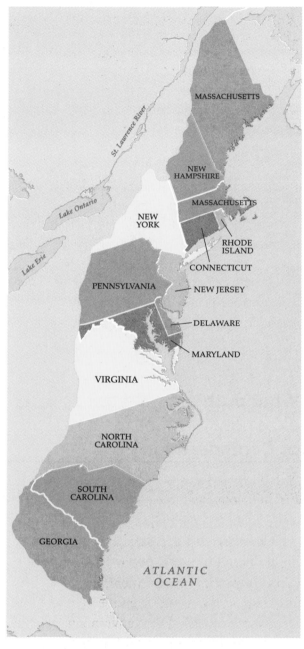

Looking at this map, why would some Founders fear that some states would have more power in a national government than others?

How did the Articles of Confederation organize the national government?

The Founders did agree that the states needed a central government. Their solution to fears of a strong national government was to create a weak one. The national government under the Articles of Confederation was simply a legislature, Congress; there were no executive or judicial branches.

The states were afraid that Congress might be able to control them. So they made sure that Congress was weak and its powers limited. The Articles left most of the powers of government with the states. The national government had little power over the states and their citizens. Every action taken by Congress had to be with the consent, approval, and cooperation of the states.

To solve the problem of representation, the Articles gave each state one vote in Congress. The more populous states did not have more than one vote. The Articles also provided that on important matters, such as declaring war, nine states would have to agree. This way, the seven less populated states could not outvote the six larger states.

state have one vote? Would states with greater population or wealth have more votes than the other states? Decisions in the Congress would be made by majority vote. Some leaders were afraid that the majority would use its power for its own interest at the expense of those who were in the minority.

Why did the Founders keep the power of the national government weak?

What did the national government achieve under the Articles of Confederation?

Although the national government was weak under the Articles of Confederation, it was responsible for a number of important achievements.

- It successfully waged the war for independence against Great Britain.

- It negotiated the Treaty of Paris, the peace treaty that ended the American Revolution.

- It provided that each state recognize the laws of the other states. For example, a marriage in one state would be valid in all other states. A citizen could travel freely from one state to another. Criminals who had crossed state borders could be sent back to the state in which they committed their crime.

Why was public education important in the new American territories?

- It passed the **Northwest Ordinance** of 1787. This was the most important law passed by Congress under the Articles. It gave people in the Northwestern lands the right to organize their own governments. Once they had done this, they could ask to be admitted as new states with the same rights as the original thirteen states. The law also provided for public education and forbade slavery. The Western settlers were guaranteed freedom of worship, the right to trial by jury, and due process of law.

These were major accomplishments. There were serious problems with the national government, however, that led to the decision to develop a new constitution.

What problems did the country experience under the Articles of Confederation?

Governing the nation under the Articles of Confederation was difficult. Here is a list of some problems the nation experienced:

- **Congress did not have any money and it did not have the power to raise money** Congress had no power to tax. All Congress could do was to ask the states to pay certain amounts to support the costs of the national government. The states argued about paying their fair shares of government expenses. Some states refused to pay. Congress could do nothing to force a state to pay its fair share.

- **Congress had no power over the state governments or their citizens** State governments and individual citizens often ignored the laws passed by Congress. Congress had no way to make people obey its laws. For example, at the end of

What problems did Congress face without the financial support of the states?

the Revolutionary War Congress signed a treaty with Great Britain. In the treaty, Congress promised to respect the rights of the Loyalists and ensure that they were treated fairly. Some state governments refused to respect the treaty. Those states refused to return property they had taken away from the Loyalists. These states also refused to force payment of money owed to the Loyalists before the start of the war. Thus, the national government was unable to live up to its promise to the British.

- **Congress could not make the states live up to trade agreements with other nations** Sometimes citizens imported goods from other countries and then refused to pay for them. This made people in foreign countries unwilling to trade with the United States. Many Americans lost money because they could not sell their goods to people in other nations.

- **Congress had no power to regulate trade among the states** Congress had no power to make laws regulating trade among the states. States taxed goods going from one state to another. Trading often became impossible. Business slowed down and people lost their jobs.

- **Citizens thought that their property rights were threatened** Many people believed that the states were not protecting the property rights of their citizens. Some people in the states had formed factions to promote their own interests at the expense of the common good. These factions with special interests became the majority in some state legislatures. People accused the factions of making laws to benefit themselves while ignoring the property rights of the minority. For example, they passed laws that canceled debts for those who were members of the faction and other laws that confiscated the property of people who had been Loyalists. People who were hurt by such laws argued that the states were not protecting the property of all citizens. Many people thought that a strong national government was needed to protect property rights.

Why was Shays' Rebellion important?

By 1786, many Americans were in financial trouble. Businesses failed, trade suffered, and many people were in debt. Soldiers who had fought in the Revolution still had not been paid. Congress could not control the country and people worried about what would happen.

Farmers in Massachusetts had serious economic problems. Farm prices were low, and when farmers could not pay their debts, many lost their farms and homes. Some were even put in prison. Many people claimed that the new state taxes had put them in debt. As a result, they felt that the state was not protecting their interests.

Then a dramatic series of events that became known as **Shays' Rebellion** finally convinced many Americans that it was time for a change. In an attempt to keep the state from taking their farms, local farmers under the leadership of Daniel Shays began to close down the courts where their cases were heard. The action against the courts spread to other towns and into neighboring states.

In January 1787, Shays led 2,000 rebels to Springfield, Massachusetts, to raid the federal arsenal for weapons. Shays' Rebellion frightened many property owners. The rebellion failed when the governor called out the militia to put it down. However, people feared that the actions of the farmers might become widespread. People were asking how the country could continue to exist if it could not maintain law and order.

How did Shays' Rebellion force people to examine the weaknesses of the national government?

In January of 1786, Virginia had invited all the states to send delegates to a meeting to be held in Annapolis the following September. The purpose of the meeting was to consider trade problems. Only five states sent representatives to the Annapolis meeting. Without the other states present, the delegates who did attend the meeting were not able to accomplish much.

Everyone who was there, however, agreed that the regulation of trade could not be discussed separately from the larger political issues. The general discontent was leading to outbreaks of violence such as those led by Daniel Shays. The delegates decided to write a report for Congress. In the report, they asked for a convention of all the states.

After much debate, Congress agreed and invited the states to send delegates to a convention in Philadelphia. This meeting would be "for the sole and express purpose of revising the Articles of Confederation."

What did Daniel Shays and his followers hope to gain from their rebellion?

Critical Thinking Exercise

Examining positions for and against a new constitution

Suppose that you were at the meeting in Philadelphia where delegates were supposed to improve the Articles of Confederation. A heated debate is taking place. Some people argue that the Articles are fine as they are. Some people want to make changes to the Articles. Others want to throw away the Articles and write a new constitution.

The following exercise that calls for you to create arguments on each side of the issue and then take and defend your own position. You may complete this exercise by yourself or work with two or three other students to do so.

• **Position 1: Defending the Articles of Confederation** Write an argument claiming that the Articles of Confederation are the best way to organize the national government. You should rely on the arguments in favor of a weak national government and strong state governments. Examine the successes of the national government under the Articles. Argue that the Articles should be kept, but revised to make up for their weaknesses. Then propose possible revisions.

• **Position 2: Claiming a new constitution is needed** Write an argument claiming that the Articles should be discarded and a new constitution written. Examine the arguments against a weak national government and the problems with the Articles listed in this lesson. Examine the events of Shays' Rebellion as one example of problems that might arise when there is no strong national government. Explain why you believe that the nation needs a new constitution.

• **Your position** Write what position you would take on whether or not a new constitution should be developed or the Articles revised.

Reviewing and Using the Lesson

1. Why did the people in the newly independent states fear a strong national government?

2. What were the Articles of Confederation? How did the Articles organize the national government to address the fears of the people and of the states?

3. What parts of government were not included in the Articles of Confederation?

4. What did the national government achieve under the Articles of Confederation?

5. What were the weaknesses of the national government under the Articles?

6. Why was Shays' Rebellion an important event?

Activities

1. Learn more about Shays' Rebellion. Make posters illustrating the farmers' point of view.

2. Create a short play that shows one of the problems of government under the Articles of Confederation. Perform the play for your class.

3. Learn more about the Northwest Ordinance of 1787. Explain how the ordinance provided for public education or the importance of forbidding slavery in the territories.

What Happened at the Philadelphia Convention?

What Happened at the Philadelphia Convention?

UNIT PURPOSE

You now are familiar with the knowledge and experiences of the Founders of our government. This unit will help you understand why the Framers, the men who created the Constitution, wrote the Constitution as they did. You will study the major problems facing the Framers and how they solved them.

When you complete this unit, you will be able to explain how the Constitution was written. You will also be able to describe some disagreements that occurred during the Philadelphia Convention and how they were solved. Finally, you will be able to explain how the Framers allocated powers to the executive and judicial branches.

KEY CONCEPTS

- Electoral College
- enumerated powers
- equal representation
- ex post facto law
- general welfare clause
- Great Compromise

- impeach
- jurisdiction
- necessary and proper clause
- proportional representation
- writ of habeas corpus

LESSON 12

Who Attended the Philadelphia Convention?
How Was It Organized?

LESSON PURPOSE

In this lesson, you will learn about the Philadelphia Convention of 1787. You will learn about some of the Framers who attended the convention. You will also learn about the decisions that the Framers made at the start of the meeting.

LESSON OBJECTIVES

When you finish this lesson, you should be able to

❑ explain why Congress called for the Philadelphia Convention, and

❑ explain the decisions that the delegates made at the start of the meeting.

TERMS TO UNDERSTAND

• Framers
• Philadelphia Convention

Who attended the Philadelphia Convention?

Congress called for a meeting to be held in Philadelphia in 1787. The members of Congress invited each state to send delegates. This important meeting is known as the **Philadelphia Convention**.

The purpose of the convention was to search for ways to improve the Articles of Confederation. At the end of the meeting, the delegates would submit a plan for Congress to approve. As far as members of Congress were concerned, the role of the delegates was advisory. But something very different was about to happen.

Fifty-five delegates attended the meeting. These delegates are called the **Framers** of the Constitution. All were men. Most were young. The average age was forty-two. Most had played important roles in the American Revolution. About three-fourths of the delegates had served in Congress. Most were leaders in their states. Some were rich; most were not, but nobody was poor.

The lives of all the Framers are worth learning about in detail. We will mention only a few.

James Madison Madison of Virginia is known as the "Father of the Constitution." His influence during the convention was great. This was partly because Madison brought with him a plan for creating a stronger national government. Madison's ideas were the basis for discussing how to structure a new government. Much of what we know about what happened at the convention is based on Madison's notes.

George Washington Washington was probably the most respected and honored man in the country. He was convinced that a stronger national government was necessary,

Why is James Madison known as the "Father of the Constitution"?

but he did not talk about it publicly. He did not want to become involved in politics. He preferred to return to Mount Vernon, Virginia, his home, to be a farmer. He thought that he had served enough. At first, Washington refused to attend the convention. He finally agreed. Washington was afraid that if he did not attend, people might think he had lost his faith in republican government.

George Washington refused to attend the convention at first. Why do you think his attendance at the convention was important?

Benjamin Franklin Franklin was eighty-one years old and in poor health. He attended the convention as a delegate from the state of Pennsylvania. Franklin was one of the most respected men in America. He had a long and distinguished career as a printer, inventor, writer, revolutionary, peacemaker, and diplomat. Franklin's primary role during the convention was to encourage the delegates to cooperate with each other when they disagreed. He also supported the important compromises reached during the convention.

Gouverneur Morris Morris was from New York. He had served in the state militia and in the New York legislature. Morris had also been a member of the Continental Congress. He was an exceptionally good speechmaker during the convention. He played an important role in writing the Constitution and prepared its final draft.

Critical Thinking Exercise

Organizing a constitutional convention

Imagine that the teachers and principal in your school have called for a convention to create a new constitution for the school. They have asked each class to send delegates to the convention. A **delegate** is a person who represents other people at a meeting. In this case, the delegates represent the people of each class. The delegates are to recommend a new constitution that will set forth the way the school is to be governed. It will include rules for students, teachers, and administrators. It will also include a list of rights of each group.

Write your answers to the following questions. If possible, work with one or more partners to develop your answers. Be prepared to share and explain your ideas.

❶ What qualifications should a delegate have to represent your class at a constitutional convention?

❷ How should these delegates be selected?

❸ What rules would you establish for the delegates to follow during the convention?

❹ Would you keep the rest of the school informed about what was happening at the convention? Why or why not?

What qualifications should a student have to represent your class as a delegate?

Who did not attend the convention?

Some important Americans did not attend the Philadelphia Convention. Thomas Jefferson was in France. John Adams was in England. Both men were in Europe representing the United States.

Patrick Henry refused to attend the convention. He is quoted as saying, "I smell a rat." He was against the idea of a strong national government. Henry thought that the delegates would not work on improving the Articles of Confederation. He suspected that the delegates would instead write a new constitution that would result in a strong national government. After the convention, Patrick Henry worked hard to get the people to reject the new Constitution.

Not all segments of the American population were represented at the Philadelphia Convention. There were no women among the delegates. There were no African Americans or American Indians. Poor farmers, like those who took part in Shays' Rebellion, were not present either.

The Rhode Island state legislature refused to send delegates to the convention. Citizens there were fiercely independent and hostile to the idea of a new constitution.

What rules did the Framers agree to follow during the convention?

By May 25, 1787, delegates from eleven states had arrived at the convention. We call the delegates **Framers** because they framed, or shaped, and wrote the U.S. Constitution. The Framers all agreed that George Washington should preside over the meetings.

At the start of the convention, the Framers agreed on three things. They agreed they would

Patrick Henry said he did not attend the convention because he "smelled a rat." What do you think he meant by this?

- not try to find ways to improve the Articles of Confederation as Congress had asked them to do. The Framers thought the problems were too serious to try to correct them. Instead, the Framers decided to write a new constitution.

- keep the record of what was said at the convention a secret for thirty years. The reason for secrecy was that the Framers wanted to develop the best constitution possible. Many feared that if their discussions were made public, the delegates would not express their opinions freely. Also, the Framers did not want people from the outside trying to influence what they were doing. Finally, the Framers wanted the new constitution to be accepted. A new constitution would have a greater chance of being approved if people did not know about the arguments that went on during the convention.

- give each state one vote in the convention proceedings, no matter the size of a state's population. The reason for this decision was to gain the cooperation of the small states.

Delaware, for example, had threatened to withdraw from the convention if states with large populations were given more votes than states with small populations.

What ideas about government did the Framers agree to include in the new constitution?

The Framers agreed that certain basic ideas about government should be included in the new constitution. These included the idea that

- the national government should be a constitutional government, that is, a government of limited powers,

- the purpose of government should be to protect fundamental rights and promote the common good,

- a strong national government was needed to protect fundamental rights,

Why did the Framers keep the proceedings of the Philadelphia Convention secret?

This is a reproduction of the first page of the original Constitution of the United States. Why do you think it was important to the Framers to make "We the People" so prominent at the top of the document?

- a republican form of government of elected representatives was needed to make sure that government served the common good, and

- a system of separation of powers and checks and balances was needed to prevent the abuse of power.

Because of their agreement on basic ideas about government, the Framers were able to write a new constitution. In less than four months, they created a constitution that has lasted, with some revisions, for more than two hundred years.

Reviewing and Using the Lesson

1. What did Congress ask the delegates to do during the Philadelphia Convention? Did the delegates accomplish what Congress asked them to do? Explain your answer.

2. In what ways were the delegates at the Philadelphia Convention representative of the American people? In what ways were they not representative?

3. What rules did the Framers establish for the convention? What was the purpose of these rules?

4. What basic ideas about government did the Framers agree should be included in a new constitution?

Activities

1. Find pictures of the people who attended the Philadelphia Convention. Use the pictures to create a gallery for your classroom. For each picture, write a brief biography of the Framer it represents.

2. George Washington did not want to attend the Philadelphia Convention. Conduct research to find out why Washington did not want to attend the convention, as well as why he finally changed his mind. Create a bibliography for the sources you use.

3. Create an editorial cartoon that expresses your opinion about whether the topics being discussed at the Philadelphia Convention should have been reported to the public during the time of the meeting.

How Did the Framers Resolve the Conflict about Representation in Congress?

LESSON PURPOSE

In this lesson, you will learn about the disagreement the Framers had about how many representatives each state should be able to send to Congress. You will learn what compromises the Framers reached to resolve the conflict.

LESSON OBJECTIVES

When you finish this lesson, you should be able to

☐ explain the reasons for the conflict over how many representatives each state should be able to send to Congress, and

☐ explain how this conflict was resolved.

TERMS TO UNDERSTAND

- equal representation
- Great Compromise
- New Jersey Plan
- proportional representation
- Virginia Plan

Why might people in states with smaller populations favor equal representation?

What important conflict existed between the large and small states?

One of the most important conflicts at the Philadelphia Convention was about representation. The Framers disagreed about how many representatives each state should be able to send to Congress. The conflict was between delegates from states with small populations and delegates from states with large populations.

Small states The small states feared that the states with larger populations would control the national government. To avoid this problem, the small states wanted each state to have the same number of representatives in Congress. This is called **equal representation**.

Large states The delegates from the states with larger populations thought that equal representation was unfair. A state with more people should have more votes. The large states wanted to base the number of representatives in Congress on the number of people living in a state. This is called **proportional representation**.

Critical Thinking Exercise

Examining equal and proportional representation

Examine the population figures in the map. Then answer the following questions. You may use a calculator to find some of the answers. If possible, work with one or more partners to find the answers.

1 Assume that in 1790, the small states were those with fewer than 250,000 people.

2 Assume that the number of representatives from each state in Congress is the same and each state has one vote.

- How many total votes would the small states have?
- How many total votes would the large states have?
- Explain why the small states favored equal representation in Congress.

3 Assume there is one representative in Congress for every 30,000 people and each representative has one vote.

- How many total votes would the large states have?
- How many total votes would the small states have?
- Explain why the large states favored proportional representation.

4 Explain why the disagreement about representation in Congress was so important to the states.

5 Which alternative is consistent with the principle of "one person, one vote"?

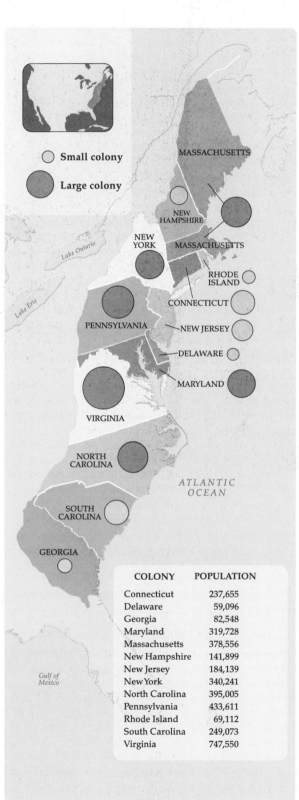

COLONY	POPULATION
Connecticut	237,655
Delaware	59,096
Georgia	82,548
Maryland	319,728
Massachusetts	378,556
New Hampshire	141,899
New Jersey	184,139
New York	340,241
North Carolina	395,005
Pennsylvania	433,611
Rhode Island	69,112
South Carolina	249,073
Virginia	747,550

Under the Virginia Plan, from where would the federal and state governments get their power?

What was the Virginia Plan?

Before the convention started, James Madison had drafted a plan for a national government. He called it the **Virginia Plan**.

- The Virginia Plan proposed a strong national government.

- Under the Virginia Plan, two governments would govern the people. There would be individual state governments and the national government. Both state and national governments would get their power from the people. This is what we now call a federal system.

- The national government would have the power to make and enforce its own laws. It would have the power to collect its own taxes.

- The Virginia Plan divided the government into legislative, executive, and judicial branches.

- The national legislature was to have two houses: the House of Representatives and the Senate.

- The number of representatives in each house would be proportional.

There was considerable debate in the convention about the different parts of the Virginia Plan. The part that created the biggest problem was representation. The larger states favored proportional representation in both houses of Congress. The small states opposed the idea. The smaller states said that unless they had an equal voice in Congress, the larger states would dominate them.

By the middle of June, the debate about representation was no longer making progress. The delegates from the small states asked for time to come up with an alternative to the Virginia Plan.

What was the New Jersey Plan?

William Paterson of New Jersey led the group of small states to develop a new plan for representation. Their plan was called the **New Jersey Plan**. The New Jersey Plan followed the framework of the Articles of Confederation.

- It favored a weak national government.

- It called for only one house of Congress.

- Each state would have equal representation.

- Congress would have the power to collect taxes on products and stamps, as well as to levy fines and collect money from the states if they refused to pay their taxes.

- Congress also would have the power to regulate trade among the states and with other nations.

- The New Jersey Plan also proposed executive and judicial branches of government. Congress would appoint several persons to serve in the executive branch. The executive branch would appoint the members of a U.S. Supreme Court.

The convention debated the New Jersey Plan. The Framers saw that neither the Virginia Plan nor the New Jersey Plan solved the problem of representation. The convention remained divided on this issue. Neither side was willing to accept the position of the other. Tension was growing. Some delegates threatened to quit and go home.

Finally, the convention decided to appoint a special committee to try to solve the conflict. One delegate from each state was asked to serve on the committee.

How did the New Jersey Plan differ from the Virginia Plan? How were they the same?

Should Congress have one or two houses? What are the advantages and disadvantages of each approach?

Critical Thinking Exercise

Work with a group of five students. Imagine that each group is a committee formed to solve the problem of representation in Congress. Each committee should have students who represent small states and students who represent large states. The task of each committee is as follows.

❶ Examine the descriptions of the Virginia Plan and the New Jersey Plan in this lesson. Decide whether Congress should have one or two houses. Then decide on the number of representatives each state should send to Congress. To resolve the problem, you may need to write a new plan.

❷ Select a spokesperson to present your plan to the entire class. All members of the committee may help clarify the plan and defend it against criticisms by members of the other committees.

❸ Each committee may revise its plan if it wishes. Then, put the plan on the board or chart paper and display it in your class.

❹ Finally, the entire class should compare the plans developed by each committee. The class should try to reach an agreement on the question of representation. Compare the plan you have developed with the plan arrived at by the Framers.

How did the Great Compromise solve the problem of representation?

The committee appointed to solve the problem of representation came up with the Connecticut Compromise. It is now called the **Great Compromise**. The Great Compromise has three parts.

❶ Congress would have two houses: the Senate and the House of Representatives.

❷ Membership in the House would be based on proportional representation. The House would have the power to develop all bills dealing with taxes and government spending. As you learned in Lesson 5, a bill is a proposed law.

What were the most important elements of the compromise that solved the problem of representation in Congress?

3 Membership in the Senate would be based on equal representation. At first, the Senate only had power to accept or reject bills related to taxes and spending passed in the House. This power was later modified to let the Senate make changes to bills involving taxes and spending developed in the House.

As in most compromises, each side received a little and each gave up a little. The small states got equal representation in the Senate. The large states got proportional representation in the House. Also, the House would have important powers related to taxing and spending.

The compromise meant that the large states would have slightly more influence over issues of taxes and spending. In the Senate, the small states could check the large states by changing or rejecting taxes and spending bills passed in the House. The Great Compromise was hotly debated. It finally passed by one vote.

Critical Thinking Exercise

Taking a position on representation in the Senate of the United States

The Great Compromise resulted in the Senate of the United States having two senators from each state no matter how small or large it is. This means that people in a small state like Wyoming, which has less than one million people, have two senators to represent them. It also means that people in a large state like California, which has more than 38 million people, also have two senators to represent them.

Is it fair to have equal representation in the U.S. Senate? Why or why not?

The Supreme Court has ruled that both houses of state legislatures must follow the principle of "one person, one vote." This means that representation in each house must be in proportion to the population, that is, for example, you cannot have one representative for 100,000 people from one area and one representative for 1 million people from another area.

1 Is there any principle in the Declaration of Independence that is relevant to this issue?

2 How, if at all, is the principle of majority rule and minority rights relevant to this issue?

3 What might be the consequences of establishing proportional representation in the Senate?

4 Should the Constitution of the United States be changed to provide for proportional representation in the Senate as is required in the state legislatures? Why or why not?

Reviewing and Using the Lesson

1. What is the difference between equal representation and proportional representation? Why did the small states want equal representation? Why did the large states want proportional representation?

2. What was the Virginia Plan?

3. What was the New Jersey Plan?

4. How did the Great Compromise solve the conflict about representation?

5. What did the small states and the large states gain or lose as a result of the Great Compromise?

6. What did individual citizens gain or lose as a result of the Great Compromise?

Activities

1. Find out who represents your state in the U.S. Senate. Visit their Web pages on the Internet. Write brief biographies of your senators to share with your class.

2. For purposes of representation in the House of Representatives, each state is divided into congressional districts. There is one representative for each district. Find the number of congressional districts in your state. Find the name of the person who represents your congressional district. Visit his or her website. Write a brief biography of your representative in the House to share with the class.

How Did the Framers Resolve the Conflict between the Northern and Southern States?

LESSON PURPOSE

The states of the North and South had different economies and different economic interests. These differences led to another conflict at the Philadelphia Convention. The sources of this disagreement were protective tariffs and slavery.

LESSON OBJECTIVES

When you finish this lesson, you should be able to

❑ explain the conflicts about protective tariffs and slavery, and

❑ explain how they were resolved.

TERMS TO UNDERSTAND

- fugitive slave clause
- tariff
- three-fifths clause

How were the economies of the North and South different?

The economy of the South was almost completely agricultural. The Southern states grew products such as cotton, tobacco, and indigo.

The large farms in the Southern states used enslaved people to grow their crops. The farm owners depended on slave labor to make their goods more profitable. Slaves were treated as if they were property that could be bought or sold. People held in slavery were not citizens. They could not claim the rights of citizens.

Southern farmers shipped most of their products to Great Britain and other nations in Europe. They sold some in the Northern states. People in the South bought the manufactured goods they needed from Great Britain.

The economy of the North was more diverse than that of the South. Some people were farmers, fishers, merchants, or bankers. Other people manufactured goods or worked as laborers. The North's economy did not depend on slave labor.

The North was also a center for shipbuilding and trade with other nations. The North had to compete for business with Great Britain's shipping and manufacturing industries.

Why did the states disagree about the need for tariffs?

The economic differences between the North and South caused a conflict among the Framers at the Philadelphia Convention. One area of disagreement was the issue of tariffs. A **tariff** is a tax on goods and products imported from other nations. The purpose of a protective tariff is to raise the cost of the imports to protect local farmers and businesses against outside competition. The Northern and Southern delegates held different opinions about tariffs.

The Northern position

The Northern states believed that tariffs were necessary for their businesses to

Why was agriculture profitable in the South?

Why did the North believe tariffs were necessary?

How did economics affect the position of the South on slavery?

prosper. Tariffs on British products would make those products cost more than similar ones made in America. As a result, Americans would be more likely to buy goods made in their own country instead of those made in other countries.

The Framers who came from the Northern states wanted to give the new national government the power to control trade between the states and trade with foreign nations. This included the power to pass tariffs.

The Southern position
The South argued that tariffs would increase the cost of the manufactured goods that they bought from European nations. Southerners argued that tariffs unfairly favored the North. Southerners also feared that Great Britain might place its own tariffs on agricultural products grown in the South. This would make those products harder to sell in Europe.

The Southern states had fewer citizens than did Northern states. Southerners were afraid they would be a minority in Congress. They thought they might have less power in the new national government to decide issues of trade. So, the Framers who came from the Southern states opposed giving the national government power to regulate trade.

Why was there a conflict between Northern and Southern Framers about slavery?

Why was there a conflict about slavery?

The conflict about slavery was more complicated than the issue of tariffs. Slavery began in the colonies soon after the first settlements were established, but most of the Northern states had put an end to the practice, at least officially. Most of the Framers from the Northern states were opposed to slavery, as were some Framers from Southern states.

Many Southern farmers, however, were still financially dependent on slavery and wanted it to continue. The Southerners believed that each state had a right to decide the issue for itself. The delegates from three Southern states said they refused to be part of a union of states that denied them the right to own and import slaves.

The Framers who opposed slavery faced a dilemma. They wanted all the states to be part of one country, but they did not want to allow slavery to continue.

Critical Thinking Exercise

Developing plans to deal with issues of tariffs and slavery

Work with a group of six students. Divide the groups into two committees each. Each committee should have three students who represent the Northern states and three who represent the Southern states. The task of each committee is as follows:

1 Develop a plan for dealing with the issues of tariffs and slavery. Your plan should be agreeable to the representatives of all the states.

2 Select a spokesperson to present your committee's plan to the entire class.

All members of the committee may help to clarify and defend the plan.

3 Each committee may then revise its plan, if it wishes, and display it on the board or chart paper.

4 The entire class should then compare the plans made by the committees and try to reach an agreement on one plan. After you have completed this exercise, compare the plan you have developed with the plan arrived at by the Framers.

What ideas did your class present to resolve the issues of slavery and tariffs?

How did the Framers resolve the conflicts about tariffs and slavery?

After a long and sometimes bitter debate, the Framers reached a compromise over the issues of tariffs and slavery. Read the following parts of Article I, Sections 8 and 9 of the Constitution.

The Congress shall have the power:

Section 8

1 To lay and collect Taxes, Duties, Imposts, and Excises.

2 To regulate Commerce with foreign Nations, and among the several States, and with the Indian Tribes;

Section 9

1 The Migration or Importation of such Persons as any of the States now existing shall think proper to admit, shall not be prohibited by the Congress prior to the Year one thousand eight hundred and eight.

What arguments were there over the three-fifths clause?

As you can see, the Constitution gave Congress the power to place tariffs on imports. Congress also was given the power to control both interstate and foreign trade. To get this agreement from the Southern delegates, the Framers from the North agreed to Southern demands on the issue of slavery.

The Framers reached the following agreements about slavery.

- The national government would not end the slave trade before 1808.

- They included the three-fifths clause in Article I, Section 2, Clause 3. The **three-fifths clause** states that in deciding how many representatives a state could send to the House of Representatives, the numbers would be determined by counting free persons, indentured servants, and "three-fifths of all other persons" [slaves]. Congress was to use the same count for collecting direct taxes from the states. Native Americans were excluded.

- Finally, the Framers agreed to include the fugitive slave clause in Article IV, Section 2. The **fugitive slave clause** states that persons who escaped from slavery to a state where slavery was prohibited "shall be delivered up on Claim of the Party to whom such Service or Labour may be due."

The compromise on slavery was designed to satisfy the demands of some of the Southern states. It was accepted by a majority of the Framers to get the support of North Carolina, South Carolina, and Georgia. These states would not have supported the Constitution without this agreement. In spite of strong criticisms, the compromise was not as controversial in 1787 as it became in the 1800s and later.

Although the delegates agreed to the compromise, many people in both the North and the South were strongly opposed to slavery. For example, one Framer, Gouverneur Morris, denounced slavery as "the curse of Heaven on the states" where it existed. It is also interesting to note that nowhere in the Constitution did the writers use the words *slave* or *slavery*. Some people say that this is because the Framers were ashamed of slavery.

What Do You Think?

1 What compromises did the Framers reach on the issues of tariffs and slavery?

2 What reason did the Framers have for compromising on the issue of slavery? Do you agree or disagree that the compromise violated fundamental principles that you have been studying in this text? Why?

Reviewing and Using the Lesson

1. In what ways were the economic interests of the Northern and Southern states different?

2. What was the position of the Northern states on the issue of tariffs? What was the position of the Southern states?

3. What was the position of the Northern states on the issue of slavery? What was the position of most of the Southern states?

Activities

1. Go to your library or use the Internet to find some of the Framers' speeches about slavery. George Mason's is of particular interest. Share the speech with your class.

2. Research the use of tariffs today. Create a drawing that illustrates how tariffs are employed. Write a paragraph explaining the point of view your drawing expresses on the issue.

How Did the Framers Resolve the Conflict about the Powers of the Legislative Branch?

LESSON PURPOSE

One problem facing the Framers at the Philadelphia Convention was how much power to give to the legislative branch. In this lesson, you will learn about the debates that the Framers had concerning which powers to delegate to Congress.

LESSON OBJECTIVE

When you finish the lesson, you should be able to explain the powers that the Constitution gives to Congress.

TERMS TO UNDERSTAND

- bill of attainder
- enumerated powers
- ex post facto law
- general welfare clause
- necessary and proper clause
- unconstitutional
- writ of habeas corpus

How much power should Congress have?

Under the Articles of Confederation, Congress was unable to deal with the trade and economic problems of the country. More importantly, Congress was not strong enough to control the actions of state governments. The Framers were convinced that the state legislatures were passing laws that violated the property rights of many citizens.

A basic problem with the Articles of Confederation was that Congress did not have the power to act directly on the people. When Congress passed laws, it had to depend on the states to enforce them. Congress could not raise taxes to support itself; it could only ask the states for money. Many states ignored congressional requests for funds.

What was the problem facing the Framers regarding the powers of the three branches of the national government?

Most of the Framers agreed that there was a need for a stronger national government. There were still some areas of disagreement, however. The American experience with the British government had caused many of the Framers to be suspicious of a central government and executive power.

The compromises about representation and slavery reduced resistance to increasing the power of the national government. The delegates, however, still disagreed about how much power to give to each of the three branches of the national government. The problem facing the Framers was how to create a national government that was strong enough to protect the rights of the people, and yet not so strong that it would endanger those rights.

How should the Constitution be written to give power to Congress?

James Madison argued that the new Congress should keep the powers that it had under the Articles of Confederation. He also wanted Congress to make the laws that the state legislatures were prevented from making. He thought that Congress should also be given the power to reject or turn down laws made by state legislatures.

Madison's recommendations would have given the national government great power over the states and the people. To give all this power to the national government meant that the new constitution would have to be written in very general language. For example, the constitution might say, "Congress shall have the power to make all laws that are necessary."

Many of the Framers disagreed with Madison. They saw a problem with general language in the new constitution. General language could be understood to mean that government was given the power to do almost anything it wanted to do. It does not provide a good way to limit the powers of government.

Many delegates also opposed giving Congress the power to veto laws made by state legislatures. Under British rule, royal governors and Parliament had vetoed acts of the colonial legislatures. The Framers did not want to give this power to Congress.

An alternative was to write the new constitution in very specific language. Specific language meant writing down exactly what powers Congress would have. For example,

"Congress shall have the power to collect taxes." The Framers wanted a government of enumerated powers. **Enumerated powers** are powers that are specifically listed in a constitution. The problem with enumerated powers was that a constitution might leave out important powers needed by Congress to deal with unforeseen situations.

The solution was to use both general and specific language. The new constitution would give specific powers to Congress and place limitations on these powers. It would also include two general clauses that would give Congress the power to deal with unexpected situations.

How did the Framers solve the problem of distributing power between the state governments and the national government?

Why did the Framers give the power to declare war to Congress, rather than to the president?

What are the enumerated powers of Congress?

Article I deals with the legislative branch. Article I alone makes up more than half of the Constitution. It shows just how important the legislative branch was to the Framers.

Article I, Section 8 includes seventeen enumerated powers. Some of these powers give Congress the right to

- impose and collect taxes and duties,

- borrow money,

- regulate commerce with foreign nations and among the states,

- coin money,

- establish post offices,

- declare war, and

- raise and support an army and navy.

What are the general powers of Congress?

Article I, Section 8 also includes two general statements of power given to Congress. These are the power of Congress to

- "provide for the common Defense and general Welfare [common good] of the United States." This is called the **general welfare clause**.

- "make all Laws which shall be necessary and proper" for carrying out the other powers that the Constitution grants to Congress. This is called the **necessary and proper clause**. For example, under the enumerated powers, Congress has the power to raise and support an army. To exercise this power, it might be necessary and proper that Congress pass a law requiring citizens to serve in the armed forces.

Neither of these general clauses caused any disagreements at the convention. They did cause strong disagreements in the states about whether to approve the Constitution. Both clauses were the source of conflicts in the early years of the new government. You will learn more about these conflicts in later lessons.

What part of Article I, Section 8 of the Constitution gives Congress the power to conduct a space exploration program?

What limits are there on the powers of Congress?

The Constitution includes several limits on the powers of Congress. Article I, Section 9 prohibits Congress from doing any of the following:

- Banning the slave trade before 1808.

- Suspending the privilege of the **writ of habeas corpus** except in emergencies. In Latin, *habeas corpus* means to "have the body." A writ of habeas corpus orders government to deliver a person it has arrested to a court of law. Government must explain why that person has been arrested and held. If government cannot show that the person has broken the law, the person must be set free.

- Passing **ex post facto laws**. This is a law that makes an act a crime even though the act was legal when it took place.

- Passing **bills of attainder**. This is a legislative act that declared a person guilty of violating the law and set the punishment without a court trial.

- Taxing anything exported from a state.

- Taking money from the treasury without first passing a law to do so.

- Granting titles of nobility.

In this way, the Framers tried to balance the need for a strong government with the need to limit its powers. Those limits were included to make sure that government did not become a threat to the people's rights.

How might the right to habeas corpus protect people from the abuse of power by government?

How do the other branches check the power of Congress?

Remember that Congress is divided into two "houses." This arrangement is a check on the power of Congress to pass laws. For example, when the House of Representatives passes a bill, it must be sent to the Senate. The bill must also pass the Senate by a majority vote before it can become law.

The executive and judicial branches also have checks, or controls, on Congress. If a bill passes in both houses of Congress, the bill must be sent to the president for approval and signature. When the president signs the bill it becomes a law.

The president may refuse to sign a bill and send it back to Congress. This is the president's power to veto a bill passed in Congress. When the president vetoes a bill, the bill can only become law if approved by a two-thirds majority in both houses of Congress.

The U.S. Supreme Court has the power to declare a law made by Congress unconstitutional. **Unconstitutional** means that the law or action is not permitted by the Constitution. The Court may say that the Constitution does not give Congress the right to pass such a law. In this case, the law can no longer be carried out or enforced. You will learn more about this power of the U.S. Supreme Court in a future lesson.

How does the judicial branch check the executive and legislative branches?

Critical Thinking Exercise

Taking positions on the constitutionality of bills

A bill is a proposed law. Members of Congress create bills and try to get a majority of both houses to vote for them.

Your class should be divided into congressional committees of about five members each. Complete the following activity and report your findings to the entire class.

Your committee wants to introduce six bills in Congress. Review the general and enumerated powers granted to Congress. For each bill in the next column, identify which of these two types of powers enables Congress to pass it. Support your opinion.

Answer these two questions as part of your discussion:

- If you used only the enumerated powers of Congress to decide whether to pass a law, what problems might arise?

- If you used only the general powers of Congress to decide whether to pass a law, what problems might arise?

Bills under consideration to become laws. A law to

1 allow government to keep watch over websites on the Internet to protect children from potentially harmful material,

2 allow government to draft citizens to serve in the armed forces,

3 provide money to pay the expenses of the army and navy,

4 allow the executive branch to conduct a space exploration program,

5 allow government to impose fines as punishment for industries that pollute the air, or

6 require government to use tax money to provide medical assistance.

Reviewing and Using the Lesson

1. What disagreements about the powers of Congress did the Framers have? How did they resolve these disagreements?

2. What enumerated powers does Article I, Section 8 grant to Congress?

3. What general powers does Article I, Section 8 grant to Congress? Why are these general powers necessary?

4. What limits does Article I place on the powers of Congress? Explain how these limitations protect the rights of citizens.

5. Explain some ways in which the executive and judicial branches can check the powers of Congress.

Activities

1. Draw three illustrations. Each one should show how the limits on Congress protect the rights of citizens. Make one illustration focus on a writ of habeas corpus, one on ex post facto laws, and one on bills of attainder.

2. Article IV gives Congress power to create new states from the territories. Find out how a territory can become a state.

3. Sometimes it becomes necessary to make changes to the Constitution. This has happened twenty-seven times in the history of the United States. Read Article V in the Constitution. Explain the process for amending the Constitution.

4. Research an attempt to amend the Constitution that failed. Why did it fail? Would it be more successful today? Has the issue that the amendment was meant to correct been addressed in other ways?

How Much Power Should Be Given to the Executive and Judicial Branches?

LESSON PURPOSE

In this lesson, you will learn about the powers that the Constitution gives to the executive and judicial branches. You will learn how the legislative and judicial branches check the power of the executive branch. You also will learn about the system that the Constitution established for electing a president.

LESSON OBJECTIVES

When you finish this lesson, you should be able to

❏ explain the powers of the executive and judicial branches of government, and

❏ explain the process for electing the president of the United States.

TERMS TO UNDERSTAND

- advice and consent
- appellate jurisdiction
- Electoral College
- impeach
- jurisdiction
- original jurisdiction
- Twenty-second Amendment

What challenge did the Framers face in creating the executive branch?

In 1787, Americans still remembered how much trouble they had experienced with the executive branch of the British government. Americans believed that the king and his royal governors and other officials had violated their rights.

With this experience in mind, the Framers faced the problem of creating an executive branch of government. They wanted an executive branch with enough power to carry out its responsibilities yet not strong enough to overwhelm the other branches. An executive branch with too much power could endanger the rights of the people.

What powers does the Constitution give to the executive branch?

Article II of the Constitution created the executive branch. The Framers wrote Article II in more general terms than they did Article I. As a result, Article II is shorter.

The list of powers it gives to the president is brief. These include the powers to

- carry out and enforce laws made by Congress,

- make treaties with foreign nations,

- appoint certain important government officials,

- act as commander in chief of the armed forces, and

- veto laws passed by Congress.

Is it important that the commander in chief of the armed forces is a civilian? Why or why not?

Why would the Constitution require the president and Congress to share power when negotiating treaties with other nations?

The president also can send and receive ambassadors to and from other countries. The president has the power to pardon people convicted of crimes against the United States.

How does the Constitution limit the powers of the executive branch?

The Constitution limits the powers of the executive branch by making it share most of its powers with Congress. Here are some examples of how this works.

❶ **Appointments** The president has the power to nominate people for important jobs in government with the advice and consent of the Senate. **Advice and consent** is the term used for this process. The president also nominates people to serve in the executive and judicial branches of the national government.

The Senate has the power to approve or reject the president's nominations.

❷ **Treaties** The president has the power to negotiate treaties with another nation. The Senate has the power to approve or reject these treaties.

❸ **War** Although the president can conduct a war as commander in chief, only Congress can declare war. In addition, only Congress has the power to provide money to conduct a war.

❹ **Veto** The president may veto laws passed by Congress. Congress, however, may override the veto by a two-thirds vote of both houses.

The Constitution provides another important way to limit the power of the president and prevent the abuse of power. It gives the House of Representatives the power to impeach the president. To **impeach** means "to bring to trial." This means the House can accuse the

Why did the Framers allow presidents the power to veto laws passed by Congress?

Why did the Framers allow for the impeachment of presidents?

president of serious crimes. The Senate then holds a trial. If the Senate finds the president guilty, he or she can be removed from office. While it is rarely used, impeachment is an important power that Congress has for checking the power of the executive branch.

How should the president be selected?

The Framers had given important powers to the president. It is not surprising that the Framers were concerned about how to select people to fill this position. The Framers took it for granted that George Washington would be the first president. Washington was patriotic, honest, devoted to the public good, and not interested in using power for his own advantage.

The Framers wanted a way of selecting future presidents who would be as qualified as Washington. The Framers discussed the problem for some time. They also discussed how long a president should be able to stay in office.

The Framers finally agreed that a president would serve for four years and could be reelected any number of times. This was changed in 1951 by the **Twenty-second Amendment**. The president can now be reelected only once.

A few Framers wanted the people to elect the president directly. But James Madison thought that in such a large country the people would not know enough about the candidates to make good choices. Madison also believed that the people might not always have the wisdom to select the best person for president. Most Framers agreed with Madison.

What qualifications should a person have to become president of the United States?

In most states, the head of the executive branch was chosen by the state legislature. But the Framers thought that if Congress chose the executive, Congress would control the president. The result would be a weak executive branch. The Framers also thought that if the president were to be selected by the state governments, then the states would control the president. This too would result in a weak executive branch. Neither of these choices would have helped the Framers create a stronger national government.

The method the Framers finally created for electing the president is complicated. They decided that an **Electoral College** would be created once every four years to choose the president. Each state would have electors equal to the number of senators and representatives it had in Congress. Each state would decide how to select persons to serve as their electors in the college. The candidate who received a majority of votes in the Electoral College would become president.

But what if no candidate got a majority of votes in the Electoral College? In that case, the House of Representatives would select the president by majority vote. Each state would have one vote.

We still use the Electoral College today. But it does not work the way the Framers originally planned.

Critical Thinking Exercise

Determining qualifications for the presidency

Examine Article II of the Constitution and review what you learned in this lesson to help you complete the following chart. You might cooperate with one or more students to do so.

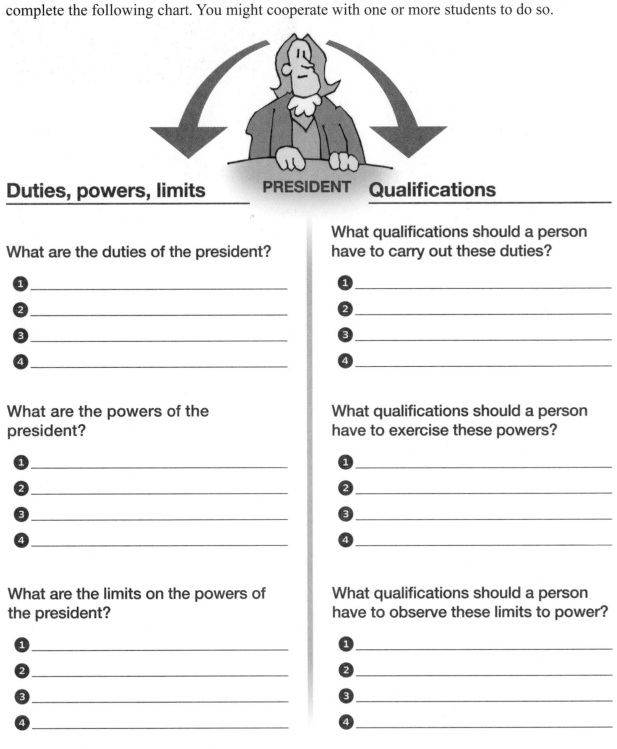

Duties, powers, limits

PRESIDENT

Qualifications

What are the duties of the president?

1. _____
2. _____
3. _____
4. _____

What qualifications should a person have to carry out these duties?

1. _____
2. _____
3. _____
4. _____

What are the powers of the president?

1. _____
2. _____
3. _____
4. _____

What qualifications should a person have to exercise these powers?

1. _____
2. _____
3. _____
4. _____

What are the limits on the powers of the president?

1. _____
2. _____
3. _____
4. _____

What qualifications should a person have to observe these limits to power?

1. _____
2. _____
3. _____
4. _____

What powers does the Constitution give to the judicial branch?

To complete the system of separation of powers, the Framers planned for a judicial branch. A national judiciary was needed to decide disputes between state governments and between citizens of two or more states; it was also needed for disputes between the national government and a state or a citizen.

The Framers had few problems agreeing on the powers of the judicial branch. Article III of the Constitution establishes the judicial branch. Article III includes the following ideas about a national court system.

1 Judges should be appointed, not elected. Thus, judges would be independent of politics. They could use their best judgment to decide cases and not worry about the influence of political pressures.

2 Judges should keep their positions "during good Behavior." Judges cannot be removed from office unless they are impeached. Then the judge would have to be tried and convicted of "Treason, Bribery, or other high Crimes and Misdemeanors." This means that judges should be able to make decisions without fear of losing their jobs. It also means that judges can keep their jobs for life.

3 There should be a single U.S. Supreme Court with two types of jurisdiction. **Jurisdiction** means the power or authority to hear cases and make decisions. The types of jurisdiction are original and appellate.

- The U.S. Supreme Court has original jurisdiction in cases involving a state government or an ambassador. **Original jurisdiction** means that these cases go directly to the U.S. Supreme Court. A lower court does not try these cases first.

Why do you think the Framers wanted Supreme Court justices to be appointed, rather than elected?

- In all other cases, the U.S. Supreme Court has **appellate jurisdiction**. The case is tried first in a lower court. Then the decision of the lower court is appealed to the U.S. Supreme Court. The Supreme Court may decide whether to hear a case on appeal.

The Constitution clearly gave the U.S. Supreme Court the power to overrule state laws that violate the Constitution or the laws made by Congress. The power is based on the supremacy clause in Article VI. You will study the supremacy clause in Lesson 17.

The national government is supreme in those areas where the Constitution gives it the power to act. For example, suppose a state passes a law allowing factories to pollute the air. Then Congress passes a law controlling the pollution a factory can produce. The national government's laws would have to be obeyed over state laws.

Washington, Madison, and the other Framers who agreed with them got the strong national government they wanted. But the battle was not yet won. Many people in the United States were still afraid of a strong national government. They believed that it would be a threat to their rights and to their state governments.

Reviewing and Using the Lesson

① What challenges did the Framers face in creating the executive branch?

② What powers does the Constitution grant to the president?

③ Explain how the system of checks and balances limits the powers of the president. Give specific examples.

④ Explain the process for selecting a president.

⑤ What are the powers of the judicial branch? Do you think it is important that judges are appointed to office rather than elected? Why? Do you think judges should stay in office unless they are impeached or that their terms should be limited? Why?

⑥ What branch of the federal government has the power to overrule state laws that violate the U.S. Constitution?

Activities

① Only two presidents have faced impeachment: Andrew Johnson and William Jefferson Clinton. Richard Nixon faced the threat of impeachment, but he resigned from office. Learn more about the impeachment process and what happened with each of the three presidents listed. Share what you learned with your class.

② Find out how electors to the Electoral College are selected in your state. Share what you learned with your class.

③ Examine the Twenty-fifth Amendment to the Constitution. Draw a chart that illustrates who is next in line to become the president if a president dies while in office or otherwise cannot carry out his or her duties.

④ Learn more about John Jay and John Marshall, two justices of the U.S. Supreme Court. You can find information about these important men in your library or on the Internet.

How Was the Constitution Used to Establish Our Government?

4

How Was the Constitution Used to Establish Our Government?

UNIT PURPOSE

Why is our nation's Constitution so short? The Framers wrote the Constitution as a general framework, or plan, for the new government. They left out many details because they knew that future presidents and members of Congress would add them.

In this unit, you will discover how government was organized under the Constitution. You will be able to explain the positions of the Founders who supported the Constitution and the positions of those who were against it. You will also learn about some unexpected developments that have influenced the way our nation is governed today.

KEY CONCEPTS

- Anti-Federalists
- confederation
- federal system
- Federalists
- judicial review
- political parties
- supremacy clause

How Did the Constitution Create a Federal System of Government?

LESSON PURPOSE

The Constitution organized government in a new way. It created a federal system of government. The Constitution gives certain powers only to the national government and certain powers only to the state governments. There are also certain powers that they share. All other powers are kept by the people.

LESSON OBJECTIVES

When you finish this lesson, you should be able to

❏ explain what a federal system is,

❏ explain how a federal system differs from other forms of government, and

❏ explain what powers the Constitution gives to the federal government and what powers it gives to the state governments.

TERMS TO UNDERSTAND

- confederation
- federal system
- federalism
- sovereign
- supremacy clause
- unitary government

This is the Swiss Bundeshaus, or parliament. What form of government does Switzerland have? How does it differ from our form of government?

How do some other nations organize their governments?

Not all nations organize government in the same way. Some nations have a unitary form of government. A **unitary government** is one in which a central government controls the state and local governments. The central government acts directly on the people. The power of state and local governments comes from the central government, and it can be taken away at any time. As a result, the central government is much stronger and more powerful than the state and local governments. The United Kingdom, France, and Sweden are examples of unitary government.

Some nations have a form of government called a confederation. In a **confederation**, the states are independent and have control of anything that affects their citizens and territory. In a confederation, the central government only handles those things that are of common concern. The states can withdraw from the confederation at any time. The central government acts on the states, not directly on the people. The United States under the Articles of Confederation had a confederate form of government. Switzerland is a modern example of a confederation.

Before the Framers created the Constitution, most nations had either a unitary or confederate form of government. The kind of government that the Framers created in our Constitution is a federal system of government.

What is a federal system of government?

According to natural rights philosophy, the people have a right to create a government. The people delegate to government the right, or authority, to govern them. In return, government is responsible for protecting the people's rights to life, liberty, and property.

The Constitution begins with the words "We the People of the United States." The people have created a government and have given it the authority to govern them. Power flows upward from the people to their government. The people remain sovereign at all times. **Sovereign** means to have the highest rank of authority. The people have ultimate authority to control government.

At the time the Framers wrote the Constitution, the people in most other nations were not sovereign. Governments held authority over the people. In some countries, the king was sovereign.

In a **federal system** of government, the sovereign people decide how to delegate their authority. When creating the Constitution, the Framers decided to delegate the power of the people to more than one government. They delegated some powers only to the national government. They delegated other power to the state governments. Some powers, they decided, should be shared by the state and national governments. Finally, all other powers, or rights, are kept by the people.

A federal system of government may also be described as a government that is based on the principle of federalism. **Federalism** refers to the practice of dividing and sharing the powers of government between a central government and regional governments such as state governments.

How do these three types of government differ in their distribution of power?

141

What powers are delegated to the state and federal governments?

As citizens of the United States, the people delegate certain powers to the federal, or national, government. These powers are in the Constitution. They include the power to

- create post offices,
- regulate interstate and foreign trade,
- declare and conduct war, and
- create a national currency.

As citizens of the various states, the people delegate certain powers to their state governments. These powers are in each state's constitution. They include the power to

- regulate trade within the state,
- establish public schools,
- create traffic and motor vehicle laws, and
- regulate marriage and divorce practices.

The state and federal governments share certain powers. These include the powers to

- make their own laws,
- tax the people,
- borrow money,
- create their own court systems, and
- provide for the health and welfare of the people.

Finally, the people have kept certain rights or powers and have not delegated them to any government. These include the right to

- believe what we wish,
- form or join organizations,
- select our careers and live our lives as we choose,

- choose our friends,
- travel where we wish to go inside or outside the country, and
- raise a family.

This is President Franklin Roosevelt signing the congressional declaration of war against Japan on December 8, 1941. Why do you think that only the federal government has the authority to engage in war?

Why do you think state governments are not allowed to tax imports or exports? Why is the federal government not allowed to tax exports?

What powers does the Constitution deny to the federal and state governments?

A constitutional government means that the powers of government are limited. The U.S. Constitution limits the powers of both the federal and state governments.

Limits on the Power of the Federal Government

The federal government may not
- tax exports,

- spend money in a way that is not approved by law,

- enact laws that favor trade in one state over the others,

- exercise powers that belong to the states, or

- suspend the right to a writ of habeas corpus, except in a national emergency.

Limits on the Power of the State Governments

The state governments may not
- coin or print money,

- enter into treaties with other nations,

- tax imports or exports,

- keep an army or navy in time of peace, or

- engage in war unless invaded or in immediate danger of being invaded.

Limits on Both the Federal and State Governments

Neither the federal nor state governments may
- deny the right to trial by jury,

- enact ex post facto laws or bills of attainder, or

- grant titles of nobility.

The Bill of Rights places other limits on federal and state governments. You will examine these in the next unit.

Critical Thinking Exercise

Determining which level of government, if any, has the power to pass certain types of laws

Work with a partner. Imagine that you want to encourage a legislature to pass laws to do each of the things listed below. First, you need to decide which level of government, state or national, has the power to create the law you want. Examine each item. For each item, indicate whether the power to pass the law you propose belongs to the national government, the state governments, both, or neither.

1 You want a law to help control what people can put on the Internet for children to see and read.

2 You want to increase the age at which people may buy tobacco to twenty-five.

3 You want a law that helps to control who may or may not buy and sell guns.

4 You want a law to limit driving privileges for people over eighty-five years of age.

5 You think that we no longer need a one-cent coin. You want a law to end the minting of pennies.

6 You want a law to stop the sale of sports shoes made by children who work long hours for little pay in some other countries.

7 You want a law to make it more difficult for parents of very young children to get a divorce.

8 You think that the leader of another country is not able to run the government of that country. You want a law to punish anyone who supports this leader.

9 You want a treaty that requires all nations to pass laws to clean up the air and water.

10 You want a law to raise the minimum age requirement for children to remain in school.

Which part of government would negotiate treaties among nations requiring them to pass laws to clean up the air and water?

What is the supremacy clause?

There were disagreements among the Framers over what powers the federal government should have. The Framers did agree that the powers of the federal government were to be greater than the powers of the state governments. As you learned in Lesson 16, this is clearly stated in the supremacy clause of Article VI. The **supremacy clause** says,

> *This Constitution, and the Laws of the United States ... shall be the supreme Law of the Land.*

The states cannot make laws that conflict with the Constitution or laws made by Congress.

The supremacy clause gives the courts the power to decide disagreements between the states and the federal government. It does not change the fact, however, that the Constitution limits the powers of both the federal and state governments.

What might be the advantages and disadvantages of the supremacy clause?

How do local laws affect education?

How has the relationship between federal and state governments changed?

The Framers created a new and very complicated form of government. They could not predict exactly what powers the state and federal governments would eventually have. Early in our history, the state governments were very powerful. Today, the federal government has far more power over the state governments than most of the Framers could have imagined.

In thinking about the relationship between the federal and state governments, it is important to understand the following things:

- In spite of the increase in the power of the federal government, most of the laws that affect us directly are state or local laws. These include laws regarding education, most property, contracts, families, and criminal behavior.

- Congress makes most of the decisions about how much power is left to the states. Congress decides whether the federal or state governments should carry out certain responsibilities.

This complicated system is sometimes not as efficient as a unitary system of government. But the Framers did not see this as a disadvantage. In fact, the Framers thought that the separation of powers between the federal and state governments was one way to protect the rights of the people.

Reviewing and Using the Lesson

1. Explain the major differences between a unitary form of government and a confederation.

2. What is a federal system?

3. What powers does the Constitution delegate to the federal government?

4. What powers belong to the states?

5. What powers do the state and federal governments share?

6. What powers did the people keep for themselves?

7. What powers does the Constitution deny to the federal government?

8. What powers does the Constitution deny to the state governments?

9. What is the supremacy clause? Why is it important?

Activities

1. Draw a diagram that shows how the federal system works in the United States. Your diagram should show the powers that belong to the states and powers that belong to the national government. Your diagram should also show the powers that the states and the national government share.

2. Look in a newspaper to find articles that illustrate how the federal system works. You may find articles that illustrate federal powers, state powers, and powers that both levels of government share.

3. Plan a short play. Suppose you and a few friends were in a situation like that of the Framers. You must organize a government. Explain to your classmates, the "people," what you think might be some advantages and disadvantages of a federal system of government.

   • Which responsibilities and powers would you give to the national government?

   • Which powers would you give to the state governments?

   • Which powers would you keep for the people?

How Did the People Approve the New Constitution?

LESSON PURPOSE

In this lesson, you will learn about the struggle to get the Constitution ratified. You will learn how the Framers planned to have the people decide whether or not to approve the Constitution. You will also examine the arguments made by the Anti-Federalists and the Federalists for and against the new Constitution.

LESSON OBJECTIVES

When you finish this lesson, you should be able to

❏ explain why the ratification process was important, and

❏ describe the arguments for and against approving the Constitution.

TERMS TO UNDERSTAND

- Anti-Federalists
- Federalists
- ratify
- *The Federalist*

How did Madison plan to get the people to approve the new Constitution?

Why did the Framers want the people to ratify the Constitution?

The Framers did not believe they had created a perfect plan of government. The four months they spent creating the Constitution had been filled with disagreements. A few delegates had walked out of the convention. Some delegates refused to sign the Constitution. The great majority of Framers, however, thought they had done a good job.

After creating the Constitution, the Framers knew that they had to get it approved. James Madison was afraid that the Constitution would be rejected if either the Congress or the state legislatures were asked to ratify it. To **ratify** means to approve. To avoid rejection, Madison developed a plan. His plan was to get the voters to ratify the Constitution at special conventions to be held in each state. The delegates to these conventions would be elected by popular vote of the people for the sole purpose of approving the Constitution.

Madison based his plan on the idea in the Preamble to the Constitution. The first words in the Preamble are "We the People ... do ordain and establish this Constitution." The people who were to be governed by the new national government would consent to its creation and agree to obey its decisions. This was the method for establishing a government set forth in natural rights philosophy and in the Declaration of Independence. Thus, the Framers used the idea of a social contract to get the Constitution approved. It was to be approved by an agreement among the people to create a national government.

The Framers approved Madison's plan. Article VII said that the Constitution would be in effect after it had been ratified by the conventions of nine of the thirteen states. The Framers required approval of the voters of nine states because they were afraid they would not get the approval of all thirteen.

What do you think?

Work with two or three partners to write brief responses to each of the following questions.

1 What reasons might some delegates have given for leaving the convention and refusing to sign the Constitution?

2 Why do you suppose Congress or the state legislatures might have rejected the Constitution if they had been asked to ratify it?

3 Why do you suppose Madison wanted to have the Constitution ratified by delegates to state conventions elected directly by the people?

4 In what way was Madison's plan an example of a social contract?

5 In 1789, the Constitution was ratified by nine states. The people gave their consent to a social contract to create a national government and obey its decisions. Are people today responsible for honoring that contract? Why?

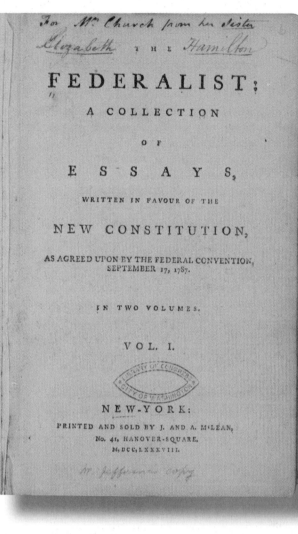

What is The Federalist? *Who wrote it? Why is it important?*

Who were the Federalists and Anti-Federalists?

Once the Philadelphia Convention ended, the Federalists went to work. The **Federalists** were the people who supported ratifying the Constitution. The Federalists asked the states to organize their ratifying conventions as quickly as possible. They knew that their opponents had not had much time to prepare their arguments. By contrast, the supporters of the Constitution had worked on it for four months. They knew the arguments for and against it.

To explain the new Constitution to the people, Alexander Hamilton, James Madison, and John Jay wrote a series of articles for a New York newspaper supporting ratification. These collected articles are called *The Federalist*. *The Federalist* was read in other states as well. Today, *The Federalist* remains one of the most important explanations of constitutional government ever written.

The **Anti-Federalists** were the people who opposed ratifying the Constitution. Anti-Federalist leaders included George Mason, Edmund Randolph, and Elbridge Gerry. Each had attended the Philadelphia Convention but refused to sign the Constitution. Although John Hancock, Samuel Adams, and Richard Henry Lee had all signed the Declaration of Independence, they too were against ratification. Patrick Henry had always opposed the idea of a strong national government. Henry became a leading Anti-Federalist. Mercy Otis Warren, a playwright, also was against ratification.

She wrote pamphlets explaining why she did not support the Constitution.

Most Americans were very suspicious of government, but the Anti-Federalists were especially mistrustful of government in general and strong national government in particular. This mistrust was the basis of their opposition to the Constitution. They feared it had created a government the people could not control. The Anti-Federalists feared that flaws they saw in the Constitution would be a threat to their natural rights. During the ratification debates, the Anti-Federalists put up a strong fight.

Do you think a bill of rights would cause intense debate today? Why or why not?

What issues related to the new Constitution did the people debate?

The debates in the states lasted ten months. It was an intense and sometimes bitter political struggle.

Both the Federalists and Anti-Federalists made many arguments for and against the Constitution. However, the most intense arguments were about three basic issues:

1 Whether the Constitution would maintain republican government

2 Whether the national government would have too much power

3 Whether a bill of rights was needed in the Constitution

The next three sections will help you see both sides of the debate. They summarize how the Federalists and Anti-Federalists responded to each of the three issues.

Does the national government have too much power?

ANTI-FEDERALISTS	FEDERALISTS
The Constitution gives the national government too much power at the expense of the state governments. It gives government the power to tax citizens. It gives government the power to raise and keep an army during peacetime. This army could be used by government to suppress the people.	The national government will have greater power than it did under the Articles of Confederation. But its powers are limited to solving problems that face the entire nation, such as trade and defense. The recent history of the states shows that a stronger national government is needed to deal with such problems.
The supremacy clause means that all the national government's laws are superior to laws made by the states. It will only be a matter of time until the state governments are destroyed.	The Constitution provides protections for the state governments by specifically reserving certain powers for the states. This will prevent the states from being destroyed by the national government.
The necessary and proper clause is too general. It gives too much power to the national government. It is dangerous not to list all the powers of government in order to put clear limits on them.	The necessary and proper clause and general welfare clause are needed if the national government is to do the things it is responsible for doing.
The Constitution gives too much power to the executive branch of government. It will soon become a monarchy.	A strong executive branch is necessary. It is needed if the national government is to fulfill its responsibilities. Congress and the U.S. Supreme Court have checks on the use of power by the executive branch. The executive branch cannot become a monarchy. The powers of the national government are separated and balanced among the three branches. No one branch can dominate the others. This system makes it impossible for any person or group to take complete control of government.

Does the system of checks and balances make it impossible for any one branch of government to dominate the others? Why or why not?

Does the Constitution provide for republican government?

ANTI-FEDERALISTS	FEDERALISTS
Throughout history, the only places where republican governments worked were in small communities. There, the people had similar wealth and the same values. People who are not too rich or too poor are more likely to have civic virtue. Such people are more likely to agree on what is best for their common good. The new nation would be too large and diverse. The people will not be able to agree on their common welfare.	History has proven that selfish groups destroyed all the small republics of the past. The civic virtue of the citizens was not enough to keep people from seeking their own interests. People did not work for the common good. A large republic where power is divided between the national and state governments is a better solution. It is also better to organize government based on checks and balances. Under such a government, it will be more difficult for special interests to work against the common good.
Free government requires the active participation of the people. The national government will be located far from where most people live. People will be unable to participate in government. As a result, the only way government will be able to rule will be with military force. The result will be a tyranny.	The national government cannot become a tyranny. The limits placed on government by the system of separation of powers and checks and balances will prevent it. Government will be so good at protecting the rights of the people that it will soon gain their loyalty and support.

Is a bill of rights needed for the Constitution?

ANTI-FEDERALISTS	FEDERALISTS
The Constitution does not include a bill of rights. A bill of rights is necessary to protect people against the power of the national government. There is no mention of freedom of religion, speech, press, or assembly. Since these freedoms are not in the Constitution, government is free to violate them. Americans recently fought a war to secure their fundamental rights. They do not want a constitution that places those rights in jeopardy.	A bill of rights is not needed. The Constitution is the ultimate protection for people's rights and the people are the ultimate sovereigns. The Constitution does not give government the power to deprive people of their rights. It gives government only limited power to do certain things. A bill of rights will give the impression that the people can expect protection only for the rights that are actually listed. The Constitution protects a number of rights by requiring writs of habeas corpus, and prohibiting ex post facto laws and bills of attainder.

What compromise did the Federalists finally agree to make in order to get enough support for the Constitution to be ratified?

Why did the Federalists agree to add a bill of rights to the Constitution?

A compromise was reached on the issue of a bill of rights. The Federalists made this compromise to get enough support for the Constitution to be ratified. They agreed that when the first Congress was held, it would draft a bill of rights. As a result, by 1789, the required nine states had ratified the Constitution.

The agreement to add a bill of rights was a victory for the Anti-Federalists. It was an important addition to the Constitution and has been of great importance in the protection of the basic rights of the American people.

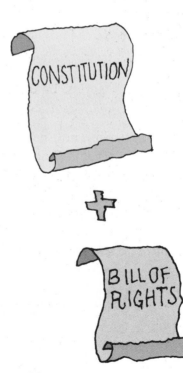

Critical Thinking Exercise

Arguments for and against ratification of the Constitution

Evaluating arguments of the Federalists and Anti-Federalists

You have read the arguments the Federalists and Anti-Federalists gave regarding the ratification of the Constitution. Evaluate those arguments in response to the following questions. Work with one or more partners to discuss and complete the exercise.

- Does the Constitution give the national government too much power?

    - What were the Federalists' best arguments on this question?

    - What were the Anti-Federalists' best arguments on this question?

- Does the Constitution provide for republican government?

    - What were the Federalists' best arguments on this question?

    - What were the Anti-Federalists' best arguments on this question?

- Does the Constitution need to have a bill of rights?

    - What were the Federalists' best arguments on this question?

    - What were the Anti-Federalists' best arguments on this question?

Debating ratification

Imagine that your class is one of the original thirteen states. You are holding a ratifying convention to decide if your state will approve the new constitution. The students in your class are delegates to the state convention. The class should be divided into two groups. One group represents the Anti-Federalists. The other group represents the Federalists.

Apply what you have learned from this text to help you prepare your arguments. You may want to divide your group into three smaller groups, so that each smaller group can prepare responses for one of the questions listed to the right.

Participating in the debate

Before the debate begins, establish a few rules. Decide upon the amount of time each group gets to speak and how many turns each group should get. Decide which group gets to speak first on each of the three questions.

Select one student from your group to moderate the debate. He or she should read the questions aloud to the class, call on groups to speak, and keep track of time limits.

At the end of the debate, each group should give a short summary of its arguments. Finally, everyone in the class should vote on whether or not to ratify the new constitution.

Evaluating the decision

Your class should discuss the results of the debate.

1. What do you think were the best arguments for ratifying the Constitution?

2. What were the best arguments against ratifying the Constitution?

3. What might have happened to the country if the states had not ratified the Constitution?

Reviewing and Using the Lesson

1. Why did the Framers oppose submitting the Constitution to the existing Congress or state governments for ratification?

2. What process did the Framers select for ratifying the Constitution? How did the Preamble to the Constitution help them decide on this method?

3. What arguments did the Anti-Federalists make against ratifying the Constitution?

4. How did the Federalists respond to the criticisms of the Constitution made by the Anti-Federalists?

5. The Anti-Federalists lost their battle to prevent adoption of the Constitution. Their struggle, however, permanently shaped the new Constitution. Explain how the ideas and concerns of the Anti-Federalists accomplished this. Why was this struggle important? Why is it relevant today?

6. Explain how the ratification process provided a widespread public debate about an important political decision.

Activities

1. Learn more about *The Federalist*. Find information in your library or on the Internet. Write your own *Federalist* paper. Read it to your class.

2. Imagine that you are an Anti-Federalist. Make a collage that illustrates your point of view about the Constitution. Include references to actual Anti-Federalist writings. Be prepared to defend your design before the class.

3. Imagine that people in 1787 drove cars like ours. Create a bumper sticker that reflects either a Federalist or Anti-Federalist point of view about the new constitution.

How Did Congress Organize the New Government?

LESSON PURPOSE

The U.S. Constitution is a plan for government. Once the Constitution was ratified, it was the job of the first Congress to use this plan to organize the new government. In this lesson, you will read about some of the decisions made by the first Congress. You will learn how Congress organized the executive branch. You will also learn how Congress established a system of federal courts below the U.S. Supreme Court. Finally, you will learn how the Bill of Rights was added to the Constitution.

LESSON OBJECTIVES

When you finish this lesson, you should be able to

❑ explain how the first Congress organized the executive and judicial branches of government, and

❑ explain how the Bill of Rights was added to the Constitution.

TERMS TO UNDERSTAND

- appellate court
- cabinet
- federal district court
- Judiciary Act of 1789
- Ninth Amendment
- Tenth Amendment

Who was elected the first president?

When the votes in the Electoral College were counted, George Washington, as expected, was elected president unanimously. John Adams of Massachusetts was elected vice president. Washington took the oath of office on April 30, 1789.

Washington did not really want to be president. He would have preferred to remain at Mount Vernon, his home, and take care of his plantation. But Washington had a strong sense of civic responsibility and felt that it was his duty to serve his country. He wrote, "when I had judged ... that it was my duty to embark again on the tempestuous and uncertain Ocean of public life, I gave up all expectations of private happiness in this world."

Why was accepting the presidency so difficult for George Washington?

Washington knew that the Founders who were against the Constitution were afraid that it gave too much power to the president. He knew he should not do anything that added to their fears. Yet, he also knew that he had to be a strong leader.

By May of 1789, members of the new Congress of the national government were at work in New York City, the nation's temporary capital. Many people in Congress were worried about how Washington would use his power. They even disagreed on what they should call the president. Some people said he should be called "His Highness, the President of the United States of America." Congress decided that because America was not a monarchy, Washington should simply be addressed as "the President of the United States."

How did Congress and the president organize the executive branch?

The Constitution gives Congress the power to organize the executive branch. Washington could not run the executive branch alone. To help Washington fulfill his responsibilities, Congress created three departments.

- **Department of State.** Thomas Jefferson was selected to serve as Secretary of State to be responsible for the foreign relations of the nation.

- **Department of the Treasury.** Alexander Hamilton, as Secretary of the Treasury, guided the new government in money matters.

- **Department of War.** Henry Knox, as the Secretary of War, handled military affairs and defense.

This is a view of Federal Hall in New York City, which is where Congress first met. How did Congress help the executive branch of government deal with its responsibilities?

In addition, Congress created the office of attorney general, whose job was to give the president legal advice. Washington appointed Edmund Randolph to this position.

Washington used these officials as advisers to help him make decisions. These officials became known as the president's **cabinet**. Today, the cabinet positions have grown from the original four to the present number of fifteen. In fact, the executive branch of the federal government has grown far beyond the expectations of the Framers.

How did Congress organize the judicial branch?

Congress set up the judicial branch of government under Article III of the Constitution. Article III provided for a U.S. Supreme Court and said that Congress could establish lower courts as needed.

In 1789, Congress passed a law that organized the court system for the new nation. This law was the **Judiciary Act of 1789**. It stated that the U.S. Supreme Court was to have a chief justice and five associate justices. Over time, Congress has increased the size of the Court to nine justices.

Why do you think Congress created three levels of federal courts?

The lower courts that were authorized by the Judiciary Act include two kinds of courts—**federal district courts**, which hear cases involving the Constitution and federal laws, and appellate courts. **Appellate courts** handle those cases that have been tried first in **district court** and have been appealed. The appellate court is a higher court than a district court. But the U.S. Supreme Court is the highest court of appeals in the nation. In addition to the federal courts, each state has its own courts to rule on state laws.

How did Congress add the Bill of Rights to the Constitution?

When the Constitution was sent to the states for ratification, the Anti-Federalists opposed it. They felt that the Constitution should include a bill of rights. The Federalists claimed that a bill of rights was not necessary. They said that the Constitution organized government in such a way that it would be impossible to violate people's rights. They also argued that listing individual rights might make people think that these were the only rights guaranteed by government.

Finally, a compromise was reached. The Federalists agreed that when the first Congress met, they would draft a bill of rights to add to the Constitution.

The Bill of Rights was passed by the first Congress. It contains ten amendments. The first eight amendments list basic protections already guaranteed in most state constitutions. These include the following:

- Freedom of religion

- Freedom of the press

- Freedom of speech

- The rights of assembly and petition

- The right to a speedy, public trial by jury

The **Ninth Amendment** to the Constitution says that the listing of certain rights does not mean that these are the only rights the people have. Finally, the **Tenth Amendment** says that the powers not delegated to the federal government nor forbidden to the states belong to the states or to the people.

Congress proposed the Bill of Rights in 1789. It was ratified by the necessary eleven states on December 15, 1791. The Bill of Rights has proved to be very important to the protection of the basic rights of the American people. You will learn more about the Bill of Rights in the next unit.

How did the Bill of Rights become part of the Constitution?

Reviewing and Using the Lesson

1. The Constitution describes the organization of the executive and judicial branches only in general terms. Explain how the first Congress and the president organized the executive branch.

2. How did the first Congress organize the judicial branch?

3. What is the president's cabinet and what does it do?

4. What was the purpose of the Bill of Rights? Why was it included in our Constitution?

5. What rights are guaranteed in the Ninth and Tenth Amendments? How do these amendments differ from the other amendments in the Bill of Rights?

Activities

1. Find out the process for amending the U.S. Constitution.

2. The idea of having one person serve as president was developed when our nation had fewer than four million people. Today we have more than 300 million people. Do you think it is still a good idea to have only one person head the executive branch? Why or why not? What alternatives can you suggest? Make a chart showing how your ideas might improve our government.

3. Visit the website of the executive branch of our national government, www.whitehouse.gov. Find a list of the fifteen cabinet positions and the functions of each. Which is the newest cabinet position? Why was it created? Write an essay explaining what you learn.

Federalists   Republicans

How Did Political Parties Develop?

LESSON PURPOSE

The new nation faced a number of problems. Differing ideas about how these problems should be resolved led to the rise of political parties. In this lesson, you will learn what political parties are and how they began in American politics.

LESSON OBJECTIVE

When you finish the lesson, you should be able to describe the two original political parties, their leaders, and the issues that divided them.

TERMS TO UNDERSTAND

- Alien and Sedition Acts
- currency
- Federalist Party
- political party
- Republican Party

Why were the Framers of the Constitution concerned about factions? This cartoon from 1798 shows a fight between two members of Congress.

Why were the Framers of the Constitution against political parties?

When George Washington was elected as the first president, he received every electoral vote. One reason for this was the great respect people had for him. Another reason was that there were no political parties to run candidates against him.

The Framers were opposed to the idea of political parties. A **political party** is a group of people who join together because they have similar views about government. The Constitution does not include rules for forming or regulating political parties.

The Framers believed that political parties were factions. As you learned in Lessons 3 and 10, a faction is usually a dissatisfied group formed within a larger group. The Framers

thought that factions might fight to promote the interests of their own members. The Framers feared that the strongest faction would then control government. In such a case, government would not protect equally the rights and interests of all the people. Instead, government would promote the interests of the party in power.

When Washington took office, the new nation faced many problems. The country was in debt and needed to create good relations with other nations. People had different ideas about how to solve these problems. As President Washington and his advisers tried to deal with the issues, disagreements arose. These disagreements eventually led to the rise of political parties.

Why was the disagreement about the meaning of the words in the Constitution important?

President Washington chose Alexander Hamilton and Thomas Jefferson to be his advisers. Hamilton was the Secretary of the Treasury. Jefferson was the Secretary of State. The views of Hamilton and Jefferson about the powers of the federal government were often in conflict.

Hamilton wanted a strong federal government. He favored taking a broad view of the meaning of the words in the Constitution. The Constitution does not always use clear terms to describe the power of the federal government. Take, for example, the necessary and proper clause. What does *necessary* mean? Hamilton believed that necessary meant that which is needful or useful to solve a problem. He argued that the Constitution created government to solve national problems. As long as a problem was national, the federal government could and should deal with it.

On the other hand, Thomas Jefferson believed in small, local government. He favored taking a narrow view of the meaning of the words in the Constitution. To Jefferson, *necessary* meant "absolutely necessary." The federal government could not do whatever it wanted. Government could not exercise power just because it was convenient to do so. If government were free to define its own powers, it would threaten the liberty of the people.

The conflict about the meaning of the words in the Constitution was an important one. Hamilton would give more power to the federal government. Jefferson would limit it strictly to its enumerated powers.

The people who supported the views of Hamilton eventually became the **Federalist Party**. The people who supported Jefferson became the **Republican Party**. This is not the same Republican Party of today.

What role for the federal government did Thomas Jefferson favor?

Critical Thinking Exercise

The conflict over the necessary and proper clause in the Constitution

The Constitution gives Congress the power to make any laws it thinks are "necessary and proper" for carrying out the enumerated and other powers it has, including the "general Welfare." Work with one or more partners to answer the following questions.

1 What were the differences between Hamilton's and Jefferson's positions on this power?

2 What do their positions reveal about their differences about the role and powers of the national government?

3 What might happen if Congress did not have the power to make any laws it thinks are "necessary and proper" to promote the "general Welfare"?

4 What threats to the liberty of the people, if any, result from giving Congress the power to make any laws it thinks are necessary and proper to promote the general welfare?

5 What position would you take on whether or not the necessary and proper and general welfare clauses should be included in the Constitution?

How did Alexander Hamilton propose to strengthen the nation's economy? Why were some people opposed to his plans?

Why was the disagreement about the nation's economy important?

As Secretary of the Treasury, Alexander Hamilton wanted to strengthen the nation's economy. To do this, he wanted to create a strong currency. **Currency** is the form of money that a country uses.

He also wanted to encourage people to manufacture goods on a large scale. At that time, most Americans were farmers. The factories that did exist were small, family-owned businesses.

Hamilton also wanted to solve the problem of the national and state debts. Most of the debt was the result of borrowing to pay for the Revolutionary War. The federal government owed $54 million and the state governments owed about $25 million. Hamilton believed that solving the problem of the debt would strengthen the economy and would establish the public credit of the United States.

To achieve his goals, Hamilton came up with a plan to create a government bank. The bank, Hamilton said, was needed to help collect taxes, make loans to private citizens, and issue paper money. Gold and silver coins were in short supply. Paper money would increase the amount of currency available.

The problem was that the people did not trust paper money. They believed that it would not hold its value. The value of coins was based on the amount of gold or silver in the coin. Thus, the federal government would need to guarantee the value of paper money.

This building in Philadelphia was the site of the First Bank of the United States from 1795 to 1811. What were Jefferson's and Hamilton's opinions on establishing the bank?

167

Hamilton advised President Washington that the necessary and proper clause gave government the power to create a bank. He argued that a bank was necessary to allow government to carry out its enumerated powers to collect taxes and regulate trade.

Thomas Jefferson was against the use of federal power to create a bank. He believed that the necessary and proper clause only allowed government to do those things that were absolutely necessary. Creating a bank did not pass the test.

George Washington listened to the arguments for and against the bank. He then signed the bill from Congress creating the Bank of the United States. The effect of the new law was to increase the power of the federal government. People began to take sides on whether the federal government had acted in accord with the Constitution.

Why was the disagreement about foreign affairs important?

In 1793, war broke out between France and Great Britain. This event raised the level of tension between the Federalists and the Republicans.

Thomas Jefferson wanted a close relationship with France. Many Americans had strong feelings for France. After all, the French had supported the colonies during the Revolutionary War.

During this time, the British were seizing American ships on the high seas. They were searching for British sailors they claimed were deserters. But sometimes they captured American sailors and forced them to serve in the British navy. The British also refused to leave the forts they still occupied on land that now belonged to the United States. The Republicans wanted the United States to take strong measures against the British.

Alexander Hamilton wanted a close relationship with Great Britain. Most of the colonists had come from Britain and still had links with people in that nation. In addition, the United States carried on more trade with Great Britain than it did with France. The Federalists wanted the United States to side with the British.

President Washington had sent United States Chief Justice John Jay on a mission to Great Britain. He negotiated a treaty that confirmed that the British would leave the forts they still held in the United States.

John Jay was quoted as saying that he could travel from Boston to Philadelphia by the light of his burning effigies. Why was his treaty with the British unpopular?

They agreed to increase trade with the Americans. They did not agree to stop searching American ships for goods going to the enemy, France. The treaty was unpopular and the Republicans were greatly angered.

Washington did not want to take sides in the war between Great Britain and France. To do so, he thought, would be harmful to the United States. He declared that the American government would be neutral. When Washington left the presidency, he cautioned the new nation against entering into any permanent agreements with foreign governments.

What were the Alien and Sedition Acts?

George Washington served two terms as president. When he left office, he warned the Americans about the harmful effect of political parties.

By the election of 1796, there was serious hostility between the Federalists and the Republicans. Each party wanted one of its own people to win the presidential election. John Adams, a Federalist, was elected president. Thomas Jefferson, a Republican, was elected vice president.

The Alien and Sedition Acts prevented the press from speaking out against the government. What limits, if any, should be placed on the people's right to criticize the government?

	Thomas Jefferson of Virginia	Aaron Burr of New York	John Adams of Massachusetts	Charles Cotesworth Pinckney of South Carolina	John Jay of New York
New Hampshire			6	6	
Massachusetts			16	16	
Rhode Island			4	3	1
Connecticut			9	9	
Vermont			4	4	
New York	12	12			
New Jersey			7	7	
Pennsylvania	8	8	7	7	
Delaware			3	3	
Maryland	5	5	5	5	
Virginia	21	21			
Kentucky	4	4			
North Carolina	8	8	4	4	
Tennessee	3	3			
South Carolina	8	8			
Georgia	4	4			
	73	73	65	64	1

This is the tally of electoral votes from the election of 1800. How was the president selected when Thomas Jefferson and Aaron Burr tied for votes in the Electoral College?

Jefferson and the Republicans were very critical of the way Adams ran the government. The Republicans organized their opposition. They used the newspapers to build public support for their views.

Adams and the Federalists in Congress were able to pass two laws called the **Alien and Sedition Acts**. The Alien Act gave the president broad powers over aliens entering the country. The Sedition Act made it a crime for newspaper editors, writers, or speakers to criticize the government.

The Alien and Sedition Acts outraged the Republicans. They knew that the laws were intended to silence them. Several newspaper editors and a member of Congress were fined and put in jail for writing and speaking against the government.

Why was the presidential election of 1800 important?

The election of 1800 was the first time that political parties backed candidates for president. The Federalists worked to re-elect John Adams. The Republicans supported Thomas Jefferson.

Adams and Jefferson did not campaign the way it is done in modern elections. Instead, the parties ran the campaign, and it was a bitter one. Both parties accused each other of wishing to destroy the Constitution. The Republicans cited the Alien and Sedition Acts as proof that the Federalists were not fit to govern.

The election of 1800 was very important. Even though it had been a bitter campaign, the parties accepted the result.

Thomas Jefferson and Aaron Burr, also a Republican, tied for votes in the Electoral College. So, according to the Constitution, the House of Representatives was obliged to select the winning candidate. After thirty-six ballots, Jefferson was chosen.

For the first time in modern history, control of a government was transferred from one political party to another as the result of a democratic election. Thomas Jefferson later called it the "revolution of 1800."

Over the long term, the Federalist Party could not compete with the Republicans. Other parties arose to take its place. The modern Democratic Party claims its roots lie with the Republican Party of Thomas Jefferson. The modern Republican Party claims its roots lie with the Republican Party of Abraham Lincoln.

What is the role of political parties today?

Political parties are active today at the local, state, and national levels. Despite the fears of the Framers, they are an important part of the political system. The following list states some ways political parties may be useful.

- Political parties give people a way to join with others of similar interests to try to influence their government.

- People, working through their parties, can nominate candidates for public office, raise money for their candidates, and encourage people to vote for them.

- Political parties can and do get many people involved in the process of government.

- Political parties give people a choice of candidates and programs.

- The political party that is not in power can debate and criticize the party in power.

What role do political parties play in the American system of government?

Reviewing and Using the Lesson

1. Why were the Framers of the Constitution against having political parties?

2. What was the disagreement over the meaning of the words in the Constitution?

3. What was the disagreement about the creation of the Bank of the United States?

4. What was the disagreement about foreign affairs?

5. What were the Alien and Sedition Acts? Why were they passed?

6. Explain how the disagreements about how to solve the new nation's problems led to the rise of political parties.

7. Why was the election of 1800 important?

Activities

1. Draw a cartoon that illustrates the disagreements between the Federalist and Republican parties.

2. Presidents and vice presidents were elected differently in 1800 than they are today. Make a chart showing what the differences are. Find out which Amendment to the Constitution was passed to correct the problems that occurred in the 1800 presidential election.

3. Use the Internet to do a research activity. Find current information about the Democratic and Republican parties. Learn what each party believes about how government should be run. Then study a policy issue that interests both parties. Create a chart that illustrates their differences of opinion over the issue.

4. Find information about the beliefs of third parties, such as the Libertarian Party, the Reform Party, or the Green Party. Write a campaign speech that explains the role of third parties in elections today. Give the speech to your classmates.

LESSON 21

How Does the U.S. Supreme Court Use the Power of Judicial Review?

LESSON PURPOSE

Even in our nation's earliest years, people such as Alexander Hamilton and Thomas Jefferson disagreed about exactly what the words in the Constitution meant. Who should decide which reading of the Constitution is correct? The Constitution gives the U.S. Supreme Court the final say about the meaning of the Constitution. This lesson explains how the Supreme Court established its power to decide whether acts by other branches of the federal government or by state and local governments violate the Constitution. This power of the Court is called the power of judicial review. This power is not mentioned in the Constitution.

LESSON OBJECTIVES

When you finish this lesson, you should be able to

☐ explain what is meant by judicial review, and

☐ explain how the U.S. Supreme Court established its power of judicial review in one of the most important cases in our nation's history.

TERMS TO UNDERSTAND

- judicial review
- *Marbury v. Madison*
- null and void
- opinion of the Court

Does the Supreme Court have the power of judicial review over laws passed by state governments? Why or why not?

Minnesota governor Mark Dayton (right) signs a bill into law with Secretary of State Mark Ritchie (left) in July 2011.

What is judicial review?

Judicial review is the power of the courts to decide whether laws and actions of government are allowed under the Constitution. When a court decides that a law or action is not allowed, it orders that the law or action be considered null and void. A law that is **null and void** may not be enforced. Such a law is considered unconstitutional and not acceptable as a law at all.

How does judicial review apply to laws passed by state governments?

The Framers wanted to be sure that the states obeyed the laws of the federal government. So, in Article VI of the Constitution, they said that the U.S. Constitution, federal laws, and treaties are the supreme law of the land. As we discussed in Lessons 16 and 17, this is the supremacy clause. The Constitution, the laws passed by Congress, and treaties are the nation's highest laws and must be obeyed by the states. If state laws conflict with those of the federal government, the U.S. Supreme Court can order that the state laws not be enforced.

The U.S. Supreme Court first used its power of judicial review over state governments in 1796. After the Revolutionary War, the United States signed a peace treaty with Great Britain. As part of this treaty, Americans agreed to pay all debts they owed to British citizens. The state of Virginia passed a law that canceled all debts that its citizens owed to the British. Because this law violated the peace treaty, the Supreme Court ruled that the law could not be enforced. The citizens of Virginia would have to pay their debts.

Why do you think the Constitution does not explicitly state that the Supreme Court has the power of judicial review over the legislative and executive branches of the federal government?

Does the U.S. Supreme Court have the power of judicial review over acts of the federal government?

The Framers clearly meant that the U.S. Supreme Court should have the power of judicial review over acts of the state governments. The Constitution does not state that the U.S. Supreme Court has the power of judicial review over the legislative and executive branches of the federal government.

Critical Thinking Exercise

Examining the Supreme Court's power of judicial review over acts of Congress

Imagine that you must decide whether the U.S. Supreme Court should have the power of judicial review over laws passed by Congress. Read the two opinions below. Consider each position and its possible results.

Work with one or more partners. Use the questions below to help you decide which position your group would support.

Opinion 1

Give the U.S. Supreme Court the power to declare that a law passed by Congress is unconstitutional.

Possible result Some laws, even though they were passed by a majority of representatives in Congress—people elected by citizens to represent their interests—would not be carried out and enforced.

1. How is this position related to the principles of representative government and majority rule?

2. Is this position more democratic than the position explained in Opinion 2? Why or why not?

3. What effect might this position have on the basic rights of the individual?

4. What effect might this position have on protecting the minority from the whims of the majority?

Opinion 2

Deny the U.S. Supreme Court the power to declare laws passed by Congress unconstitutional.

Possible result All laws passed by a majority of representatives in Congress—people elected by citizens to represent their interests—would be carried out and enforced.

1. How is this position related to the principles of representative government and majority rule?

2. Is this position more democratic than the position explained in Opinion 1? Why or why not?

3. What effect might this position have on the basic rights of the individual?

4. What effect might this position have on protecting the minority from the whims of the majority?

How did the U.S. Supreme Court decide the case of *Marbury v. Madison?*

The U.S. Supreme Court established its power of judicial review over the other branches of the federal government in one of the most famous cases in our history. This case, *Marbury v. Madison*, was decided in 1803.

During the last weeks that John Adams was president, he appointed a number of people to office. There had not been enough time to deliver the proper papers to all the appointees before the next president, Thomas Jefferson, took office. Without the proper papers, the appointees could not take the jobs that Adams gave them. When Jefferson did take office, he ordered his secretary of state, James Madison, not to deliver the appointments that were left.

One person who did not receive his appointment was William Marbury. Marbury believed that he was entitled to have the job. Marbury took his case directly to the U.S. Supreme Court because the Judiciary Act of 1789 stated he had that right.

What was Chief Justice John Marshall's argument for the Supreme Court's power of judicial review?

Chief Justice John Marshall wrote the opinion for the U.S. Supreme Court. The **opinion of the Court** is the Court's decision and the reasoning behind the decision. The Court ruled that Marbury did have a right to his job. But they also said that the part of the Judiciary Act that gave Marbury the right to bring his case directly to the U.S. Supreme Court was unconstitutional.

The Constitution clearly limits the cases that can go directly to the U.S. Supreme Court without being first heard in a lower court. Marbury's case did not fit within these limits. Congress had changed the Constitution when it passed that part of the Judiciary Act. Congress by itself does not have the power to change the Constitution. So, the section of the Judiciary Act that increased the Court's power was ruled unconstitutional.

By declaring part of a law passed by Congress unconstitutional, the U.S. Supreme Court assumed the power of judicial review over the legislative and executive branches. Justice Marshall argued that the people of this nation had adopted the Constitution as the supreme law of the land and consented to be governed by its rules.

These rules include important limits on the powers of Congress. When Congress violates those limitations, it has violated the will of the people.

Marshall said that if the U.S. Supreme Court could not strike down such acts, there would be no effective way to enforce the constitutional limits on the powers of Congress. Its powers would be unlimited, and we would no longer have a constitutional government. Since the decision of *Marbury v. Madison*, the U.S. Supreme Court has exercised the power of judicial review over the federal government.

Reviewing and Using the Lesson

1. What is judicial review?

2. How does judicial review apply to the laws passed by state governments?

3. What was the case of *Marbury v. Madison*? How did the U.S. Supreme Court decide this case?

4. Why was *Marbury v. Madison* such an important case?

5. How does judicial review protect the rights of the people?

6. How might judicial review override the will of the majority?

Activities

1. In the history of our country, there have been several important justices on the U.S. Supreme Court. Learn more about one of the justices listed below. Share what you learned with your class.

   * Oliver Wendell Holmes Jr.
   * John Jay
   * John Marshall
   * Thurgood Marshall
   * Roger B. Taney
   * Earl Warren

2. Find an article in the newspaper that explains a case or constitutional issue before the U.S. Supreme Court. Be prepared to explain the article to your class.

3. With your teacher, invite an attorney or judge to come to your classroom to discuss how our court system works. Prepare questions you want to ask the guest during the visit.

4. Almost every trial in the United States is open to the public. With your teacher, visit your local courthouse. Talk with one of the judges. Observe a trial. This will allow you to see for yourself how our justice system operates.

How Does the U.S. Supreme Court Determine the Meaning of the Words in the Constitution?

LESSON PURPOSE

Some parts of the Constitution are clear and easy to understand. Other parts are much more difficult. What is the best way to decide what the Constitution means? In this lesson, you will learn about some of the more common approaches the U.S. Supreme Court has used to decide what the Constitution means.

LESSON OBJECTIVES

When you finish this lesson, you should be able to

❑ describe common approaches the U.S. Supreme Court has used to decide the meaning of the Constitution, and

❑ give arguments in favor or against each of these methods.

TERMS TO UNDERSTAND

- interpret
- Second Amendment

What characteristics should justices of the U.S. Supreme Court have? Why are these characteristics important?
Chief Justice John G. Roberts Jr. and Justice Elena Kagan

Why is it difficult to understand the meaning of some parts of the Constitution?

Deciding what the Constitution means has been a continuous process throughout our history. Even the justices of the Supreme Court sometimes disagree about the best method of deciding what the Constitution means.

Some parts are easy to understand. For example, Article II says, "The executive Power shall be vested in a President of the United States of America." This is a very specific statement about the head of the executive branch. Not all parts of the Constitution are so clear. For example, the meaning of the

following statements in the Constitution is not specific:

- Congress shall have the power to make laws that are "necessary and proper" to carry out its responsibilities.

- Citizens are protected against "unreasonable searches and seizures."

- No state shall "deprive any person of life, liberty, or property without due process of law."

Critical Thinking Exercise

Interpreting the Constitution

Read the following example of language found in the Constitution and answer the questions that follow. Work with one or more partners to discuss and complete this exercise.

> ### Example
>
> **The Fourth Amendment protects citizens against "unreasonable searches and seizures."**

If you were a member of the U.S. Supreme Court, how would you decide what makes a search or seizure unreasonable?

Read the five methods that follow. Identify the advantages and disadvantages of each method presented. Then, determine which method you think would be best for deciding the meaning of the Constitution. Be prepared to explain your opinion to the class.

❶ Look up *unreasonable* in a dictionary to find out what it means.

❷ Try to find out how the Framers might have explained the word *unreasonable*.

❸ Examine the word *unreasonable* in relation to such basic ideas as natural rights and limited government?

❹ Examine the word *unreasonable* in relation to the historical, political, and social changes that have occurred since the Constitution was written.

❺ Rely upon previous Court rulings on "unreasonable" searches and seizures.

If you were a member of the Supreme Court, how would you decide what makes a search or seizure unreasonable?

How does the U.S. Supreme Court decide what the words in the Constitution mean?

When deciding constitutional cases, the justices of the U.S. Supreme Court have to interpret the Constitution. To **interpret** means to decide what the words or phrases actually mean.

There are four basic methods that the U.S. Supreme Court has used to interpret the Constitution. Each method has its advantages and disadvantages.

❶ **The plain meaning of the words in the Constitution** Using this method, the justices consider the literal, or plain, meanings of the words. Sometimes they study what the words meant at the time they

The Constitution only grants Congress the authority to establish an army and a navy. What argument can you make that the Constitution also grants Congress the authority to establish an air force?

were written. With this method, the Court bases its decisions, as closely as possible, on how the Framers meant the Constitution to be interpreted. If the meaning of the words is clear, then this is the best way to know what the Framers meant.

The problem is that at the Philadelphia Convention there was disagreement about the meaning of some words. Another problem is that some questions are not answered at all. For example, the Constitution gives Congress the power to establish an army and a navy. Does this mean that Congress does not have the power to establish an air force?

② **The intention of the Framers** This method is based on the idea that the Constitution by itself does not always have an obvious meaning. Therefore, we should look at the intentions of the people who wrote it. Those who believe in this method say that the justices should base their decisions on how the Framers would have decided. They claim that it is the approach most faithful to the ideas in the Constitution.

The problem is that it is extremely difficult, if not impossible, to figure out what the Framers intended on some issues. There were differences of opinion among the thirty-nine Framers. How can you determine who had the correct view? This method of interpretation also gives no guidelines about types of situations that did not exist when the Constitution was written.

③ **Fundamental principles** The Constitution is based on some fundamental principles of government. These principles include natural rights philosophy, constitutionalism, and republican government. As the nation matures so does our understanding of these basic principles. This method says that the justices should make their decisions based on these basic principles and values.

④ **Today's social values and needs** This method says that the justices should use today's social values in interpreting the Constitution. People who hold this view believe that the justices should not ignore the realities of our society today. Justices, they argue, should not hold back social progress by sticking to outmoded interpretations.

The problem with methods 3 and 4 is that these approaches might give the justices too

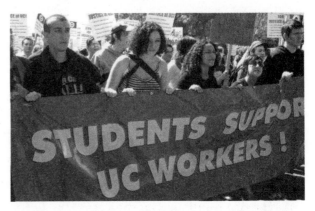

What arguments can you make for and against using today's social values and needs to interpret the Constitution?

What colonial experiences might have led Americans to believe that the right to keep and bear arms was an important check against tyranny?

much freedom to decide cases according to their own political ideas and personal beliefs. The justices can simply alter the Constitution as they please.

In deciding a case, U.S. Supreme Court justices are influenced by a number of things. They consider the literal meaning of the words in the Constitution as well as the intention of the Framers. Justices consider the basic principles of the Constitution as well as the previous decisions of the Court. The justices are also aware of the current political, social, and economic situation in the country. Finally, the justices are influenced, as is everyone, by their own personal beliefs.

The U.S. Supreme Court's decisions often raise much controversy—especially when the Court has attempted to define and protect certain basic rights. In the next unit, we will look at some of these controversies.

Critical Thinking Exercise

Interpreting the Second Amendment

Senator Orrin Hatch has written: "When our ancestors forged a land 'conceived in liberty,' they did so with musket and rifle…as a nation of armed freemen…[and] they devoted one full amendment out of ten to nothing but the protection of their right to keep and bear arms against governmental interference."

Using library and Internet resources, work in small groups to answer the following questions. Share your answers with the class.

1. In 1791, when the Second Amendment was passed, why did the nation seek to protect liberty by protecting the right to keep and bear arms? What historical background and circumstances led them to this conclusion?

2. Do you think the Second Amendment is as important today as it was in the eighteenth century? Explain your answer.

3. In a 1998 U.S. Supreme Court case, Justice Ruth Bader Ginsburg pointed out that the text of the **Second Amendment** refers to the right to keep *and bear* arms. Since to *bear* arms means to carry them—not just to possess them—should citizens in every state be allowed to carry firearms on their person? Should they be able to keep them in vehicles? Why or why not?

Reviewing and Using the Lesson

1. Why is it sometimes difficult to determine the meaning of the words in the Constitution?

2. What does it mean "to interpret" the Constitution?

3. What are the four methods that justices might use to interpret the Constitution? What are the advantages and disadvantages of each method?

Activities

1. Imagine that you are a member of the U.S. Supreme Court. The Court has agreed to hear a case involving government agencies watching which sites citizens visit on the Internet. This technology did not exist when the Constitution was written. What method for interpreting the Constitution might you use to determine whether the practice is unconstitutional? Explain your reasons.

2. Examine the following two statements by former justices of the U.S. Supreme Court. What does each statement mean? Do you agree with these statements? Why or why not?

"We are under a Constitution, but the Constitution is what the judges say it is."

Charles Evans Hughes, Chief Justice of the United States, 1930–1941
Associate Justice of the U.S. Supreme Court, 1910–1916

"As a member of this court I am not justified in writing my opinions into the Constitution, no matter how deeply I may cherish them."

Felix Frankfurter, Associate Justice of the U.S. Supreme Court, 1939–1962

How Does the Constitution Protect Our Basic Rights?

How Does the Constitution Protect Our Basic Rights?

UNIT PURPOSE

You have learned that one of the most important purposes of government is to protect the basic rights of the people. The addition of the Bill of Rights to the Constitution was intended to achieve that purpose.

Adding the Bill of Rights, however, did not automatically guarantee these valued rights to all the people. In this unit, you will learn about five fundamental rights and how they have been extended to many people who were denied them in the past.

KEY CONCEPTS

- due process of law
- equal protection clause
- establishment of religion clause
- free exercise of religion clause
- freedom of expression
- freedom of religion
- suffrage

How Does the Constitution Protect Freedom of Expression?

LESSON PURPOSE

In this lesson, you will learn about how the Constitution protects freedom of expression. You will also learn why freedom of expression is important to you as an individual and to the preservation and improvement of our constitutional democracy.

LESSON OBJECTIVES

When you finish this lesson, you should be able to

☐ explain the importance of freedom of expression, and

☐ describe situations in which it might be reasonable and fair to place limitations on this freedom.

TERMS TO UNDERSTAND

- abridging
- assemble
- First Amendment
- freedom of expression
- redress of grievances

What rights are the people in this photograph exercising?

What is freedom of expression?

One of the main purposes of government is to protect our freedom. The **First Amendment** to our Constitution protects our freedom of expression. This is what the First Amendment says about freedom of expression:

> Congress shall make no law ... **abridging** the freedom of speech, or of the press; or the right of the people peaceably to **assemble**, and to petition the government for a **redress of grievances**.

As you can see, this section of the First Amendment includes several important freedoms. **Freedom of expression** is freedom of speech, of the press, of assembly, and of petition. The right of assembly is the right to meet with others to discuss your beliefs, ideas, or feelings.

It is important to understand that the First Amendment limits the powers of Congress. It prevents Congress from placing unreasonable and unfair limits on freedom of expression. That is why the Amendment begins with the phrase, "Congress shall make no law ..."

What are some benefits of freedom of expression?

The Founders of our nation believed that the right to hold and express one's beliefs was essential if citizens were to participate in the affairs of government. The following arguments highlight the importance of freedom of expression.

❶ Individual development and human dignity It is important for your growth as a person to have the right to present your ideas and to consider other points of view. Your dignity as a person should be respected by allowing you the freedom to say what you think and to hear what others think.

❷ Advancement of knowledge It is easier for new discoveries to be made when ideas can be discussed freely. Even if you disagree with someone, that person may say something that helps you test your knowledge and increase your understanding.

❸ The maintenance of representative democracy Individual citizens participate in running our country by electing their representatives to Congress and other government officials. Citizens can also participate in making decisions about government policies. To make wise choices, you need to have good information. Free expression does not guarantee complete or accurate information, but it increases the chances of getting such information.

❹ Peaceful social change Freedom of expression allows you to try to influence public opinion by persuasion without feeling you have to resort to violence to make changes. Also, if you have the opportunity to express your opinions freely, you might be more willing to accept government decisions, even decisions you do not agree with.

How does freedom of expression help maintain representative democracy?

Should there be limits to freedom of expression?

Many people believe that freedom of expression is necessary for the protection of all our individual freedoms. Does this mean there should be no limits to freedom of expression? Should you have the right to yell "Fire!" in a crowded theater when there is no fire? Such an action may cause bodily harm to others when they run to safety.

Other situations are more complicated. What if you wanted to convince other people that we should change our type of government? Should government be able to keep you from doing so? What if you are part of an unpopular group that wants to have a public demonstration in the streets? Should government be able to stop you because of the possibility of a riot?

Over the years, the courts in our country have developed guidelines to use in limiting freedom of expression. The courts use these guidelines to decide when the right to free expression interferes with other important rights and interests.

Suppose your right to freedom of expression in a particular situation is dangerous to public safety, national security, or some other important interest. If the danger is great enough, the courts sometimes allow freedom of expression to be limited.

Also, one person's right to freedom of expression may conflict with someone else's rights. The right to a free press might conflict with someone's right to a fair trial in a court of law. For this reason, we accept limitations that are intended to protect everyone's rights.

What limits, if any, should there be on freedom of expression? Can you name some situations where freedom of expression might endanger people?

Critical Thinking Exercise

Freedom of expression in schools

When should students' freedom of expression be limited? The following is a summary of an important U.S. Supreme Court case that dealt with this question. Read the summary and complete the exercise that follows it. The exercise will ask you to take a position on whether you agree or disagree with the decision of the U.S. Supreme Court.

Tinker v. Des Moines School District (1969)

This case involved a few high school students who wore black armbands to school. They were protesting American involvement in the Vietnam War. The school principal told the students to remove their armbands. The students refused and were suspended from school. The suspension was to last until they agreed to come back without the armbands. The parents took the case to court. They argued that the school was depriving the students of their right to freedom of expression.

The school argued that they were justified in suspending the students. They said the suspension had been necessary to prevent any disturbance that could be caused by wearing the armbands.

The U.S. Supreme Court ruled that the school's action was an unnecessary limitation on freedom of expression. The Court said that a school cannot limit a student's right to freedom of expression unless the student's exercise of that right disrupts the educational process. The Court said there was "no evidence whatever of … interference … with the school's work or … with

Do you agree with the Supreme Court's decision in the Tinker *case? Why or why not?*

Mary Beth Tinker was a junior high school student when she was suspended from school for wearing a black armband to protest the Vietnam War. Tinker now teaches young people about the case.

the rights of other students to be secure and to be let alone."

Justice Abe Fortas wrote the opinion for the Court. He said,

> "Any word spoken, in class, in the lunchroom or on the campus, that deviates from the views of another person, may start an argument or cause a disturbance. But our Constitution says we must take this

risk … and our history says that it is this sort of hazardous freedom—this kind of openness—that is the basis of our national strength and of the independence ... of Americans."

The Court said that students do not give up their "constitutional rights to freedom of speech or expression at the schoolhouse gate." Freedom of expression should be protected unless it clearly violates other important rights and interests.

Work with one or more partners to discuss and develop your responses to the following questions.

❶ Do you agree with the opinion of the Supreme Court in this case? Why?

❷ What rules do you think would be reasonable and fair to make to limit students' freedom of expression in school?

Should students have the same right to freedom of expression as adults? Why or why not?

Critical Thinking Exercise

Balancing rights and interests

The following U.S. Supreme Court case involves a situation about the need to balance freedom of expression with other important rights and interests. Read the summary and work with one or more partners to complete the exercise that follows it. The exercise will ask you to take a position on whether you agree or disagree with the decision of the U.S. Supreme Court.

Hazelwood School District v. Kuhlmeier (1988)

The journalism class in Hazelwood East High School wrote and published the high school's newspaper. In one issue of the paper, students planned to print an article about teenage pregnancy. The principal of the school thought that the story was not appropriate for younger students.

In the same issue of the paper, the students also planned to run a story in which a student wrote about divorce and made negative remarks about her father. The principal said that the newspaper had not given the father a chance to respond to his daughter's remarks. The principal ordered both stories to be removed from the paper before it was printed and distributed.

When the case was appealed to the Supreme Court, five justices voted to support the action of the principal and three voted to support the students' right to freedom of expression.

1. What are the conflicting rights and interests in this case?

2. In what ways is this case similar to the *Tinker* case? In what ways is it different?

3. Examine each of the two opinions and respond to the questions that follow them.

Opinion 1

A school does not need to tolerate student speech that is inconsistent with its basic mission to educate young people. The public schools are not like the streets, parks, and other public places that are used for purposes of assembly, communicating thoughts between citizens, and discussing public questions. Accordingly, the principal had a right to regulate the contents of the school newspaper in any reasonable manner. It is this standard, rather than the decision in *Tinker*, that governs this case.

- Do you agree or disagree with this opinion? Why?

Opinion 2

The school principal removed the articles from the newspaper not because the article would interfere with school discipline. He removed the articles because he considered them inappropriate, personal, and unsuitable for student consumption. The principal's action violated the First Amendment's prohibitions against censorship of any student expression that neither disrupts class work nor denies the rights of others.

- Do you agree or disagree with this opinion? Why?

Reviewing and Using the Lesson

1 How would you define freedom of expression?

2 What are the benefits of freedom of expression to the individual and to society?

3 What are some circumstances that might cause government to limit the right to freedom of expression?

4 What rights and interests are involved when limiting freedom of expression in the public schools?

Activities

1 Learn about the policies in your school district or the rules at your school that regulate how students may exercise freedom of expression. Make a computer presentation so you can share what you learned with your class.

2 Take photographs that illustrate the four parts of the right to freedom of expression. Make a collage of your photos showing the benefits of freedom of expression.

3 Suppose that an unpopular group wants to hold a demonstration in a public park in your community. Most people do not agree with the views of this group. People fear that the demonstration might become disorderly and disturb the peace. Work with a partner to create a skit. One of you should be in favor of allowing the group to hold the demonstration. The other should be opposed. Both of you should act out your views in front of the class and let them decide the issue.

4 Find a newspaper article that discusses someone exercising the right to freedom of expression in your community. Write an editorial based on the article for your school newspaper. In your essay, explain the benefits of this right to you and your community.

How Does the Constitution Protect Freedom of Religion?

LESSON

24

LESSON PURPOSE

In this lesson, you will learn about freedom of religion. You will learn about the difference between religious beliefs and religious practices. You will learn why there are no limits on beliefs but some limits on religious practices. Finally, the lesson will examine issues about the relationship between religion and public education.

LESSON OBJECTIVES

When you finish this lesson, you should be able to

❑ explain the importance of freedom of religion,

❑ describe situations in which religious practices may be limited, and

❑ explain some of the guidelines the U.S. Supreme Court has used to decide issues related to religion and the public schools.

TERMS TO UNDERSTAND

• establishment clause
• free exercise clause

Why did some of the colonists' ideas about religious tolerance change?

How does the First Amendment protect freedom of religion?

The very first part of the First Amendment says that "Congress shall make no law respecting an establishment of religion, or prohibiting the free exercise thereof." The meaning of these words in the First Amendment is explained below.

- **Establishment of religion** Congress may not establish, that is, institute, an official religion for our country or favor any one religion over others. We call this the **establishment clause**.

- **Free exercise** Congress may not stop you from holding any religious beliefs you choose or having no religious beliefs at all. Government may not unfairly or unreasonably limit your right to practice any religious beliefs you wish. We call this the **free exercise clause**.

Why did freedom of religion become an important principle in America?

Few of the early English colonies in North America permitted religious freedom. In several colonies, one religious group controlled the whole colony. Everyone living there had to follow the same religious ideas. People who disagreed were often persecuted or forced to leave the colony.

By the end of the colonial period, things had changed. For one thing, there were more religious groups, such as Baptists, Catholics, Jews, Quakers, and others. Most people's attitudes had also changed. More people practiced different religions. People became more accepting of each other's religious differences. Over time, people came to believe strongly that everyone has a right to his or her own religious beliefs.

In addition, men like Thomas Jefferson and James Madison were greatly concerned about the dangers of religious intolerance. They were well aware that throughout history, religious intolerance had often led to conflict and to the violation of individual rights. They thought religious intolerance was a danger to the community and harmful to religion.

The freedom of religion clause in the first part of the First Amendment illustrates the strong belief in America that government should not interfere with religion.

Why do conflicts about freedom of religion exist today?

Americans strongly believe that freedom of religion is an important right. But that does not mean that we have no disagreements about this issue today. Today's conflicts about freedom of religion focus on the following issues:

- **The establishment clause** This clause sets forth the idea that government is to be separated from religion. The meaning of the establishment clause is a continuing source of conflict among Americans. Does it mean that government may not be involved with religion in any way?

Is the federal government violating the establishment clause by providing chaplains to the armed forces? Why or why not?

A military chaplain celebrates Catholic mass aboard a U.S. Navy ship.

• **The free exercise clause** Each person has an absolute right to believe in any religion or in no religion at all. Freedom of belief is an inalienable right that cannot be interfered with by government in any way. The free exercise clause also means that your right to practice your religious beliefs is protected. But does the free exercise clause mean that all religious practices are protected? Can government prohibit a religious practice that endangers public health or safety?

Sometimes there are conflicts between the principles in the establishment and the free exercise clauses. For example, if government pays for prison chaplains, it is supporting religion. On the other hand, to prohibit government from doing this would interfere with the right of prisoners to practice their religion.

Disagreements like these about the relationship between government and religion have caused a number of important cases to be brought before the U.S. Supreme Court. In each case, the Supreme Court has had to decide how the freedom of religion clauses of the First Amendment should be interpreted.

Under what conditions, if any, should the government be able to control the practice of religious beliefs?

Can government limit your right to practice your religious beliefs?

In certain cases, government can limit the way you practice your religious beliefs. The U.S. Supreme Court has ruled that certain religious practices may be forbidden without violating constitutional rights. The Court has said that religious practices may be limited if they are contrary to public morals, endanger health, or harm the common good.

U.S. Supreme Court decisions have said that religious practices involving polygamy may be forbidden. Government can also require that children be vaccinated against certain contagious diseases before being admitted to public school. They may require vaccination even if it violates a family's religious beliefs.

Critical Thinking Exercise

What limits, if any, do you think should be placed on freedom of religion?

Work with two or more partners to develop answers to the following questions.

1 The First Amendment says that "Congress shall make no law respecting the establishment of religion … " Should this be interpreted to mean that the government cannot be involved in religion in any way? For example, should it be interpreted to mean that government cannot pay for chaplains to serve in the armed forces? Should it be interpreted to mean that schools may not observe religious holidays? What limits regarding the establishment of religion do you think should be placed on government? Explain your answer.

2 The First Amendment says that "Congress shall make no law respecting the … free exercise of religion … " Should this be interpreted to mean that the government cannot place any limits on your right to practice any religious beliefs? For example, should it be interpreted to mean that government cannot prohibit sacrificing animals for religious purposes? Should it be interpreted to mean that the government cannot require students attending public schools to be vaccinated against contagious diseases even if it violates a family's religious beliefs? What limitations regarding the free exercise of religious beliefs do you think the government should be allowed to make? Explain your answer.

How can we decide issues about religion in the public schools?

At the time the Constitution was written, public schools as we know them did not exist. Children who attended school usually received a great deal of religious training. In fact, their parents expected the schools to give religious instruction.

There has been growing disagreement about whether religious teaching should be supported in public schools. During the past seventy years especially, the U.S. Supreme Court has heard many cases dealing with this subject. Some questions the Court has tried to answer are as follows:

• Should tax money be used to support religious schools?

Should students be required to say the Pledge of Allegiance even if they object to doing so for religious reasons?

• Should public schools be allowed to provide periods of time when students can attend special classes to receive religious instruction from their own minister, priest, or rabbi?

• Should public schools be allowed to require students to take part in prayers or read the Bible during regular school hours?

The establishment clause requires that government be neutral toward religion. Government cannot support one type of religion over another type, nor can it support religion over nonreligion.

The courts follow guidelines when deciding whether government is complying with the establishment clause. They look at three factors.

❶ The courts examine whether government is actively endorsing religion.

❷ The courts examine whether government is compelling people to participate in religious activities or to accept religious beliefs.

❸ The courts examine whether government is providing special treatment to one type of religion that it is not providing to other types of religion.

If government fails any one of these factors, it is in violation of the establishment clause. In a recent case, for example, the U.S. Supreme Court ruled that a high school could not require its students to participate in a prayer at their graduation ceremony. The Court concluded that the high school, by requiring the prayer, was endorsing religion and compelling the students to participate in the prayer.

Critical Thinking Exercise

Deciding issues concerning religion in public schools

Work with one or more partners to complete this exercise. Read each of the following situations. Use the guidelines discussed in the previous section to decide whether the laws and actions described should be declared unconstitutional. Be prepared to explain your decisions to the class.

1 Your state passes a law allowing your public school principal to post the Ten Commandments in every classroom.

2 Your state passes a law that gives parents who send their children to religious schools a tax deduction for tuition, transportation, and educational materials.

3 Your state allows your public school's algebra teacher to spend part of his class day at a church school, giving instruction to students having difficulty with math.

4 There is an unused classroom at your public school. The student council requests permission to use it after school hours for voluntary prayer meetings. The principal refuses to make the classroom available.

How do the courts determine whether government is complying with the establishment clause?

Reviewing and Using the Lesson

1. What is the establishment clause?

2. What is the free exercise clause?

3. Why was freedom of religion an important principle in early America?

4. What conflicts exist over the freedom of religion clauses in the First Amendment? Give examples of each.

5. Can government limit your right to freedom of belief? Why or why not?

6. Can government limit your right to practice your religious beliefs? If so, under what circumstances?

7. What conflicts exist between freedom of religion and public education?

Activities

1. Some people have suggested adding an amendment to the Constitution that would allow public schools to set aside time for voluntary prayer. Use the Internet or your school library to find more information about this proposal. Then decide if you would support such an amendment. Write a brief essay explaining why or why not.

2. Thomas Jefferson and James Madison had strong opinions about the separation of church and state. Write an essay comparing and contrasting your opinions on this issue with those of Jefferson and Madison.

3. Make an illustration in the style you think might be found in eighteenth-century schoolbooks. In your drawing, show your understanding of the establishment clause.

How Has the Right to Vote Expanded Since the Constitution Was Adopted?

25

LESSON PURPOSE

The Constitution originally left it up to the state governments to decide who should have the right to vote. In the early years of our nation, the states limited the right to vote to white men who owned property. In 1789, white men who did not own property, members of certain religious groups, freedmen, Native Americans, slaves, and women were not allowed to vote.

In this lesson you will learn about how the right to vote has been expanded in the last two hundred years to achieve a basic ideal of our representative democracy—the constitutional right of all adult citizens to vote.

LESSON OBJECTIVE

When you finish this lesson you should be able to explain how voting rights were extended by changes in state voting laws, amendments to the Constitution, acts of Congress, and decisions of the U.S. Supreme Court.

TERMS TO UNDERSTAND

- civil rights movement
- Civil War Amendments
- grandfather clause
- literacy test
- poll tax
- register
- suffrage
- Voting Rights Act
- Thirteenth Amendment
- Fourteenth Amendment
- Fifteenth Amendment
- Nineteenth Amendment
- Twenty-fourth Amendment
- Twenty-sixth Amendment

How was the right of suffrage extended before the Civil War?

The colonial limits on who could vote did not change much during the early years of the new nation. Many colonies only allowed white men who owned property and belonged to a particular religious group to vote.

After the Revolution, an increasing number of people objected to these limits on voting rights. States began to do away with property and religious restrictions. In addition, new states joining the Union placed fewer limitations on suffrage. **Suffrage** means the right to vote. In the early 1800s, for example, six new Western states gave the vote to all adult white males.

Although the states took steps before the Civil War to extend suffrage to more people, change was not easy. For example, as late as 1842 in Rhode Island, only men with property were allowed to vote. This situation caused an armed rebellion. The rebellion failed. But the following year, Rhode Island adopted a new state constitution that gave voting rights to all male citizens who paid a tax of at least one dollar a year.

Before the Civil War, a large part of the population—including African American men and all women—still could not vote. In the remaining sections of the lesson, you will learn how these groups, Native Americans, and others gained the right to vote.

What criteria should be used to determine who should be eligible to vote?

How did African American men gain the right to vote?

Although many black men fought in the Revolutionary War, the right to vote was not extended to African Americans. In 1860, only six of the thirty-four states allowed freedmen to vote.

After the Civil War, the states approved the Thirteenth, Fourteenth, and Fifteenth Amendments to the Constitution. These amendments are known as the **Civil War Amendments**. The **Thirteenth Amendment** abolished slavery. The **Fourteenth Amendment** granted full citizenship to African Americans. The **Fifteenth Amendment** guaranteed the right to vote to men regardless of their "race, color, or previous condition of servitude."

Adding these Civil War Amendments to the Constitution was only the start of an effort to guarantee voting rights to African Americans. Many people in the Southern states did not want black people to vote or hold public office. Some states passed laws that made it impossible for African Americans to vote. Some examples of these laws follow.

Were the Civil War Amendments enough to guarantee the right of African Americans to vote? Why or why not?

What was unfair about these voting requirements?

Democracy's Turnstile

What was the poll tax? Why was it used?

- **Literacy tests** A **literacy test** requires a person to prove that he or she is able to read and write. Some states required all men to pass these tests before being allowed to vote. Because most African American men had been denied an education they could not pass the test. Often the people who gave the test behaved unfairly. They made it impossible for even educated African American men to pass the test.

- **Grandfather clause** Some states had voting laws with wording that we call **grandfather clauses**. A grandfather clause said that a person had the right to vote only if his grandfather had had the right to vote. Few African American men could qualify. Their grandfathers had been slaves and had been denied the right to vote.

- **Poll tax** A **poll tax** is a fee that a person must pay in order to vote. Some states charged all people a poll tax. Since most former slaves were very poor, they could not afford to pay the tax and, therefore, could not vote.

People fought to get these state laws changed, but it took a long time. In 1915, the U.S. Supreme Court said that grandfather clauses were unconstitutional. Some states, however, continued to use literacy tests and poll taxes until the 1960s in order to keep African Americans from voting.

In the 1950s, more and more people began to demand that the federal government protect the right of African Americans to vote. People of all races worked together to change unfair state laws. People gave speeches and marched in the streets. These actions became known as the **civil rights movement**.

As a result of the civil rights movement, the **Twenty-fourth Amendment** was added to the Constitution in 1964. The amendment says that the right to vote in national elections shall not be denied because a person fails to pay a poll tax or any other tax. The U.S. Supreme Court later said that the Twenty-fourth Amendment also applied to state elections.

Congress passed a law called the **Voting Rights Act** in 1965. The law protected the right to vote for all citizens. The law forced the states to obey the Constitution. It made it clear that the right to vote could not be denied because of a person's color.

How did women gain the right to vote?

In 1848, a convention was held at Seneca Falls, New York, that launched a national movement by women to win the right to vote. Although suffrage for women had many supporters among men, the battle was a difficult one. In those days it was common to believe that women should not participate in government. This idea made it harder for women to achieve their goal.

In 1876, Susan B. Anthony led a delegation of women to Philadelphia to celebrate the one-hundred-year anniversary of the Declaration of Independence. While there, the women publicly protested their lack of suffrage by reading the Women's Declaration of Rights.

Gaining the right to vote for women was a long, slow process. The earliest gains were made in the western part of the country. The territory of Wyoming granted women the right to vote in 1869. By 1900, Colorado, Utah, and Idaho had followed Wyoming's lead.

It was not until 1912 that the movement to give women the right to vote gained national recognition. Presidential candidate Theodore Roosevelt's Bull Moose Progressive Party supported the movement. In 1913, women were granted the right to vote in the territory of Alaska.

In 1920, the states ratified the **Nineteenth Amendment** to the Constitution, which gave women the vote. One hundred and thirty years after the signing of the Constitution, women had finally gained the right to vote.

What contributions did Elizabeth Cady Stanton (left) and Susan B. Anthony (right) make to the movement to recognize women's right to vote?

President Calvin Coolidge with a group of Native Americans after the signing of the Indian Citizenship Act of 1924. What rights were realized by Native Americans with the passage of this law?

How did Native Americans gain the right to vote?

American Indians governed themselves by their own tribal laws, treaties with the U.S. government, and by special laws passed by Congress. These laws did not recognize American Indians to be citizens of the United States. As a result, they did not have the right to vote.

The first attempt to grant Native Americans citizenship came in 1887 when Congress passed the Dawes Act. The Dawes Act granted a tract of land and citizenship to those who were willing to give up their allegiance to their tribe. The law was strongly resented by most tribes.

Finally, Congress passed a law in 1924 called the Indian Citizenship Act. This law fully recognized Native Americans as citizens of the United States. The law also gave Native Americans the right to vote in federal elections.

How did eighteen-year-olds gain the right to vote?

In the 1960s and 1970s, the government drafted thousands of young men to fight in the Vietnam War. Many of these young men were too young to vote. They did not have a voice in the elections for government officials responsible for deciding America's role in that war. The voting requirement at that time was twenty-one years of age.

Congress passed a law in 1970 lowering the voting age to eighteen. The U.S. Supreme Court then ruled that Congress could only regulate federal elections. At that time, only four states allowed eighteen-year-olds to vote. Following the Court's decision, steps were taken to amend the Constitution so that suffrage would be extended to eighteen-year-olds in both state and federal elections.

In 1971, the **Twenty-sixth Amendment** was added to the Constitution. The amendment grants the right to vote to any citizen who is eighteen years of age or older.

What are voting requirements today?

The states, although limited by the Constitution and the federal Voting Rights Act, still make some decisions regarding voting rights. All states have laws saying only citizens have the right to vote, although the Constitution does not require this. Every state requires that persons must live in the state for a period of time before they can vote, and all states except North Dakota require citizens to register before voting. To **register** to vote means to have your name added to a list. Voters are required to register to ensure that they are qualified to vote and to keep people from voting more than once.

Why should people who are old enough to serve in the armed forces also have the right to vote?

Throughout our history we have used our Constitution to achieve nearly universal adult suffrage. Today, almost every American of voting age has the right to vote. This has made the United States one of the most democratic nations on earth. Americans can use the power of the ballot box to choose more public officials at more levels of government than can voters in any other democracy.

As the right to vote has expanded, though, the willingness of American citizens to participate has decreased. In recent years, there has been a steady decline in voter

Should young people learn about their obligation to vote before they are eighteen? Why or why not?

turnout for elections. The United States now ranks eleventh among the world's democracies in the percentage of eligible voters who exercise the right to vote.

Many people worry about the unwillingness of so many Americans to use this most fundamental right and duty of citizenship. They fear that not voting may reflect a growing feeling of being disconnected from government. However, if the United States is to be a country that is truly of, by, and for the people, it is essential that the people exercise their right to vote competently and responsibly. Responsible voting is essential to democracy.

Critical Thinking Exercise

Suggesting ways to increase participation in elections

Generally, better-off and better-educated citizens use their right to vote to a much greater extent than do poor or uneducated citizens. Voter turnout is also related to age. Older Americans are almost twice as likely to vote than are young Americans. Work with one or more partners to develop answers to the following questions.

1 Why do you think that older Americans might be more interested in government policies than younger Americans?

2 What political issues motivate younger citizens to get involved with public life? Give examples.

3 Some countries increased voter participation by holding elections on Sundays. What other methods can you suggest to increase voter turnout?

4 In some countries, voter participation is mandatory. What effect might this have on elections? Do you think this is a good way to increase citizen participation in elections?

Do you think something should be done to increase voter turnout? Why or why not?

Reviewing and Using the Lesson

1. What were some of the restrictions on voting rights that kept various groups of people from voting?

2. Explain how each of the following groups of people gained the right to vote.

   - African Americans
   - eighteen-year-olds
   - Native Americans
   - women

3. What amendments were added to the Constitution so that more people would have the right to vote?

4. What laws did Congress pass to protect the constitutional right of citizens to vote?

5. What actions did citizens take to expand the right to vote to most Americans?

Activities

1. With help from your teacher, invite someone from the League of Women Voters to come to your class to discuss elections in your state. Prepare questions to ask your guest during the visit.

2. Use the Internet to find information about the requirements for voting in your state. Obtain a copy of a voter registration form and a sample ballot from a recent election. Your community library, county clerk, or registrar's office should be able to help you. Share the information you find with your class.

3. Follow a political campaign in your community or state. Learn about the candidates. Keep articles from the newspaper. Keep a journal where you record your impression about the election process.

4. Write a story that shows how one person's vote can determine the outcome of an election. Share your story with the class.

How Does the Constitution Safeguard the Right to Equal Protection of the Law?

LESSON PURPOSE

In this lesson you will be introduced to one of the most important parts of the Fourteenth Amendment to the Constitution—the equal protection clause.

LESSON OBJECTIVES

When you finish this lesson, you should be able to

❏ explain the purpose of the equal protection clause, and

❏ describe some of the steps that Congress, the executive branch, the U.S. Supreme Court, and citizens have taken to end unfair discrimination in our nation.

TERMS TO UNDERSTAND

- boycott
- Civil Rights Act of 1964
- equal protection clause
- Jim Crow laws
- segregation
- separate but equal

Why did the passage of the Thirteenth Amendment fail to end unfair treatment of African Americans?

How did the Constitution end unfair treatment of citizens by government?

Although the Thirteenth Amendment abolished slavery in 1865, it did not end unfair treatment of African Americans by government. Many states in the South passed laws that discriminated against black people. State and local laws required that public facilities such as restrooms, theaters, and parks have separate areas for black people and white people.

Congress adopted the Fourteenth Amendment in 1868. The **equal protection clause** is stated in Section 1 of the amendment. It is the most important constitutional protection that the people have against unfair discrimination by state and local governments. The equal protection clause says that

no State shall...deny to any person within its jurisdiction the equal protection of the laws.

At the time it was ratified, this clause was intended to prevent discrimination against African Americans and guarantee them the rights that go along with citizenship.

The Fourteenth Amendment did not by itself prevent discrimination, however. The states continued to pass laws requiring African Americans to go to separate schools and to use separate public facilities. These laws came to be called **Jim Crow laws**. The states claimed that such laws did not violate the equal protection clause because the separate schools and facilities for blacks were equal to those provided for whites. This is known as the **separate but equal** argument. The U.S. Supreme Court considered this argument in two famous cases: *Plessy v. Ferguson* (1896) and *Brown v. Board of Education* (1954).

How did the Supreme Court rule in Plessy v. Ferguson? *What case overturned the "separate but equal" doctrine?*

How did the U.S. Supreme Court interpret the equal protection clause in two separate cases?

Case One: *Plessy v. Ferguson* (1896)

The state of Louisiana passed a law requiring railroad companies to provide separate, similar cars for white passengers and black passengers. A group of African American leaders decided to challenge the law.

Homer Plessy bought a railroad ticket and took a seat in a car set aside for whites. Plessy was arrested when he refused to move. The Louisiana state court found him guilty of violating state law. Plessy took his case to the U.S. Supreme Court, arguing that the Louisiana law violated the equal protection clause.

The Supreme Court ruled against Plessy. The Court said that separating the races did not mean that one race was inferior to the other. Because the state law required the facilities to be separate but equal, the Supreme Court said there was no discrimination.

The decision in this case, *Plessy v. Ferguson* (1896), allowed states to practice **segregation**, separation of the races, for almost sixty years. Then, in the case of *Brown v. Board of Education* (1954), the U.S. Supreme Court changed its interpretation of the equal protection clause.

Case Two: *Brown v. Board of Education* (1954)

Linda Brown was a seven-year-old child who lived five blocks from an elementary school. Linda was forced to attend a school for African American children twenty-one blocks away from her home. Linda's parents, along with twelve other parents, brought a lawsuit against the school board of Topeka, Kansas, saying their children had been deprived of equal protection of the law.

One of the lawyers for the parents was Thurgood Marshall, an attorney for the National Association for the Advancement of Colored People. Marshall later became the first African American justice of the U.S. Supreme Court. He argued that segregated schools could not be equal. This time the Court agreed. It said that placing African American children in schools separate from white children denied them the equal protection of the laws guaranteed by the Fourteenth Amendment. The Court said,

To separate [children] *... solely because of their race generates* [causes] *a feeling of inferiority ... that may affect their hearts and minds in a way unlikely ever to be undone.*

What was Thurgood Marshall's argument against segregation? How did the Supreme Court rule in the case?

What do you think?

Work with a partner to read each of the following situations. Then explain why you think each is or is not unfair treatment by government.

- In your state, there is a law that says students belonging to a certain race must go to schools that are separate from those that other students attend.

- Your city has a regulation requiring people with particular religious beliefs to live in a special section of town.

- Your state has a law that says people must marry within their own race.

- Your city fire department will not hire women as firefighters.

- You and a friend of the opposite sex work for the state. You both do the same jobs. Yet you are each paid at a different rate.

How did Congress, the executive branch, and citizens work to end unfair discrimination by government?

The Court's decision in *Brown v. Board of Education* was the first important step in ending school segregation. Although the *Brown* case was a turning point in the fight against discrimination, it dealt only with segregated schools. The Court decision by itself did not end discrimination. Many states resisted the Court's order to integrate their schools. As late as 1957, the governor of Arkansas tried to

What means did leaders of the civil rights movement use to obtain their goals?

stop black students from entering a white high school in Little Rock. In response, President Dwight Eisenhower ordered federal troops to escort the students and enforce the law.

The civil rights movement started in the 1950s. It was a time when many people of both races worked to end unfair treatment by government. People marched in the streets.

They wrote letters to Congress asking for stronger laws. They held boycotts. A **boycott** means that they refused to buy from or deal with stores and companies that practiced racial discrimination.

One of the earliest boycotts began in 1955. Rosa Parks was a working woman who lived in Montgomery, Alabama. She was on her

Who was Rosa Parks? Why did African Americans begin a boycott of buses in Montgomery, Alabama, in 1955?

way home one day when the bus she was riding became crowded. Parks refused to give up her seat to a white man. She was arrested for violating a city law. The African American community boycotted the city buses until the city changed the law. The boycott lasted more than a year.

In August of 1963, thousands of Americans marched in Washington, D.C. They wanted to show their support for the civil rights movement. Dr. Martin Luther King Jr. was an important civil rights leader. It was here that Dr. King gave his famous "I Have a Dream" speech. King told the crowd, "I have a dream that my four little children will one day live in a nation where they will not be judged by the color of their skin, but by the content of their character." One day, he hoped, all people would join hands and be "free at last."

In 1964, Congress passed the Civil Rights Act. The **Civil Rights Act of 1964** ended segregation in public places such as restaurants and hotels. The law also said that employers could not discriminate against people because of their race, national origin, religion, or gender.

When African Americans won these civil rights after years of struggle, other groups began to call for equal protection. Women, disabled people, older people, and other groups worked to get laws passed guaranteeing their right to equal protection of the laws. In response to their efforts, Congress and state legislatures have passed laws prohibiting unfair discrimination against these groups.

What events contributed to the passing of the Civil Rights Act of 1964 by Congress and President Lyndon B. Johnson's signing it into law?

Reviewing and Using the Lesson

1. What was the purpose of the Thirteenth and Fourteenth Amendments to the Constitution?

2. What is the meaning of the equal protection clause? Why is this clause important?

3. What did the U.S. Supreme Court decide in the *Plessy v. Ferguson* case? What effects did the decision have on the lives of African Americans?

4. What did the U.S. Supreme Court decide in the *Brown v. Board of Education* case? Why was this an important decision?

5. What actions did ordinary citizens take to help end unfair discrimination?

6. What laws did Congress pass to help end unfair discrimination?

7. What actions did the executive branch take to help end unfair discrimination?

Activities

1. Research information about Martin Luther King Jr. Read his *Letter from Birmingham City Jail*. What kinds of inspiration did he have for his ideas about nonviolence? Share what you learned with the class.

2. "Equal treatment" continues to be an important issue in the United States today. Find information about issues of equality that organized groups are seeking to address today. Explain what these issues are in a report to your class.

3. Create a timeline of historical events in the struggle to gain equal protection by various groups in America. Each student should research one event to include in a classroom poster commemorating the struggle for equal rights.

How Does the Constitution Protect the Right to Due Process of Law?

LESSON PURPOSE

In this lesson, we will look at another part of the Constitution that is concerned with fairness. This is the idea of due process of law. The due process clause is intended to guarantee that government will use fair procedures when gathering information and making decisions that affect our rights to life, liberty, or property.

LESSON OBJECTIVES

When you finish this lesson, you should be able to

- explain in general terms what due process means, and

- explain how due process applies to the rights of juveniles who are accused of breaking the law.

TERMS TO UNDERSTAND

- due process
- Fifth Amendment
- procedure

What is due process of law?

It is difficult to define due process of law exactly. We may say that **due process** is the right to be treated fairly by government. There are two important ways this meaning is applied.

❶ Due process means that the **procedures**, or methods used to conduct hearings and to apply and enforce the law, must be fair and reasonable. All branches of the federal and state governments must use fair procedures when carrying out their responsibilities.

❷ Due process also means that the content of laws that legislatures pass must be fair and reasonable. Congress and the state legislatures cannot pass laws that place unfair or unreasonable limitations on people's rights to life, liberty, or property.

The ideas of due process can be found in the body of the Constitution and several amendments. The Fifth and Fourteenth Amendments specifically use the term *due process of law*.

The Fifth Amendment does not mention state governments. Therefore, this amendment applies only to actions of the federal government. The **Fifth Amendment** says

No Person shall ... be deprived of life, liberty, or property, without due process of law.

In what way does due process limit the powers of government?

The Fourteenth Amendment includes actions by the states. The Fourteenth Amendment says

nor shall any State deprive any person of life, liberty, or property, without due process of law.

In the remainder of this lesson we focus on the first meaning of due process: members of all branches of government must use fair procedures when fulfilling their responsibilities.

We will concentrate on the rights of persons suspected or accused of crimes. We examine the procedures that were followed in a situation that led to a famous U.S. Supreme Court case called *In re Gault* (1967). This case concerns the treatment of a juvenile accused of a crime.

In re Gault (1967)

Gerald Gault was fifteen years old. On the morning of June 8, 1964, the sheriff of Gila County, Arizona, arrested Gerald and a friend, Ronald Lewis. The sheriff took the boys to the Children's Detention Home.

The boys were accused of telephoning a neighbor, Mrs. Cook, and saying offensive and obscene things to her. Mrs. Cook had then called the sheriff.

While the boys were in detention, Officer Flagg, a deputy probation officer, questioned them. The boys admitted making the calls. Each boy blamed the other.

At the time that Gerald was arrested, his parents were at work. The sheriff who arrested the boys did not tell the parents that Gerald was being taken to a detention home. No one from the sheriff's office called the Gault home.

When Gerald's mother arrived home that evening, she sent her older son to look for Gerald. At the home of Ronald Lewis, he learned that Gerald was being held in the detention home.

Mrs. Gault went to the detention home and Officer Flagg explained why the sheriff had arrested her son. Officer Flagg informed Mrs. Gault that there would be a hearing in juvenile court the next afternoon.

Gerald, his mother, Officer Flagg, and the judge were the only ones at the hearing. Mrs. Cook was not present. During the hearing, no one was asked to swear to tell the truth. No record was made of what was said. No lawyers were present.

At later hearings, the judge, Mrs. Gault, and Officer Flagg agreed on some things that were said at the first hearing but disagreed about others. They agreed that the judge had

asked Gerald about the telephone call. They disagreed about what Gerald answered.

His mother remembered that Gerald said he had dialed Mrs. Cook's number and then handed the telephone to Ronald. Officer Flagg said that Gerald had admitted making one insulting remark.

Two or three days later, Officer Flagg drove Gerald home. On that day, Gerald's mother received a note from the court that was written on plain paper. The note said, "Mrs. Gault, Judge McGhee has set Monday, June 15, 1964, at 11 a.m. as the date for further hearings on Gerald's delinquency."

On June 15, the Gaults appeared in court. Mrs. Gault had requested that Mrs. Cook be present, but she did not attend. The judge, who had not spoken with Mrs. Cook, said that it was not necessary that she be in court. Again, no one was asked

to swear to tell the truth and no record was made of this hearing.

During the hearing, Officer Flagg handed the judge a report saying that Gerald had made insulting phone calls. The Gaults had never seen the report.

In the end, the judge ruled that Gerald was guilty of violating a state law that said that a person who "in the presence or hearing of any woman or child … uses vulgar, abusive, or obscene language, is guilty of a misdemeanor." The judge sentenced Gerald to the State Industrial School for juvenile delinquents until he reached age 21.

If Gerald had been 18, he would have been tried in a regular criminal court. There, the maximum penalty for making "vulgar, abusive, or obscene" calls would have been a $5 to $50 fine or not more than two months' imprisonment.

The Gaults appealed the case and it eventually reached the U.S. Supreme Court. Gault's lawyers argued that the procedure used in Gerald's case had denied him due process under the Fourteenth Amendment. Attorneys for the state argued that the informal proceedings under the juvenile court system were intended to help juveniles, rather than treat them as regular criminals. They said that this system would be undermined if the Court gave young offenders all the specific guarantees in the Bill of Rights.

Critical Thinking Exercise

Due process protections of juveniles

After reading the summary of the *Gault* case, work with one or more partners to write answers to the following questions:

1 What procedures used by government officials in do you think were unfair? Why were they unfair?

2 What parts of the Fifth, Sixth, Eighth, and Fourteenth Amendments to the Constitution apply to this case?

3 What position do you think the U.S. Supreme Court should have taken in this case? Explain the position.

4 Read the summary of the decision in the *Gault* case by the U.S. Supreme Court at www.oyez.org/cases/1966/116. How does the Court's position compare with yours? How, if at all, would you change your position? Why?

What responsibilities do members of Congress have when conducting hearings? What responsibilities do members of the executive branch have when answering questions posed to them by members of Congress?

How can the rights of the individual and the rights of society conflict?

Problems of due process involve two government responsibilities. These responsibilities are to

1 protect the rights of an individual who may have broken the law, and

2 protect everyone else from people who break the law and endanger the lives, liberty, or property of others.

These responsibilities sometimes conflict. Balancing them is a difficult job. It is the duty of government and the courts to balance these responsibilities.

Protecting the individual from unfair treatment by government is among the most important protections of our constitutional democracy.

We have discussed due process of law as it applies to the rights of someone accused of a crime. It is important to remember that the right to due process means the right to be treated fairly by all the agencies of government, not just the courts and law enforcement.

Due process of law has been called the "primary and indispensable [necessary] foundation of individual freedom" because it protects the individual from government wrongdoing. Due process applies to local school board hearings, to congressional hearings, and to hearings of the administrative agencies of your state and federal governments.

What do you think?

Some people claim that if a government is allowed to violate the right to due process of law, all of your other rights could be seriously endangered. Do you agree or disagree with this position? What other rights might be endangered? Why?

Reviewing and Using the Lesson

1 Where in the Constitution will you find the two due process clauses? In what way are the two clauses different?

2 What is the meaning of due process?

3 Why do you think the guarantee of due process is so important?

4 Why must all agencies of government protect the individual's right to due process of law?

Activities

1 With a partner, videotape an interview with your school principal or a member of your school board. Ask them about the policy in your school district regarding due process rights of students. Show the tape to your class and explain what you learned.

2 With a partner, search the Constitution to see how many references each of you can find to elements related to fair procedures and due process of law. Combine your lists and share them with the class.

3 Draw a picture or a poster. On one side of your picture, illustrate a situation in which a due process right is being violated. On the other side, illustrate the same situation but with the due process right being protected.

4 With your teacher's help, invite a police officer to your class to discuss how the police have to protect due process rights when they suspect that someone has committed a crime. Prepare questions to ask your guest during the visit.

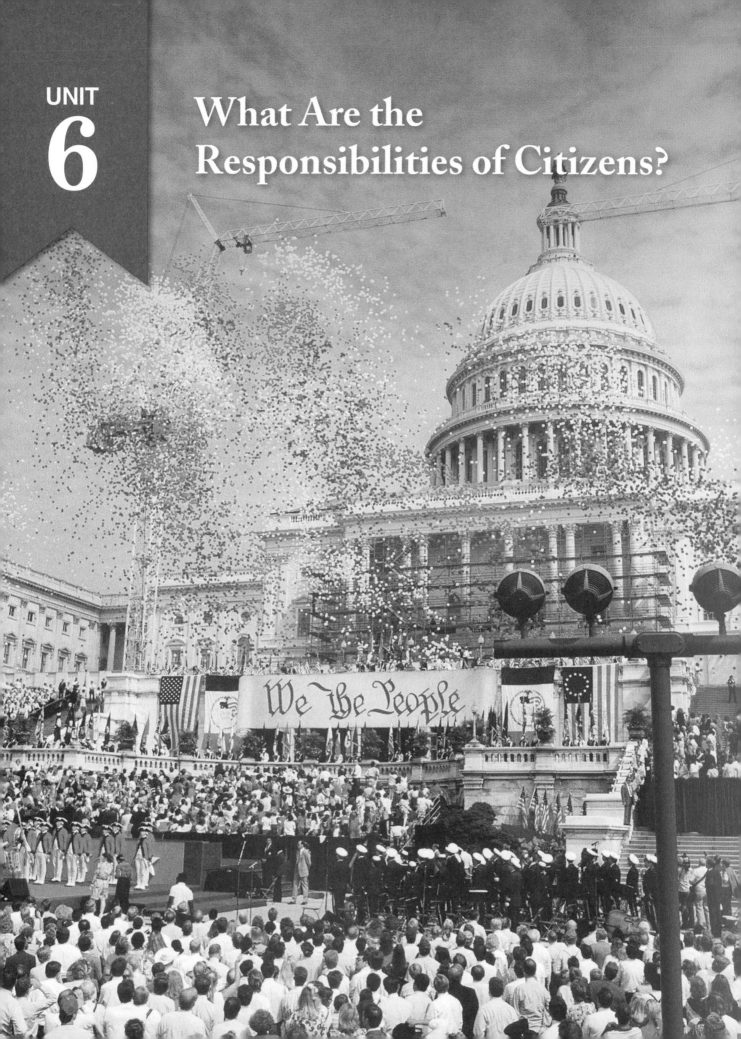

We the People

What Are the Responsibilities of Citizens?

UNIT PURPOSE

You have studied the basic ideas of our constitutional democracy. You have learned about our government's responsibility to protect the basic rights of the people and promote the common welfare. This unit deals with a question of equal or greater importance: What is the role of the citizen?

This book will not answer this question for you. The answer is one you must arrive at yourself. This unit raises some important ideas that you might find useful in deciding what your responsibilities as a citizen are.

KEY CONCEPTS

- citizen
- international law
- nation-state
- naturalized citizen
- legal permanent resident

What is the Relationship of the United States to Other Nations in the World?

LESSON PURPOSE

In this lesson, you will learn some ways in which countries interact with one another. You will also learn how the ideas about government in the Declaration of Independence and in the U.S. Constitution and Bill of Rights have influenced other countries.

LESSON OBJECTIVES

When you finish this lesson, you should be able to

explain how countries in the world interact with one another, and

explain how American ideas about freedom and government have influenced people in other countries.

TERMS TO UNDERSTAND

- humanitarian
- international law
- nation-state
- United Nations

What are nation-states?

There are many countries in the world. A country is also called a **nation-state**. The government of a nation-state claims the authority to govern the people who live within its territory.

The government of a nation-state also makes and carries out agreements with other nation-states. Today there are more than 200 nation-states in the world. Some are tiny countries such as Monaco and Singapore. Others are very large countries such as China and India.

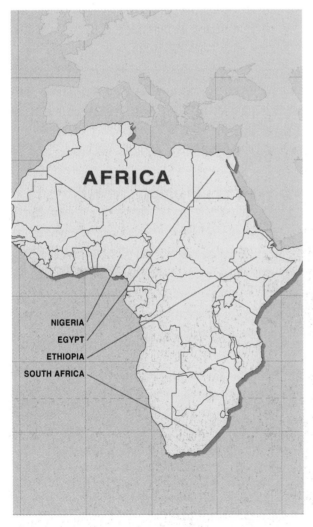

What is government's role in the nation-state?
What are some examples of nation-states?

Who has authority over nation-states?

At the international level, there is no organization with formal political power comparable to that of the nation-state. There is no international government that has authority over the world's nation-states. That is why each nation-state is said to be sovereign. By *sovereign* we mean that a country has the right to be free from outside interference within its boundaries.

Nation-states often agree to cooperate with each other. For example, letters mailed in one country arrive at their destination in another country. Telephone services function worldwide. Airplanes take off from one country and land in another. Nations trade goods and services daily. These few examples show that countries can live in peace and cooperate in their means of dealing with each other.

What is international law?

One thing that makes interactions among countries possible is a system of international law. **International law** consists of those rules that regulate how countries behave toward one another. International law is usually made by treaties that nation-states make among themselves.

It is up to each nation-state to enforce its treaties. For example, Article VI of the U.S. Constitution says, among other things,

> *This Constitution, and the Laws of the United States ... and all treaties made under the Authority of the United States, shall be the supreme law of the Land.*

This means that all treaties that the United States makes with other nations become part

In what ways might nation-states agree to cooperate with each other?

of our national laws, and they have to be enforced by the federal government.

There is no international police organization to enforce international law. This does not mean that it is impossible to make nations live up to their responsibilities to each other. Some nations use economic, political, or military pressure to keep other nations in line.

How do nations of the world interact with each other?

Today, the nations of the world are increasingly dependent on each other. Nations have many ways of interacting. Here are some common examples:

- **Cultural, science, and business exchanges** People travel all over the world. People living in different countries share ideas. Doctors, scientists, educators, and business people from many countries meet to share advances in their fields. Students and teachers live with families in other countries to learn their language and to learn about their culture. Artists show their work in the museums of other countries.

- **Humanitarian aid** The term **humanitarian** means to show concern for the pain and suffering of others. During natural

What is the role of diplomacy in international relations? What role does the president have in American diplomacy?

disasters such as floods and earthquakes, countries help the victims in other countries by giving humanitarian aid. Countries send medicine, food, and shelter to suffering people. Individuals and organizations also respond to natural disasters.

- **Trade** Countries buy and sell factory goods, farm products, and services to one another.

- **Diplomacy** As you learned in Lesson 9, the term *diplomacy* means the practice of carrying on formal relationships with governments of other countries. The official representatives of countries meet and discuss issues important to their governments. They work together in a peaceful manner to find solutions to common problems.

- **Treaties and agreements** Countries make treaties and agreements. They agree to promote trade among themselves. They agree to do certain things to protect the environment. Some agree to help each other in time of war.

- **Military force** When two or more countries cannot solve their disagreements peacefully, they sometimes threaten to use military force. Sometimes, the disagreement results in a war.

What international organizations promote interaction among nations?

There is no single organization in the world that has the power to force countries to settle conflicts peacefully. There are some organizations that help countries reach agreements without going to war. The most important worldwide

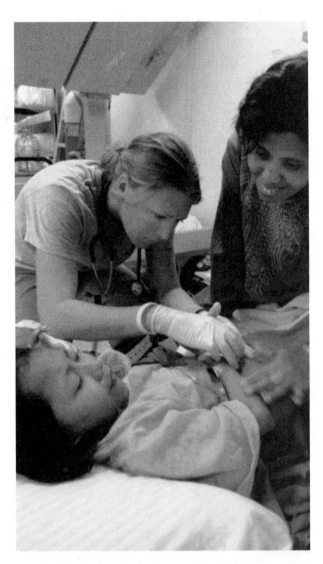

Do you think nations have a responsibility to provide humanitarian aid to the people of other nations? Why or why not?

organization is the United Nations. A treaty signed in 1945, after World War II, created the United Nations. The purposes of the **United Nations**, according to its charter, are to maintain international peace and security; develop friendly relations among nations; cooperate in solving international economic, social, cultural, and humanitarian problems; and promote respect for human rights and fundamental freedoms. Most nations of the world are members of the United Nations.

What is the United Nations? What does the United Nations do?

There are also regional treaty organizations that promote interaction among nations. These organizations deal with regional matters. The Organization of American States (OAS) promotes peace and security among all member nations in the Americas. Other examples of regional organizations are the League of Arab States and the Association of Southeast Asian Nations (ASEAN).

Many international organizations are not under direct government control. These are nongovernmental organizations, often called NGOs. Some of these organizations provide humanitarian aid, for example, the International Federation of Red Cross and Red Crescent Societies. Others, such as Amnesty International, address human rights concerns.

What do the Red Cross and Red Crescent do? Why are nongovernmental organizations important?

Which government official has the power to name ambassadors? Which branch approves such nominations? Which branch hears cases affecting ambassadors?

U.S. Ambassador to Japan Caroline Kennedy and Japanese Prime Minister Shinzo Abe

What powers does the U.S. Constitution give to government to deal with other nations?

Each branch of the U.S. government has certain powers that come from the Constitution. The Constitution gives each branch the following powers to deal with other countries.

- **Congress** Congress has the power to regulate commerce with other countries and with the Indian tribes, declare war, approve treaties, approve ambassadors, raise and support armies, and punish piracies and crimes committed on the high seas.

- **President** The president has the power to make treaties and to name ambassadors, with the approval of Congress. The president is also the commander in chief of the military forces.

- **U.S. Supreme Court** The U.S. Supreme Court has the power to hear all cases affecting ambassadors; cases in which the United States is a party; and cases involving a foreign state, its citizens, or subjects.

How have other countries influenced the United States?

Many of the ideas about government that you have studied started in other countries. The Founders learned about government from studying the histories of ancient Greece and Rome. From the Greeks and Romans, they learned about republican government, civic virtue, and the common good.

The European philosophers also had a great influence on the Founders. The theories of Baron de Montesquieu of France influenced their thinking about the separation of powers. The writings of John Locke of Great Britain guided their thinking about natural rights.

What do you think citizens of the United States gain from relationships with other countries? What do you think citizens in other countries gain from their relationships with us?

Colonial Americans also enjoyed the rights of Englishmen. Among these are the right to trial by jury, the right to be secure in one's home, and the right to express one's views about taxes through representatives in government.

How have the Declaration of Independence and the U.S. Constitution and Bill of Rights influenced other countries?

The United States has given many things to the world—advanced medical and industrial technology and the personal computer to name a few. The discoveries and inventions that we as a nation have shared with the world are important, but not as valuable or as lasting as the democratic ideals expressed in the Declaration of Independence and the U.S. Constitution and Bill of Rights. Some of these democratic ideals are listed below.

1. Power comes from the people and the people are the ultimate source of the authority of their government.

2. People in government are the servants of the people, not the masters of the people.

3. All people are political equals. No person's vote counts more than another's.

4. The people delegate their powers to their government. They consent to be governed only so long as those in power fulfill their responsibilities. They can take back those powers and change their government.

What does this illustration tell you about the American idea of the relationship between government and the people?

5 The purpose of government is to protect the people's rights to life, liberty, and property, and to promote the common good.

6 A nation's constitution should be approved by the people and serve as a higher law that everyone must obey, including the people and those serving in their government.

7 A nation's constitution should include a list of the rights of the people.

During the nineteenth and twentieth centuries, the American ideal of self-government spread around the world. People from many countries read and studied the ideas in the Declaration of Independence and in the U.S. Constitution and Bill of Rights. These documents influenced other countries to adopt similar ideas about government.

The American Revolution gave hope to many people in Europe and Latin America who wanted to promote democratic change in their own countries. The French Constitution of 1791 included many ideas from the United States. The Declaration of Independence and the U.S. Constitution and Bill of Rights also inspired Latin American leaders. In more recent years, when students in the People's Republic of China demonstrated for more freedoms from their government, they carried copies of the Declaration of Independence.

What do you think?

Work with one or more partners to discuss and develop your answers to the following questions.

1 Why do you suppose people in other countries have used ideas from the Declaration of Independence and the U.S. Constitution and Bill of Rights when demonstrating for more freedom from their governments?

2 Which of the ideas in these documents do you think are most important? Why?

3 Why is it important that countries be able to have a free exchange of ideas?

Why is it important that countries be able to have a free exchange of ideas?

Reviewing and Using the Lesson

1. What is a nation-state?

2. List some ways in which countries interact with each other.

3. What powers does the U.S. Constitution give the national government to deal with other countries?

4. List some ideas in the Declaration of Independence and the U.S. Constitution and Bill of Rights that have influenced government in other countries.

Activities

1. Learn more about the United Nations. Why and how was the United Nations established? What does the United Nations do? Share what you learned with your class.

2. Suppose you make a telephone call to a friend or relative in Mexico or in France. Suppose you send a letter to China using a stamp from the United States. Learn about international agreements that make it possible for your telephone call or letter to reach its destination. Find information about the Universal Postal Union or the International Telecommunications Union.

3. Choose one of the following countries: China, Colombia, Egypt, France, Indonesia, Israel, Mexico, Nigeria, Panama, Russia, Saudi Arabia, or Vietnam. Learn about the country's relationship with the United States in the past and today. Share what you learned with your class.

4. Find an article of clothing or other item around your home. Examine the label. Where was the item made? What international agreements exist that regulate how such items are traded on world markets? Identify some items that are manufactured in your state and exported to other countries.

5. The State Department is the cabinet position in charge of conducting our relations with other nations in the world. Who is the current Secretary of State? Explain some of his or her responsibilities. Write a brief biography of this person.

LESSON

29

What Are the Rights and Responsibilities of Citizenship?

LESSON PURPOSE

In this lesson, you will examine the meaning of citizenship and how one becomes a citizen of the United States. You will examine the rights of citizens, as well as the responsibilities that accompany our citizenship in this nation. Finally, you will develop positions on what a citizen might do when he or she thinks that a law is unjust.

LESSON OBJECTIVES

When you finish this lesson, you should be able to

- explain the meaning of citizenship and how one becomes a citizen of the United States, and

- explain some of the rights of citizens and the responsibilities that accompany those rights.

TERMS TO UNDERSTAND

- citizen
- civic responsibilities
- economic rights
- legal permanent resident
- naturalized citizen
- personal rights
- personal responsibilities
- political rights

What does it mean to be a citizen?

A **citizen** is a person who is a legal member of a self-governing community, such as a nation or state. In the United States, there are no degrees or classes of citizenship. In this country, citizenship does not depend on a person's race, gender, or ethnic origin. Every citizen is a full member of the political community.

A citizen is one person among equals. Each citizen possesses equal rights under the law. In addition, our rights as citizens come with certain responsibilities. It is also important to remember that under our federal system, Americans are citizens of both their state and the United States.

In what ways, if any, have naturalized citizens contributed to American society?

What is a citizen? Should some citizens have more rights than others? Why or why not?

How does a person become a citizen of the United States?

Every person born in the United States is a citizen of this country. A person born in another country to parents who are citizens of the United States is also a citizen of this country.

A **legal permanent resident** is someone who is not a citizen of the United States but who is legally permitted to live here. Legal permanent residents enjoy most of the rights of citizens and, like citizens, they must obey the laws and pay their taxes. They have the same rights to due process as citizens.

Legal permanent residents are not full members of the political community because there are some rights that are reserved for citizens. Only citizens may vote in national elections, hold public office, or serve on juries.

In most cases, legal permanent residents can become citizens. An adult permanent resident may apply for citizenship after living in the United States legally for five years. Before becoming a citizen, the person must pass a test to show that he or she understands the history and Constitution of the United States. The person must be of good moral character and demonstrate the ability to communicate in English. A person who gets his or her citizenship in this way is a **naturalized citizen**. The minor child of a naturalized citizen becomes a citizen of the United States when the parents do.

What are the rights of citizens?

There are three categories of rights that are important to democracy and to American citizens. These are personal rights, political rights, and economic rights.

Personal rights are those rights that allow a person to do as he or she wishes so long as those actions are consistent with the public order and do not interfere with the rights of others. The following are some personal rights:

- Freedom to associate with whomever one pleases

- Freedom of conscience and religion

- Freedom of expression for creativity

- Freedom to have children

- Freedom to live where one chooses

- Freedom to have privacy

- Freedom to travel

Political rights are those rights that allow citizens to participate in the political process. Without these rights, democracy could not exist. The following are political rights:

- Due process of law and fair procedures

- Equal protection under the law

- Freedom to examine the conduct of public officials

- Freedom of expression for political purposes

- Freedom of political association and assembly

- Freedom to seek and hold public office

- Freedom to serve on juries

- Freedom to vote in free, fair, and regular elections

Economic rights are those rights needed to earn a living and to acquire and transfer property or to produce goods and services. The following are economic rights:

- Freedom to acquire, use, and sell or give away property

- Freedom to choose one's work

- Freedom to enter into lawful contracts

- Freedom to establish and operate a business

- Freedom to join professional associations and labor unions

It is important to remember that it is reasonable and fair to place limits on most rights; they are not absolute. Most people argue that the only right that cannot be limited is freedom of belief. All other rights can be limited in certain situations. For example, you learned in an earlier lesson that freedom of expression can be limited if and when it seriously harms or endangers others.

Some rights may be limited when they conflict with other rights or with other important values and interests. For example, the right to own and use property can conflict with our interest in having a safe and healthy environment.

What responsibilities accompany the basic rights of citizens?

With the rights of citizens of the United States come certain responsibilities. Citizens do not always agree on their responsibilities. Some responsibilities that Americans have agreed upon over the years are listed below.

Personal responsibilities are obligations that each person assumes individually. The following are examples of personal responsibilities:

- Accepting the consequences of one's actions

- Adhering to moral principles

- Behaving in a civil manner

- Considering the rights and interests of others

- Supporting one's family

- Taking care of one's self

Civic responsibilities are obligations that each person has to society. The following are examples of civic responsibilities:

- Being informed about public issues

- Voting and deciding how to vote

- Keeping watch over political leaders and governmental agencies, and taking appropriate action if they do not follow constitutional principles

- Obeying the laws

- Participating in civic groups

- Paying taxes

- Respecting the rights of others

- Serving as a juror

- Serving in the armed forces

What is the difference between civic responsibilities and personal responsibilities?

Howard University volunteers participating in the International Coastal Cleanup Day along the banks of the Anacostia River in Washington, D.C.

Citizens must not only be aware of their rights. They must also learn to use their rights responsibly. Fulfilling personal and civic responsibilities is a necessity in a self-governing, free, and just society.

Must you obey a law you think is unjust?

When laws or governmental actions conflict with a citizen's views of what is right and wrong, the citizen faces a difficult decision.

In our system of government, you have a right to try to have laws changed. There are many ways that you and others can work to change laws that you think are unjust. Until you get them changed, however, you are held responsible for obeying the laws.

Suppose a law requires you to do something you believe is wrong. Must you obey the law? Some people argue that since no government is perfect, a citizen's responsibility to obey the law has limits. In their view, if a law is unjust, the citizen has no responsibility to obey it.

Deciding to disobey a law is a serious step. Disobeying the law has consequences that the citizen must be prepared to accept. Such consequences might include paying fines and even going to jail.

Throughout history, many citizens have accepted the consequences of disobeying the law. In the 1800s, the famous American philosopher Henry David Thoreau chose to go to jail rather than pay a tax to support slavery and the Mexican-American War. In the 1950s and 1960s, Dr. Martin Luther King Jr. and others chose to go to jail to protest racial segregation laws. During the Vietnam War, many young men burned their draft cards and refused to serve in the armed forces because they believed the war was unjust.

What are some examples of your responsibilities as a citizen of the United States?

What are your responsibilities as a citizen?

You have learned a great deal about our nation's government from studying this book. You also have learned about some of the rights and responsibilities of citizenship. You and all citizens will be faced with difficult decisions about your role in a democratic society.

What commitment are you willing to make to the basic principles of our government? How will you decide which of your rights, desires, or interests may have to take second place to your responsibility to the common good? It is your responsibility as a citizen to make these difficult decisions.

Why did Henry David Thoreau (pictured) and Dr. Martin Luther King Jr. practice civil disobedience? What should a citizen consider before deciding to disobey the law?

Critical Thinking Exercise

Dealing with conflicting responsibilities

The following is a hypothetical story that involves conflicting responsibilities and interests. Read the story and then complete the exercise that follows it.

A new school policy

Gail was worried. Five of her friends were going to take part in a protest during the last period of school the next day. They were planning to demonstrate against the new school policy prohibiting wearing T-shirts with controversial slogans. Like her friends, Gail believed that this situation was unfair to the students. She believed that the T-shirts were legal and not vulgar or offensive. She felt strongly that this policy should be changed.

Gail was worried about what would happen if she joined the picket line. She worried that she might be suspended from school. If this happened, it might affect her chances of being accepted by a college. She was also afraid that she might be arrested, especially if the demonstration got out of hand. An arrest on her record could keep her from getting a good job.

On the other hand, she wanted to show her views and help change what she thought was an unjust situation. What should Gail do?

Work with one or more partners to discuss and develop answers to the following questions.

1. What rights do you think Gail has in this situation?

2. What responsibilities accompany these rights?

3. What are some alternative actions that Gail might take to solve her problem or reach a decision?

4. List the advantages and disadvantages of each alternative.

5. Decide what you think should be done, considering the advantages and disadvantages of the alternatives.

6. Explain the reasons for your decision and how that decision reflects the basic principles of our government.

If you have completed this exercise in small groups, discuss the plans presented by the groups and vote to determine which plan a majority favors.

Reviewing and Using the Lesson

1. What does the term *citizen* mean?

2. Who is a citizen of the United States?

3. How can noncitizens acquire citizenship in this country?

4. What are the personal, political, and economic rights of citizens?

5. What responsibilities accompany our basic rights?

6. What are some consequences to consider when deciding whether to challenge a law that you think is unjust?

Activities

1. Write a short essay in which you describe the qualities of good citizens in a constitutional democracy. Explain why you think these qualities are necessary.

2. Debate the following questions with groups of three or four students.
   - What should a person do when he or she thinks that a law is unjust? Give examples to support your opinion.
   - Suppose you cannot agree on what is in the common good. Should you pursue your own interests or still try to consider the interests of others? Explain your answer and provide examples.

3. Learn more about resident aliens in the United States. Use the Internet to do some research. In what regions of the country do a majority of resident aliens live? What motivates resident aliens to want to live in the United States?

4. Learn more about individuals who have become naturalized citizens of the United States. Here is a list of people you might want to research in your library or on the Internet.
   - Madeleine Albright
   - Albert Einstein
   - Marcus Garvey
   - Andrew S. Grove
   - Henry Kissinger
   - Chien-Shiung Wu

5. Develop a poster that illustrates the rights of citizens and the responsibilities that those rights carry.

6. Does modern technology make the right to privacy easier or harder to protect? Write a report to share with your class that deals with the issues of privacy today.

How Might Citizens Participate in Civic Affairs?

LESSON PURPOSE

In this lesson, you will learn about one of the most important rights of citizenship. This is the right to participate in governing our nation. The different ways you might participate in our government and in voluntary organizations outside of government will be discussed. The lesson also suggests things to consider when deciding whether you should participate.

LESSON OBJECTIVE

When you finish the lesson, you should be able to support your views on whether, and to what extent, a citizen should participate in government and in voluntary organizations.

TERMS TO UNDERSTAND

- civic life
- civic participation
- constitutional principle
- influence
- monitor
- political action
- social action

What might be the advantages or disadvantages of joining volunteer organizations to influence government?

What role should citizens have in government?

As you learned in the last lesson, in the United States each citizen is a full and equal member of the political community. Each citizen has certain basic rights and responsibilities. You also learned that government and citizens are both responsible for protecting the rights of individuals. Both are also responsible for promoting the common good.

Citizens have other vital roles in our government. One important role that citizens fulfill is to **monitor** the decisions and actions of government. To monitor means to keep watch over something. Citizens monitor government to be informed about what the government is doing in their name. They also

monitor government to ensure that it serves the purposes for which it was created.

Another important role of citizens is to attempt to **influence** the decisions and actions of government. To influence means to have an effect on or to cause changes in something. It is the right of citizens to try to influence the decisions and actions of government that affect our lives.

In a sense, citizenship is an office of government. Some people might say that it is the highest office of government because citizens are the source of government's authority. Like any other office, citizenship carries important responsibilities.

Civic participation means taking part in formal political processes and taking part in community activities outside of government. Millions of Americans participate in thousands of voluntary organizations and associations. These organizations seek to improve the life of the community in many different ways. Some benefit the poor, sick, or elderly people. Other organizations are concerned with the environment, health care, or the needs of children. They deal with many other community problems and issues.

Participating in these organizations gives community members the means to deal with community issues. It also allows them to participate in the way the organizations are run.

Government must deal with some matters, such as arresting lawbreakers or establishing rules for building safety. There are other issues where government works with voluntary organizations to solve community problems. In other cases, voluntary organizations act by themselves to address community issues.

How much participation in government should citizens be willing to contribute?

Some citizens do not participate in government. They do not vote or take part in other ways. Some people, however, believe that citizens have a responsibility to participate.

Deciding whether to participate in government and how much time to spend is important. To make good decisions, you must think about such things as

1 the purposes of government,

2 how important your rights are to you, and

3 how satisfied you are with the way government is working.

How would you respond to a poorly fixed bike from the bike shop? Would you respond in a similar way to something the government had done poorly?

How can people your age participate in government?

An example might help. If you took your bike in for repairs, you would make sure that the shop repaired bicycles, not cars or toasters. Then when you claimed your bike, you would check it to make sure that they did what you had hired them to do. If you thought they did a good job but your bike broke the next week, you might bring it back, but you would check or monitor their work more closely.

Suppose the shop wanted to do more repairs than those you requested. You would want to participate in making that decision. If you were denied the right to participate in the decision, you might be very upset, especially when you got the bill.

If the shop did a poor job on the repairs again, you would not go back nor would you recommend them to your friends. You might call various agencies to complain or you might even try to force them out of the bike repair business.

The same is true of government. We should make sure that the people we elect are capable of doing the job we are choosing them for. Once they get the job, we should monitor them to make sure they are doing their job of representing us correctly. If they do a good job, we might not watch them as closely. If they do a bad job, we might check them more closely and might even decide to replace them. Because our officials make decisions that affect us, we are entitled to participate in those decisions.

Of course, not all jobs have to be accomplished by government. Americans are famous for doing many things for themselves. We organize groups to accomplish any number of things. These include building neighborhood swimming pools, discussing foreign policy issues, or improving our communities in hundreds of ways. Participating in these activities is also civic participation.

Some citizens mostly participate in formal governmental processes. Others participate mostly in volunteer groups. Many citizens take part in both forms of civic activity. Americans realize how important civic participation is. When civic participation declines, our democracy declines. It is not just others who are responsible for the civic health of our democracy. We are all responsible.

What do you think?

Reasons for participation in government

Work with one or more partners to discuss and develop your answers to the following questions.

1 What do you think the major purposes of your government should be?

2 Is it important for citizens to monitor how their government is fulfilling its purposes? Why?

3 Is it important for citizens to try to influence the way their government is fulfilling its purposes? Why?

4 What might happen if very few citizens try to monitor and influence their government?

How might citizens participate in their government?

Civic life is the public life of citizens. Civic life is different, but not necessarily separate, from private or personal life. In our personal life, we concern ourselves with our particular interests, such as getting an education or having a good job. Our civic life, on the other hand, is concerned with our own interests as well as the common affairs and interests of our community and nation.

Civic life includes the things that we do to carry out our responsibilities and roles as citizens. One example of this is monitoring and influencing the decisions of government. Sometimes our actions can be both personal and civic. These include being a decision-maker or being a participant in nongovernmental organizations. For example, we might do any of the following:

* Direct the activities or policies of organizations and associations. These could include voting for leaders or holding a leadership position yourself.

* Take part in an organization's meetings and community activities such as rallies, fundraising, or writing, or handing out pamphlets and articles.

What are some examples of civic life?

Critical Thinking Exercise

The role of citizens in American democracy

One way to understand the role of citizens in government is to think about the basic principles of our Constitution. In this case, we are discussing constitutional principles. A **constitutional principle** is an essential idea that we as a nation believe about good government. These are principles that you have learned during your study of this text. they include the following:

Constitutional principles

- Common good
- Consent of the governed
- Constitutional government
- Individual rights
- Popular sovereignty
- Representative government

Read each of the basic principles of government listed above. Then work with one or more partners to discuss and develop your answers to the following questions.

1 What is the meaning of each basic principle of government listed?

2 What do each of these principles imply about the role of citizens in their government?

3 What actions might citizens take to fulfill the roles of citizens that you have identified?

What are some different ways that citizens can serve the common good?

Critical Thinking Exercise

Participation in government to achieve personal goals

As individuals, we have personal goals that we would like to achieve, and that is one reason we participate in government.

Sometimes our personal goals are linked to the common good. A personal goal might be to get a good education. It is also in the common good that communities provide good schools so that everyone in the community can get a good education and be able to contribute to the community. Everyone should have the opportunity to realize that goal.

Suppose that you have four personal goals. They are to

- live in a safe and orderly neighborhood,

- get a good education,

- live in a healthy environment, and

- feel that you are a full member of your community and not an outsider.

Now work with one or more partners to discuss and develop your answers to the following questions.

1 Why are the personal goals listed in this exercise important to you?

2 How might these personal goals be related to the common good? In other words, how might your achievement of these goals help make our country better?

3 How might your participation in government help you attain these goals for yourself and the community?

4 How might your participation in civic life help you attain goals for yourself and the community?

What are the advantages and disadvantages of participation in civic life?

In small groups, read the list of ways in which citizens can participate in political and other forms of civic action. Then discuss the three questions in the Critical Thinking Exercise on the next page. Share your responses with your class.

How can you judge whether information you find on the Internet is accurate?

Ways citizens can participate

- Looking for information about government officials and activities in newspapers, magazines, the Internet, and reference materials and judging its accuracy

- Voting in local, state, and national elections

- Participating in political discussions

- Signing a petition

- Writing letters to elected representatives

- Contributing money to a political party or candidate

- Attending meetings to gain information, discuss issues, or lend support

- Campaigning for a candidate

- Lobbying for laws that are of special interest to you

- Taking part in marches, boycotts, sit-ins, or other forms of protest

- Serving as a juror

- Running for public office

- Holding public office

- Serving the country through military or other service

- Joining independent civic groups and attending meetings

- Holding office in and giving financial support to independent civic groups

- Taking part in solving public problems by joining voluntary groups, independent of or in cooperation with government

- Discussing civic problems and issues informally with friends and neighbors

- Becoming informed by reading, watching television programs, or doing Internet research about public problems by yourself or with others

Critical Thinking Exercise

Examining the effectiveness of different forms of participation

Thinking about the list you just read, work with one or more partners to discuss and develop your answers to the following questions.

1 Select five of the forms of participation listed in the lesson that you would be most willing to do. Explain the advantages and disadvantages of each form of participation and why you have chosen it.

2 Which of the forms of participation listed are most important in protecting our basic rights and the common good? Explain your selections.

3 In which of the activities are you most likely to participate? Why?

What is political action and what is social action?

There are two general ways that citizens can address problems in the community through participation in civic life. They are social action and political action.

Political action comes in two forms: formal and informal.

- Formal political action means voting in elections, petitioning government officials, seeking and holding public office, and similar activities.

- Informal political action means face-to-face meetings with public officials, writing to newspapers stating your opinion on issues, conducting email or telephone campaigns, attending marches and demonstrations, and similar activities.

How can you participate in your government?

There is a wide range of political actions that citizens can engage in when attempting to influence the actions of government. These actions are relevant at local, state, and national levels.

To help solve a crime problem you might meet with government officials requesting that they provide more police services to protect your neighborhood. In dealing with poverty, you might create a program such as a food bank to feed the hungry. Then you might work to get government to adopt and pay for the program.

Social action means that individuals and groups solve community problems without relying on government to do it for them. If you are dealing with crime in your neighborhood, you might form a neighborhood watch group. If you are dealing with poverty, you might work in a food bank organized by a charitable organization.

Why should I participate in the affairs of my community?

Participation in government is in our self-interest. The amount of time spent participating will probably depend on how well we think our elected officials are doing. When everything is going well, we might spend less time. If we are pleased with government, we might vote and do little else. When we are concerned that government is not meeting our needs or is violating our rights, we might spend more time. If we are dissatisfied, we might engage in a variety of types of action.

Citizens must actively participate in the civic life of their community and nation if they want their voices heard. Citizenship in a democracy is more than a legal status. Democratic citizenship is a way of life that guides our relationships with other people and with government.

Democracy can exist only if it lives in the minds and hearts of its citizens. Citizens should do more than say they are committed to democracy. They should demonstrate their commitment by their participation. It is up to each citizen to determine the level and nature of her or his participation in the civic life of the community and nation.

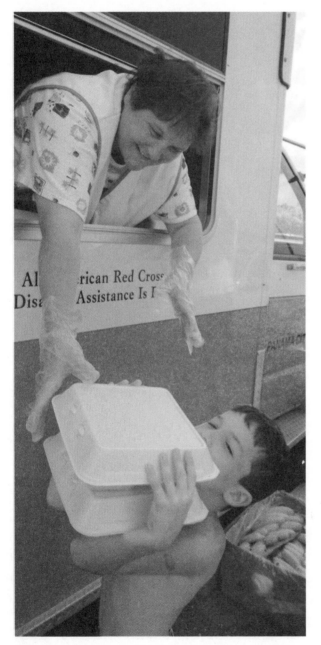

What are some examples of social action?

What do you think?

Work with one or more partners to discuss and develop your answers to the following questions.

① What is the difference between political action and social action? Why might people choose one over the other in dealing with problems in their communities?

② What does it mean to say that democracy can only exist if it lives in the minds and hearts of its citizens?

At the end of the Constitutional Convention, Mrs. Samuel Powell asked Benjamin Franklin, "Well, Doctor, what have we got, a Republic or a Monarchy?" Franklin replied, "A Republic, if you can keep it."

From the notes of James McHenry, delegate from Maryland

Reviewing and Using the Lesson

1. How is political action different from social action?

2. Why are both political and social action necessary?

3. How is citizen participation in political action related to the purposes of our government?

4. Explain why participating in government is in our self-interest.

Activities

1. Make a poster that demonstrates the different ways that citizens can participate in government. Take your own photos or use photographs from newspapers and magazines to illustrate each idea on your poster.

2. Use the Internet to find information about political action groups in your community that work to monitor and influence the decisions and actions of government.

3. Use the Internet to find information about social action groups in your community that work to address local community problems.

4. Monitor the newspaper in your community for one week. Look for articles that describe citizens participating in local, state, or national government.

5. Justice Louis Brandeis of the U.S. Supreme Court wrote, "The only title in our democracy superior to that of President is the title of citizen." Do you think that Justice Brandeis was correct? Write a short essay explaining your opinion.

Reference

THE DECLARATION OF INDEPENDENCE

July 4, 1776

The Declaration of Independence was passed by Congress on July 2, 1776, and issued on July 4, announcing the separation of the "United Colonies" from Britain and the formation of a new nation, the United States of America. The document lists reasons for the separation and a philosophical argument in defense of action.

In CONGRESS, July 4, 1776.

The unanimous Declaration of the thirteen united States of America,

WHEN in the Course of human Events, it becomes necessary for one People to dissolve the Political Bands which have connected them with another, and to assume among the Powers of the Earth, the separate and equal Station to which the Laws of Nature and of Nature's God entitle them, a decent Respect to the Opinions of Mankind requires that they should declare the causes which impel them to the Separation.

We hold these Truths to be self-evident, that all Men are created equal, that they are endowed by their Creator with certain unalienable Rights, that among these are Life, Liberty, and the Pursuit of Happiness—That to secure these Rights, Governments are instituted among Men, deriving their just Powers from the Consent of the Governed, that whenever any Form of Government becomes destructive of these Ends it is the Right of the People to alter or to abolish it, and to institute new Government, laying its Foundation on such Principles, and organizing its Powers in such Form, as to them shall seem most likely to effect their Safety and Happiness. Prudence, indeed, will dictate that Governments long established should not be changed for light and transient Causes; and accordingly all Experience hath shewn, that Mankind are more disposed to suffer, while Evils are sufferable, than to right themselves by abolishing the Forms to which they are accustomed. But when a long Train of Abuses and Usurpations, pursuing invariably the same Object, evinces a Design to reduce them under absolute Despotism, it is their Right, it is their Duty, to throw off such Government, and to provide new Guards for their future Security. Such has been the patient Sufferance of these Colonies; and such is now the Necessity which constrains them to alter their former Systems of Government. The History of the present King of Great-Britain is a History of repeated Injuries and Usurpations, all having in direct Object the Establishment of an absolute Tyranny over these States. To prove this, let Facts be submitted to a candid World.

He has refused his Assent to Laws, the most wholesome and necessary for the public Good.

He has forbidden his Governors to pass Laws of immediate and pressing Importance, unless suspended in their Operation till his Assent should be obtained; and when so suspended, he has utterly neglected to attend to them.

He has refused to pass other Laws for the Accommodation of large Districts of People, unless those People would relinquish the Right of Representation in the Legislature, a Right inestimable to them, and formidable to Tyrants only.

He has called together Legislative Bodies at Places unusual, uncomfortable, and distant from the Depository of their public Records, for the sole Purpose of fatiguing them into Compliance with his Measures.

He has dissolved Representative Houses repeatedly, for opposing with manly Firmness his Invasions on the Rights of the People.

He has refused for a long Time, after such Dissolutions, to cause others to be elected; whereby the Legislative Powers, incapable of Annihilation, have returned to the People at large for their exercise; the State remaining in the mean time exposed to all the Dangers of Invasions from without, and Convulsions within.

He has endeavored to prevent the Population of these States; for that Purpose obstructing the Laws for Naturalization of Foreigners; refusing to pass others to encourage their Migrations hither, and raising the Conditions of new Appropriations of Lands.

He has obstructed the Administration of Justice, by refusing his Assent to Laws for establishing Judiciary Powers.

He has made Judges dependent on his Will alone, for the Tenure of their Offices, and the Amount and Payment of their Salaries.

He has erected a Multitude of new Offices, and sent hither Swarms of Officers to harass our People and eat out their Substance.

He has kept among us, in Times of Peace, Standing Armies, without the consent of our Legislatures.

He has affected to render the Military independent of and superior to the Civil Power.

He has combined with others to subject us to a Jurisdiction foreign to our Constitution, and unacknowledged by our Laws; giving his Assent to their Acts of pretended Legislation:

For quartering large Bodies of Armed Troops among us:

For protecting them, by a mock Trial, from Punishment for any Murders which they should commit on the Inhabitants of these States:

For cutting off our Trade with all Parts of the World:

For imposing Taxes on us without our Consent:

For depriving us, in many Cases, of the Benefits of Trial by Jury:

For transporting us beyond Seas to be tried for pretended Offenses:

For abolishing the free System of English Laws in a neighbouring Province, establishing therein an Arbitrary Government, and enlarging its Boundaries, so as to render it at once an Example and fit Instrument for introducing the same absolute Rule into these Colonies:

For taking away our Charters, abolishing our most valuable Laws, and altering fundamentally the Forms of our Governments:

For suspending our own Legislatures, and declaring themselves invested with Power to legislate for us in all Cases whatsoever.

He has abdicated Government here, by declaring us out of his Protection and waging War against us.

He has plundered our Seas, ravaged our Coasts, burnt our Towns, and destroyed the Lives of our People.

He is, at this Time, transporting large Armies of foreign Mercenaries to compleat the Works of Death, Desolation, and Tyranny, already begun with circumstances of Cruelty and Perfidy, scarcely paralleled in the most barbarous Ages, and totally unworthy the Head of a civilized Nation.

He has constrained our fellow Citizens taken Captive on the high Seas to bear Arms against their Country, to become the Executioners of their Friends and Brethren, or to fall themselves by their Hands.

He has excited domestic Insurrections amongst us, and has endeavoured to bring on the Inhabitants of our Frontiers, the merciless Indian Savages, whose known Rule of Warfare, is an undistinguished Destruction, of all Ages, Sexes and Conditions.

In every stage of these Oppressions we have Petitioned for Redress in the most humble Terms: Our repeated Petitions have been answered only by repeated Injury. A Prince, whose Character is thus marked by every act which may define a Tyrant, is unfit to be the Ruler of a free People.

Nor have we been wanting in Attentions to our British Brethren. We have warned them from Time to Time of Attempts by their Legislature to extend an unwarrantable Jurisdiction over us. We have reminded them of the Circumstances of our Emigration and Settlement here. We have appealed to their native Justice and Magnanimity, and we have conjured them by the Ties of our common Kindred to disavow these Usurpations, which, would inevitably interrupt our Connections and Correspondence. They too have been deaf to the Voice of Justice and of Consanguinity. We must, therefore, acquiesce in the Necessity, which denounces our Separation, and hold them, as we hold the rest of Mankind, Enemies in War, in Peace, Friends.

We, therefore, the Representatives of the UNITED STATES OF AMERICA, in GENERAL CONGRESS, Assembled, appealing to the Supreme Judge of the World for the Rectitude of our Intentions, do, in the Name, and by Authority of the good People of these Colonies, solemnly Publish and Declare, That these United Colonies are, and of Right ought to be, FREE AND INDEPENDENT STATES; that they are absolved from all Allegiance to the British Crown, and that all political Connection between them and the State of Great Britain, is and ought to be totally dissolved; and that as FREE AND INDEPENDENT STATES, they have full Power to levy War, conclude Peace, contract Alliances, establish Commerce, and to do all other Acts and Things which INDEPENDENT STATES may of right do. And for the support of this Declaration, with a firm Reliance on the Protection of divine Providence, we mutually pledge to each other our Lives, our Fortunes, and our sacred Honor.

Signed by ORDER and in BEHALF of the CONGRESS, JOHN HANCOCK, PRESIDENT.

New-Hampshire

Josiah Bartlett,
Wm. Whipple,
Matthew Thornton.

Massachusetts-Bay

Saml. Adams,
John Adams,
Robt. Treat Paine,
Elbridge Gerry.

Rhode-Island and Providence, &c.

Step. Hopkins,
William Ellery.

Connecticut

Roger Sherman,
Saml. Huntington,
Wm. Williams,
Oliver Wolcott.

New-York

Wm. Floyd,
Phil. Livingston,
Frans. Lewis,
Lewis Morris.

New-Jersey

Richd. Stockton,
Jno. Witherspoon,
Fras. Hopkinson,
John Hart,
Abra. Clark.

Pennsylvania

Robt. Morris,
Benjamin Rush,
Benja. Franklin,
John Morton,
Geo. Clymer,

Jas. Smith,
Geo. Taylor,
James Wilson,
Geo. Ross.

Delaware

Casar Rodney,
Geo. Read,
(Tho M:Kean.)

Maryland

Samuel Chase,
Wm. Paca,
Thos. Stone,
Charles Carroll, of Carrollton.

Virginia

George Wythe,
Richard Henry Lee,
Ths. Jefferson,
Benja. Harrison,
Thos. Nelson, jr.,
Francis Lightfoot Lee,
Carter Braxton.

North-Carolina

Wm. Hooper,
Joseph Hewes,
John Penn.

South-Carolina

Edward Rutledge,
Thos. Heyward, junr.,
Thomas Lynch, junr.,
Arthur Middleton.

Georgia

Button Gwinnett,
Lyman Hall,
Geo. Walton.

THE CONSTITUTION OF THE UNITED STATES OF AMERICA
SEPTEMBER 17, 1787

The Constitution was adopted in Philadelphia on September 17, 1787, by the Constitutional Convention and was declared ratified on July 2, 1788.

PREAMBLE

We the People of the United States, in Order to form a more perfect Union, establish Justice, insure domestic tranquility, provide for the common defense, promote the general Welfare, and secure the Blessings of Liberty to ourselves and our Posterity, do ordain and establish this Constitution for the United States of America.

ARTICLE I
THE LEGISLATIVE BRANCH

Section 1

All legislative Powers herein granted shall be vested in a Congress of the United States, which shall consist of a Senate and House of Representatives.

Section 2

House of Representatives: Organization and Power of Impeachment

1 The House of Representatives shall be composed of Members chosen every second Year by the People of the several States, and the Electors in each State shall have the Qualifications requisite for Electors of the most numerous Branch of the State Legislature.

2 No Person shall be a Representative who shall not have attained to the Age of twenty five Years, and been seven Years a Citizen of the United States, and who shall not, when elected, be an Inhabitant of that State in which he shall be chosen.

3 [Representatives and direct Taxes shall be apportioned among the several States which may be included within this Union, according to their respective Numbers, which shall be determined by adding to the whole Number of free Persons, including those bound to Service for a Term of Years, and excluding Indians not taxed, three fifths of all other Persons.]* The actual Enumeration shall be made within three Years after the first Meeting of the Congress of the United States, and within every subsequent Term of ten Years, in such Manner as they shall by Law direct. The number of Representatives shall not exceed one for every thirty Thousand, but each State shall have at Least one Representative; and until such enumeration shall be made, the State of New Hampshire shall be entitled to choose three, Massachusetts eight, Rhode Island and Providence Plantations one, Connecticut five, New York six, New Jersey four, Pennsylvania eight, Delaware one, Maryland six, Virginia ten, North Carolina five, South Carolina five, and Georgia three.

4 When vacancies happen in the Representation from any State, the Executive Authority thereof shall issue Writs of Election to fill such Vacancies.

5 The House of Representatives shall choose their Speaker and other Officers; and shall have the sole Power of Impeachment.

Section 3

The Senate: Organization and Powers to Try Cases of Impeachment

1 The Senate of the United States shall be composed of two Senators from each State, chosen [by the Legislature thereof,]** for six Years; and each Senator shall have one Vote.

2 Immediately after they shall be assembled in Consequence of the first Election, they shall be divided as equally as may be into three Classes. The seats of the Senators of the first Class shall be vacated at the Expiration of the second Year, of the second Class at the Expiration of the fourth

---

*   *Changed by Section 2 of the Fourteenth Amendment*
**   *Changed by the Seventeenth Amendment*

Year, and of the third Class at the Expiration of the sixth Year, so that one third may be chosen every second Year; [and if Vacancies happen by Resignation, or otherwise, during the Recess of the Legislature of any State, the Executive thereof may make temporary Appointments until the next Meeting of the Legislature, which shall then fill such Vacancies.]*

3   No Person shall be a Senator who shall not have attained to the Age of thirty Years, and been nine Years a Citizen of the United States, and who shall not, when elected, be an Inhabitant of that State for which he shall be chosen.

4   The Vice President of the United States shall be President of the Senate, but shall have no Vote, unless they be equally divided.

5   The Senate shall choose their other officers, and also a President pro tempore, in the Absence of the Vice President, or when he shall exercise the Office of President of the United States.

6   The Senate shall have the sole Power to try all Impeachments. When sitting for that Purpose, they shall be on Oath or Affirmation. When the President of the United States is tried, the Chief Justice shall preside; And no person shall be convicted without the Concurrence of two thirds of the Members present.

7   Judgment in Cases of Impeachment shall not extend further than to removal from Office, and disqualification to hold and enjoy any Office of honor, Trust or Profit under the United States; but the Party convicted shall nevertheless be liable and subject to Indictment, Trial, Judgment and Punishment, according to Law.

Section 4

Elections and Meeting of Congress

1   The Times, Places and Manner of holding Elections for Senators and Representatives shall be prescribed in each State by the Legislature thereof; but the Congress may at any time by Law make or alter such Regulations, except as to the Places of choosing Senators.

2   The Congress shall assemble at least once in every Year, and such Meeting shall be [on the first Monday in December,]** unless they shall by Law appoint a different Day.

*   *Changed by Section 2 of the Fourteenth Amendment*
**   *Changed by the Seventeenth Amendment*

Section 5

Congress's Rules of Procedure, Powers, Quorum, Journals, Meetings, Adjournments

1   Each House shall be the Judge of the Elections, Returns and Qualifications of its own Members, and a Majority of each shall constitute a Quorum to do Business; but a smaller Number may adjourn from day to day, and may be authorized to compel the Attendance of absent Members, in such Manner, and under such Penalties as each House may provide.

2   Each House may determine the Rules of its Proceedings, punish its members for disorderly Behavior, and, with the Concurrence of two thirds, expel a Member.

3   Each House shall keep a Journal of its Proceedings, and from time to time publish the same, excepting such Parts as may in their Judgment require Secrecy; and the Yeas and Nays of the Members of either House on any question shall, at the Desire of one fifth of those Present, be entered on the Journal.

4   Neither House, during the Session of Congress, shall, without the Consent of the other, adjourn for more than three days, nor to any other Place than that in which the two Houses shall be sitting.

Section 6

Pay, Privileges, Limitations

1   The Senators and Representatives shall receive a Compensation for their Services, to be ascertained by Law, and paid out of the Treasury of the United States. They shall in all cases, except Treason, Felony and Breach of the Peace, be privileged from Arrest during their Attendance at the Session of their respective Houses, and in going to and returning from the same; and for any Speech or Debate in either House, they shall not be questioned in any other Place.

2   No Senator or Representative shall, during the Time for which he was elected, be appointed to any civil Office under the Authority of the United States, which shall have been created, or the Emoluments whereof shall have been increased during such time; and no Person holding any Office under the United States, shall be a Member of either House during his Continuance in Office.

Section 7

Procedure in Passing Bills, President's Veto Power

1   All Bills for raising Revenue shall originate in the House of Representatives; but the Senate may propose or concur with Amendments as on other Bills.

2   Every Bill which shall have passed the House of Representatives and the Senate, shall, before it becomes a Law, be presented to the President of the United States; if he approves he shall sign it, but if not he shall return it, with his Objections, to that House in which it shall have originated, who shall enter the Objections at large on their Journal, and proceed to reconsider it. If after such Reconsideration two thirds of that House shall agree to pass the Bill, it shall be sent, together with the Objections, to the other House, by which it shall likewise be reconsidered, and if approved by two thirds of that House, it shall become a Law. But in all such Cases the Votes of both Houses shall be determined by Yeas and Nays, and the Names of the Persons voting for and against the Bill shall be entered on the Journal of each House respectively. If any Bill shall not be returned by the President within ten Days (Sundays excepted) after it shall have been presented to him, the Same shall be a Law, in like Manner as if he had signed it, unless the Congress by their adjournment prevent its Return, in which Case it shall not be a Law.

3   Every Order, Resolution, or Vote to which the Concurrence of the Senate and House of Representatives may be necessary (except on a question of Adjournment) shall be presented to the President of the United States; and before the Same shall take Effect, shall be approved by him, or being disapproved by him, shall be repassed by two thirds of the Senate and House of Representatives, according to the Rules and Limitations prescribed in the Case of a Bill.

Section 8

Powers Delegated to Congress

The Congress shall have Power

1   To lay and collect Taxes, Duties, Imposts and Excises, to pay the Debts and provide for the common Defense and general Welfare of the United States; but all Duties, Imposts and Excises shall be uniform throughout the United States;

2   To borrow Money on the credit of the United States;

3   To regulate Commerce with foreign Nations, and among the several States, and with the Indian Tribes;

4   To establish a uniform Rule of Naturalization, and uniform Laws on the subject of Bankruptcies throughout the United States;

5   To coin Money, regulate the Value thereof, and of foreign Coin, and fix the Standard of Weights and Measures;

6   To provide for the Punishment of counterfeiting the Securities and current Coin of the United States;

7   To establish Post Offices and post Roads;

8   To promote the Progress of Science and useful Arts, by securing for limited Times to Authors and Inventors the exclusive Right to their respective Writings and Discoveries;

9   To constitute Tribunals inferior to the Supreme Court;

10   To define and punish Piracies and Felonies committed on the high Seas, and Offenses against the Law of Nations;

11   To declare War, grant Letters of Marque and Reprisal, and make Rules concerning Captures on Land and Water;

12   To raise and support Armies, but no Appropriation of Money to that Use shall be for a longer Term than two Years;

13   To provide and maintain a Navy;

14   To make Rules for the Government and Regulation of the land and naval Forces;

15   To provide for calling forth the Militia to execute the Laws of the Union, suppress Insurrections and repel Invasions;

16   To provide for organizing, arming, and disciplining the Militia, and for governing such Part of them as may be employed in the Service of the United States, reserving to the States respectively, the Appointment of the Officers, and the Authority of training the Militia according to the discipline prescribed by Congress;

17 To exercise exclusive Legislation in all Cases whatsoever, over such District (not exceeding ten Miles square) as may, by Session of particular States, and the Acceptance of Congress, become the Seat of the Government of the United States, and to exercise like Authority over all Places purchased by the Consent of the Legislature of the State in which the Same shall be, for the Erection of Forts, Magazines, Arsenals, dock-Yards and other needful Buildings;—and

18 To make all Laws which shall be necessary and proper for carrying into Execution the foregoing Powers, and all other Powers vested by this Constitution in the Government of the United States, or in any Department or Officer thereof.

Section 9

Powers Denied to Congress

1 The Migration or Importation of such Persons as any of the States now existing shall think proper to admit, shall not be prohibited by the Congress prior to the Year one thousand eight hundred and eight, but a Tax or duty may be imposed on such Importation, not exceeding ten dollars for each Person.

2 The Privilege of the Writ of Habeas Corpus shall not be suspended, unless when in Cases of Rebellion or Invasion the public Safety may require it.

3 No Bill of Attainder or ex post facto Law shall be passed.

4 [No Capitation, or other direct, Tax shall be laid, unless in Proportion to the Census or Enumeration herein before directed to be taken.]*

5 No Tax or Duty shall be laid on Articles exported from any State.

6 No Preference shall be given by any Regulation of Commerce or Revenue to the Ports of one State over those of another; nor shall Vessels bound to, or from, one State, be obliged to enter, clear, or pay Duties in another.

7 No Money shall be drawn from the Treasury, but in Consequence of Appropriations made by Law; and a regular Statement and Account of the Receipts and Expenditures of all public Money shall be published from time to time.

8 No Title of Nobility shall be granted by the United States: And no Person holding any Office of Profit or Trust under them, shall, without the Consent of the Congress, accept of any present, Emolument, Office, or Title, of any kind whatever, from any King, Prince, or foreign State.

Section 10

Restrictions on States' Powers

1 No State shall enter into any Treaty, Alliance, or Confederation; grant Letters of Marque and Reprisal; coin Money; emit Bills of Credit; make any Thing but gold and silver Coin a Tender in Payment of Debts; pass any Bill of Attainder, ex post facto Law, or Law impairing the Obligation of Contracts, or grant any Title of Nobility.

2 No State shall, without the Consent of the Congress, lay any Imposts or Duties on Imports or Exports, except what may be absolutely necessary for executing its inspection Laws: and the net Produce of all Duties and Imposts, laid by any State on Imports or Exports, shall be for the Use of the Treasury of the United States; and all such Laws shall be subject to the Revision and Control of the Congress.

3 No State shall, without the Consent of Congress, lay any Duty of Tonnage, keep Troops, or Ships of War in time of Peace, enter into any Agreement or Compact with another State, or with a foreign Power, or engage in War, unless actually invaded, or in such imminent Danger as will not admit of delay.

ARTICLE II
THE EXECUTIVE BRANCH

Section 1

President and Vice President: Election, Qualifications, and Oath

1 The executive Power shall be vested in a President of the United States of America. He shall hold his Office during the term of four Years, and, together with the Vice President, chosen for the same Term, be elected, as follows.

2 Each State shall appoint, in such Manner as the Legislature thereof may direct, a Number of Electors, equal to the whole Number of Senators and Representatives to which the State may be entitled

---

*   *Changed by the Sixteenth Amendment*

in the Congress: but no Senator or Representative, or Person holding an Office of Trust or Profit under the United States, shall be appointed an Elector.

3 [The Electors shall meet in their respective states, and vote by Ballot for two Persons, of whom one at least shall not be an Inhabitant of the same State with themselves. And they shall make a List of all the Persons voted for, and of the Number of Votes for each; which List they shall sign and certify, and transmit sealed to the Seat of the Government of the United States, directed to the President of the Senate. The President of the Senate shall, in the Presence of the Senate and House of Representatives, open all the Certificates, and the Votes shall then be counted. The Person having the greatest Number of Votes shall be the President, if such Number be a Majority of the whole Number of Electors appointed; and if there be more than one who have such Majority, and have an equal Number of Votes, then the House of Representatives shall immediately choose by Ballot one of them for President; and if no Person have a Majority, then from the five highest on the List the said House shall in like manner choose the President. But in choosing the President, the Votes shall be taken by States, the Representation from each State having one Vote; A quorum for this Purpose shall consist of a Member or Members from two thirds of the States, and a Majority of all the States shall be necessary to a Choice. In every Case, after the Choice of the President, the Person having the greatest Number of Votes of the Electors shall be the Vice President. But if there should remain two or more who have equal Votes, the Senate shall choose from them by Ballot the Vice President.]**

4 The Congress may determine the Time of choosing the Electors, and the day on which they shall give their Votes; which Day shall be the same throughout the United States.

5 No Person except a natural born Citizen, or a Citizen of the United States at the time of the Adoption of this Constitution, shall be eligible to the Office of the President; neither shall any person be eligible to that Office who shall not have attained to the Age of thirty five Years, and been fourteen Years a Resident within the United States.

6 [In Case of the Removal of the President from Office, or of his Death, Resignation, or Inability to discharge the Powers and Duties of the said

Office, the Same shall devolve on the Vice President, and the Congress may by Law provide for the Case of Removal Death, Resignation or Inability, both of the President and Vice President, declaring what Officer shall then act as President, and such Officer shall act accordingly, until the Disability be removed, or a President shall be elected.]***

7 The President shall, at stated Times, receive for his Services, a Compensation, which shall neither be increased nor diminished during the Period for which he shall have been elected, and he shall not receive within that Period any other Emolument from the United States, or any of them.

8 Before he enter the Execution of his Office, he shall take the following Oath or Affirmation:—"I do solemnly swear (or affirm) that I will faithfully execute the Office of President of the United States, and will to the best of my Ability, preserve, protect, and defend the Constitution of the United States."

Section 2

Powers of the President

1 The President shall be Commander in Chief of the Army and Navy of the United States, and of the Militia of the several States, when called into the actual Service of the United States; he may require the Opinion, in writing, of the principal Officer in each of the executive Departments, upon any Subject relating to the Duties of their respective Offices, and he shall have Power to grant Reprieves and Pardons for Offenses against the United States, except in Cases of Impeachment.

2 He shall have Power, by and with the Advice and Consent of the Senate, to make Treaties, provided two thirds of the Senators present concur; and he shall nominate, and by and with the Advice and Consent of the Senate, shall appoint Ambassadors, other public Ministers and Consuls, Judges of the supreme Court, and all other Officers of the United States, whose Appointments are not herein otherwise provided for, and which shall be established by Law: but the Congress may by Law vest the Appointment of such inferior Officers, as they think proper, in the President alone, in the Courts of Law, or in the Heads of Departments.

***

Changed by the Twelfth Amendment   *** *Changed by the Twenty-fifth Amendment*

3　The President shall have Power to fill up all Vacancies that may happen during the Recess of the Senate, by granting Commissions which shall expire at the End of their next Session.

Section 3
Duties of the President

He shall from time to time give to the Congress Information of the State of the Union, and recommend to their Consideration such Measures as he shall judge necessary and expedient; he may, on extraordinary Occasions, convene both Houses, or either of them, and in Case of Disagreement between them, with Respect to the Time of Adjournment, he may adjourn them to such Time as he shall think proper; he shall receive Ambassadors and other public Ministers; he shall take Care that the Laws be faithfully executed, and shall Commission all the Officers of the United States.

Section 4
Impeachment and Removal from Office for Crimes

The President, Vice President and all civil Officers of the United States, shall be removed from Office on Impeachment for, and Conviction of, Treason, Bribery, or other high Crimes and Misdemeanors.

ARTICLE III
THE JUDICIAL BRANCH

Section 1
Federal Courts, Tenure of Office

The judicial Power of the United States, shall be vested in one supreme Court, and in such inferior Courts as the Congress may from time to time ordain and establish. The Judges, both of the supreme and inferior Courts, shall hold their Offices during good Behavior, and shall, at stated Times, receive for their Services a Compensation, which shall not be diminished during their Continuance in Office.

Section 2
Jurisdiction of Federal Courts

1　The judicial Power shall extend to all Cases, in Law and Equity, arising under this Constitution, the Laws of the United States, and Treaties made, or which shall be made, under their Authority;—to all Cases affecting Ambassadors, other public Ministers and Consuls;—to all Cases of admiralty and maritime Jurisdiction;—to Controversies to which the United States shall be a Party;—to Controversies between two or more States; [between a State and Citizens of another State;]* between Citizens of different States;—between Citizens of the same State claiming Lands under Grants of different States;—[and between a State, or the Citizens thereof, and foreign States, Citizens or Subjects.]*

2　In all Cases affecting Ambassadors, other public Ministers and Consuls, and those in which a State shall be Party, the supreme Court shall have original Jurisdiction. In all the other Cases before mentioned, the supreme Court shall have appellate Jurisdiction, both as to Law and Fact, with such Exceptions, and under such Regulations as the Congress shall make.

3　The Trial of all Crimes, except in Cases of Impeachment, shall be by Jury; and such Trial shall be held in the State where said Crimes shall have been committed; but when not committed within any State, the Trial shall be at such Place or Places as the Congress may by Law have directed.

Section 3
Treason: Conviction Of and Punishment For

1　Treason against the United States shall consist only in levying War against them, or in adhering to their Enemies, giving them Aid and Comfort. No Person shall be convicted of Treason unless on the Testimony of two Witnesses to the same overt Act, or on Confession in open Court.

2　The Congress shall have Power to declare the Punishment of Treason, but no Attainder of Treason shall work Corruption of Blood, or Forfeiture except during the Life of the Person attainted.

ARTICLE IV
RELATIONS AMONG THE STATES

Section 1
Full Faith and Credit

Full Faith and Credit shall be given in each State to the public Acts, Records, and judicial Proceedings of every other State; And the Congress may by general Laws prescribe the manner in which such Acts, Records and Proceedings shall be proved, and the Effect thereof.

*　　*Changed by the Eleventh Amendment*

Section 2

Rights of State Citizens; Right of Extradition

1 The Citizens of each State shall be entitled to all Privileges and Immunities of Citizens in the several States.

2 A Person charged in any State with Treason, Felony, or other Crime, who shall flee from Justice, and be found in another State, shall on Demand of the executive Authority of the State from which he fled, be delivered up, to be removed to the State having Jurisdiction of the Crime.

3 [No person held to Service or Labour in one State, under the Laws thereof, escaping into another, shall, in Consequence of any Law or Regulation therein, be discharged from such Service or Labour, but shall be delivered up on Claim of the Party to whom such Service or Labour may be due.]**

Section 3

Admission of New States

1 New States may be admitted by the Congress into this Union; but no new State shall be formed or erected within the Jurisdiction of any other State; nor any State be formed by the Junction of two or more States, or parts of States, without the Consent of the Legislatures of the States concerned as well as of the Congress.

2 The Congress shall have Power to dispose of and make all needful Rules and Regulations respecting the territory or other Property belonging to the United States; and nothing in this Constitution shall be so construed as to Prejudice any Claims of the United States, or of any particular State.

Section 4

Republican Government Guaranteed

The United States shall guarantee to every State in this Union a Republican Form of Government, and shall protect each of them against Invasion; and on Application of the Legislature, or of the Executive (when the Legislature cannot be convened) against domestic Violence.

ARTICLE V
AMENDMENT PROCEDURES

The Congress, whenever two thirds of both Houses shall deem it necessary, shall propose Amendments to

** *Changed by the Thirteenth Amendment*

this Constitution, or, on the Application of the Legislatures of two thirds of the several States, shall call a Convention for proposing Amendments, which, in either Case, shall be valid to all Intents and Purposes, as Part of this Constitution, when ratified by the Legislatures of three fourths of the several States, or by Conventions in three fourths thereof, as the one or the other Mode of Ratification may be proposed by the Congress; Provided that no Amendment which may be made prior to the Year One thousand eight hundred and eight shall in any Manner affect the first and fourth Clauses in the Ninth Section of the first Article; and that no State, without its Consent, shall be deprived of its equal Suffrage in the Senate.

ARTICLE VI
SUPREMACY OF THE CONSTITUTION AND FEDERAL LAWS

1 All debts contracted and Engagements entered into, before the Adoption of this Constitution, shall be as valid against the United States under this Constitution, as under the Confederation.

2 This Constitution, and the Laws of the United States which shall be made in Pursuance thereof; and all Treaties made, or which shall be made, under the Authority of the United States, shall be the supreme Law of the Land; and the Judges in every State shall be bound thereby, any Thing in the Constitution or Laws of any State to the Contrary notwithstanding.

3 The Senators and Representatives before mentioned, and the Members of the several State Legislatures, and all executive and judicial Officers, both of the United States and of the several States, shall be bound by Oath or Affirmation, to support this Constitution; but no religious Test shall ever be required as a Qualification to any Office or public Trust under the United States.

ARTICLE VII
RATIFICATION

The Ratification of the Conventions of nine States, shall be sufficient for the Establishment of this Constitution between the States so ratifying the Same.

Done in Convention by the unanimous consent of the States present the seventeenth day of September in the year of our Lord one thousand seven hundred and eighty seven and of the Independence of the United

States of America the Twelfth. In witness whereof we have hereunto subscribed our Names,

President and deputy from Virginia
George Washington

New-Hampshire
John Langdon

Nicholas Gilman

Massachusetts
Nathaniel Gorham

Rufus King

Connecticut
William Samuel Johnson

Roger Sherman

New York
Alexander Hamilton

New Jersey
William Livingston

David Brearley

William Paterson

Jonathan Dayton

Pennsylvania
Benjamin Franklin

Thomas Mifflin

Robert Morris

George Clymer

Thomas Fitzsimons

Jared Ingersoll

James Wilson

Gouverneur Morris

Delaware
George Read

Gunning Bedford, Jr.

John Dickinson

Richard Bassett

Jacob Broom

Maryland
James McHenry

Daniel of St. Tho. Jenifer

Daniel Carroll

Virginia
John Blair

James Madison, Jr.

North Carolina
William Blount

Richard Dobbs Spaight

Hugh Williamson

South Carolina
John Rutledge

Charles Cotesworth Pinckney

Charles Pinckney

Pierce Butler

Georgia
William Few

Abraham Baldwin

Attest:
William Jackson, Secretary

AMENDMENTS TO THE CONSTITUTION OF THE UNITED STATES OF AMERICA

The first ten amendments to the U.S. Constitution are known as the Bill of Rights. The Bill of Rights lists many basic rights that the federal government may not interfere with and must protect. Nearly all these rights are now also protected from violation by state governments. Subsequent amendments were adopted shortly afterward, beginning with the Eleventh Amendment in 1795. The Twenty-seventh Amendment is the most recent to be ratified. It became a part of the Consitution in 1992.

AMENDMENT I

Congress shall make no law respecting an establishment of religion, or prohibiting the free exercise thereof; or abridging the freedom of speech, or of the press; or the right of the people peaceably to assemble, and to petition the Government for a redress of grievances.

AMENDMENT II

A well regulated Militia, being necessary to the security of a free State, the right of the people to keep and bear Arms, shall not be infringed.

AMENDMENT III

No Soldier shall, in time of peace be quartered in any house, without the consent of the Owner, nor in time of war, but in a manner to be prescribed by law.

AMENDMENT IV

The right of the people to be secure in their persons, houses, papers, and effects, against unreasonable searches and seizures, shall not be violated, and no Warrants shall issue, but upon probable cause, supported by Oath or affirmation, and particularly describing the place to be searched, and the persons or things to be seized.

AMENDMENT V

No person shall be held to answer for a capital, or otherwise infamous crime, unless on a presentment or indictment of a Grand Jury, except in cases arising in the land or naval forces, or in the Militia, when in actual service in time of War or public danger; nor shall any person be subject for the same offence to be twice put in jeopardy of life or limb; nor shall be compelled in any criminal case to be a witness against himself, nor be deprived of life, liberty, or property, without due process of law; nor shall private property be taken for public use, without just compensation.

AMENDMENT VI

In all criminal prosecutions, the accused shall enjoy the right to a speedy and public trial, by an impartial jury of the State and district wherein the crime shall have been committed, which district shall have been previously ascertained by law, and to be informed of the nature and cause of the accusation; to be confronted with the witnesses against him; to have compulsory process for obtaining witnesses in his favor, and to have the Assistance of Counsel for his defence.

AMENDMENT VII

In Suits at common law, where the value in controversy shall exceed twenty dollars, the right of trial by jury shall be preserved, and no fact tried by a jury, shall be otherwise re-examined in any Court of the United States, than according to the rules of the common law.

AMENDMENT VIII

Excessive bail shall not be required, nor excessive fines imposed, nor cruel and unusual punishments inflicted.

AMENDMENT IX

The enumeration in the Constitution, of certain rights, shall not be construed to deny or disparage others retained by the people.

AMENDMENT X

The powers not delegated to the United States by the Constitution, nor prohibited by it to the States, are reserved to the States respectively, or to the people. [The first ten amendments were ratified December 15, 1791.]

AMENDMENT XI

The Judicial power of the United States shall not be construed to extend to any suit in law or equity, commenced or prosecuted against one of the United States by Citizens of another State, or by Citizens or Subjects of any Foreign State. [Ratified February 1795.]

AMENDMENT XII

The Electors shall meet in their respective states and vote by ballot for President and Vice-President, one of whom, at least, shall not be an inhabitant of the same state with themselves; they shall name in their ballots the person voted for as President, and in distinct ballots the person voted for as Vice-President, and they shall make distinct lists of all persons voted for as President, and of all persons voted for as Vice-President, and of the number of votes for each, which lists they shall sign and certify, and transmit sealed to the seat of the government of the United States, directed to the President of the Senate;—the President of the Senate shall, in the presence of the Senate and House of Representatives, open all the certificates and the votes shall then be counted;— The person having the greatest number of votes for President, shall be the President, if such number be a majority of the whole number of Electors appointed; and if no person have such majority, then from the persons having the highest numbers not exceeding three on the list of those voted for as President, the House of Representatives shall choose immediately by ballot, the President. But in choosing the President, the votes shall be taken by states, the representation from each state having one vote; a quorum for this purpose shall consist of a member or members from two-thirds of the states, and a majority of all the states shall be necessary to a choice. [And if the House of Representatives shall not choose a President whenever the right of choice shall devolve upon them, before the fourth day of March next following, then the Vice-President shall act as President, as in the case of the death or other constitutional disability of the President .—]* The person having the greatest number of votes as Vice-President, shall be the Vice-President, if such number be a majority of the whole number of Electors appointed, and if no person have a majority, then from the two highest numbers on the list, the

Senate shall choose the Vice-President; a quorum for the purpose shall consist of two-thirds of the whole number of Senators, and a majority of the whole number shall be necessary to a choice. But no person constitutionally ineligible to the office of President shall be eligible to that of Vice-President of the United States. [Ratified June 1804.]

AMENDMENT XIII

Section 1

Neither slavery nor involuntary servitude, except as a punishment for crime whereof the party shall have been duly convicted, shall exist within the United States, or any place subject to their jurisdiction.

Section 2

Congress shall have power to enforce this article by appropriate legislation. [Ratified December 1865.]

AMENDMENT XIV

Section 1

All persons born or naturalized in the United States and subject to the jurisdiction thereof, are citizens of the United States, and of the State wherein they reside. No State shall make or enforce any law which shall abridge the privileges or immunities of citizens of the United States; nor shall any State deprive any person of life, liberty, or property, without due process of law; nor deny to any person within its jurisdiction the equal protection of the laws.

Section 2

Representatives shall be apportioned among the several States according to their respective numbers, counting the whole number of persons in each State, excluding Indians not taxed. But when the right to vote at any election for the choice of electors for President and Vice-President of the United States, Representatives in Congress, the Executive and Judicial officers of a State, or the members of the Legislature thereof, is denied to any of the male inhabitants of such State, being twenty-one years of age,** and citizens of the United States, or in any way abridged, except for participation in rebellion, or other crime, the basis of representation therein shall be reduced in the proportion which the number of such male citizens shall bear to the whole number of male citizens twenty-one years of age in such State.

---

* *Superseded by Section 3 of the Twentieth Amendment*

** *Changed by Section 1 of the Twenty-sixth Amendment*

Section 3

No person shall be a Senator or Representative in Congress, or elector of President and Vice-President, or hold any office, civil or military, under the United States, or under any State, who, having previously taken an oath, as a member of Congress, or as an officer of the United States, or as a member of any State legislature, or as an executive or judicial officer of any State, to support the Constitution of the United States, shall have engaged in insurrection or rebellion against the same, or given aid or comfort to the enemies thereof. But Congress may by a vote of two-thirds of each House, remove such disability.

Section 4

The validity of the public debt of the United States, authorized by law, including debts incurred for payment of pensions and bounties for services in suppressing insurrection or rebellion, shall not be questioned. But neither the United States nor any State shall assume or pay any debt or obligation incurred in aid of insurrection or rebellion against the United States, or any claim for the loss or emancipation of any slave; but all such debts, obligations and claims shall be held illegal and void.

Section 5

The Congress shall have the power to enforce, by appropriate legislation, the provisions of this article. [Ratified July 1868.]

AMENDMENT XV

Section 1

The right of citizens of the United States to vote shall not be denied or abridged by the United States or by any State on account of race, color, or previous condition of servitude.

Section 2

The Congress shall have the power to enforce this article by appropriate legislation. [Ratified February 1870.]

AMENDMENT XVI

The Congress shall have power to lay and collect taxes on incomes, from whatever source derived, without apportionment among the several States, and without regard to any census or enumeration. [Ratified February 1913.]

AMENDMENT XVII

The Senate of the United States shall be composed of two Senators from each State, elected by the people thereof, for six years; and each Senator shall have one vote. The electors in each State shall have the qualifications requisite for electors of the most numerous branch of the State legislatures. When vacancies happen in the representation of any State in the Senate, the executive authority of such State shall issue writs of election to fill such vacancies: *Provided*, That the legislature of any State may empower the executive thereof to make temporary appointments until the people fill the vacancies by election as the legislature may direct. This amendment shall not be so construed as to affect the election or term of any Senator chosen before it becomes valid as part of the Constitution. [Ratified April 1913.]

AMENDMENT XVIII

Section 1

After one year from the ratification of this article the manufacture, sale, or transportation of intoxicating liquors within, the importation thereof into, or the exportation thereof from the United States and all territory subject to the jurisdiction thereof for beverage purposes is hereby prohibited.

Section 2

The Congress and the several States shall have concurrent power to enforce this article by appropriate legislation.

Section 3

This article shall be inoperative unless it shall have been ratified as an amendment to the Constitution by the legislatures of the several States, as provided in the Constitution, within seven years from the date of the submission hereof to the States by the Congress. [Ratified January 1919.]***

AMENDMENT XIX

The right of citizens of the United States to vote shall not be denied or abridged by the United States or by any State on account of sex. Congress shall have power to enforce this article by appropriate legislation. [Ratified August 1920.]

***   *Repealed by the Twenty-first Amendment*

AMENDMENT XX

Section 1

The terms of the President and the Vice President shall end at noon on the 20th day of January, and the terms of Senators and Representatives at noon on the 3rd day of January, of the years in which such terms would have ended if this article had not been ratified; and the terms of their successors shall then begin.

Section 2

The Congress shall assemble at least once in every year, and such meeting shall begin at noon on the 3rd day of January, unless they shall by law appoint a different day.

Section 3

If, at the time fixed for the beginning of the term of the President, the President elect shall have died, the Vice President elect shall become President. If a President shall not have been chosen before the time fixed for the beginning of his term, or if the President elect shall have failed to qualify, then the Vice President elect shall act as President until a President shall have qualified; and the Congress may by law provide for the case wherein neither a President elect nor a Vice President elect shall have qualified, declaring who shall then act as President, or the manner in which one who is to act shall be selected, and such person shall act accordingly until a President or Vice President shall have qualified.

Section 4

The Congress may by law provide for the case of the death of any of the persons from whom the House of Representatives may choose a President whenever the right of choice shall have devolved upon them, and for the case of the death of any of the persons from whom the Senate may choose a Vice President whenever the right of choice shall have devolved upon them.

Section 5

Sections 1 and 2 shall take effect on the 15th day of October following the ratification of this article.

Section 6

This article shall be inoperative unless it shall have been ratified as an amendment to the Constitution by the legislatures of three-fourths of the several States within seven years from the date of its submission. [Ratified January 1933.]

AMENDMENT XXI

Section 1

The eighteenth article of amendment to the Constitution of the United States is hereby repealed.

Section 2

The transportation or importation into any State, Territory, or Possession of the United States for delivery or use therein of intoxicating liquors, in violation of the laws thereof, is hereby prohibited.

Section 3

This article shall be inoperative unless it shall have been ratified as an amendment to the Constitution by conventions in the several States, as provided in the Constitution, within seven years from the date of the submission hereof to the States by the Congress. [Ratified December 1933.]

AMENDMENT XXII

Section 1

No person shall be elected to the office of the President more than twice, and no person who has held the office of President, or acted as President, for more than two years of a term to which some other person was elected President shall be elected to the office of the President more than once. But this Article shall not apply to any person holding the office of President when this Article was proposed by the Congress, and shall not prevent any person who may be holding the office of President, or acting as President, during the term within which this Article becomes operative from holding the office of President or acting as President during the remainder of such term.

Section 2

This article shall be inoperative unless it shall have been ratified as an amendment to the Constitution by the legislatures of three-fourths of the several States within seven years from the date of its submission to the States by the Congress. [Ratified February 1951.]

AMENDMENT XXIII

Section 1

The District constituting the seat of Government of the United States shall appoint in such manner as the Congress may direct: A number of electors of President and Vice President equal to the whole number of Senators and Representatives in Congress to which the District would be entitled if it were a State, but in no event more than the least populous State; they shall be in addition to those appointed by the States, but they shall be considered, for the purposes of the election of President and Vice President, to be electors appointed by a State; and they shall meet in the District and perform such duties as provided by the twelfth article of amendment.

Section 2

The Congress shall have power to enforce this article by appropriate legislation. [Ratified March 1961.]

AMENDMENT XXIV

Section 1

The right of citizens of the United States to vote in any primary or other election for President or Vice President, for electors for President or Vice President, or for Senator or Representative in Congress, shall not be denied or abridged by the United States or any State by reason of failure to pay any poll tax or other tax.

Section 2

The Congress shall have power to enforce this article by appropriate legislation. [Ratified January 1964.]

AMENDMENT XXV

Section 1

In case of the removal of the President from office or of his death or resignation, the Vice President shall become President.

Section 2

Whenever there is a vacancy in the office of the Vice President, the President shall nominate a Vice President who shall take office upon confirmation by a majority vote of both Houses of Congress.

Section 3

Whenever the President transmits to the President pro tempore of the Senate and the Speaker of the House of Representatives his written declaration that he is unable to discharge the powers and duties of his office, and until he transmits to them a written declaration to the contrary, such powers and duties shall be discharged by the Vice President as Acting President.

Section 4

Whenever the Vice President and a majority of either the principal officers of the executive departments or of such other body as Congress may by law provide, transmit to the President pro tempore of the Senate and the Speaker of the House of Representatives their written declaration that the President is unable to discharge the powers and duties of his office, the Vice President shall immediately assume the powers and duties of the office as Acting President.

Thereafter, when the President transmits to the President pro tempore of the Senate and the Speaker of the House of Representatives his written declaration that no inability exists, he shall resume the powers and duties of his office unless the Vice President and a majority of either the principal office of the executive department or of such other body as Congress may by law provide, transmit within four days to the President pro tempore of the Senate and the Speaker of the House of Representatives their written declaration that the President is unable to discharge the powers and duties of his office. Thereupon Congress shall decide the issue, assembling within forty-eight hours for that purpose if not in session. If the Congress, within twenty-one days after receipt of the latter written declaration, or, if Congress is not in session, within twenty-one days after Congress is required to assemble, determines by two-thirds vote of both Houses that the President is unable to discharge the powers and duties of his office, the Vice President shall continue to discharge the same as Acting President; otherwise, the President shall resume the powers and duties of his office. [Ratified February 1967.]

AMENDMENT XXVI

Section 1

The right of citizens of the United States, who are eighteen years of age or older, to vote shall not be denied or abridged by the United States or by any State on account of age.

Section 2

The Congress shall have power to enforce this article by appropriate legislation. [Ratified July 1971.]

AMENDMENT XXVII

No law, varying the compensation for the services of the Senators or Representatives, shall take effect, until an election of Representatives shall have intervened. [Ratified May 1992.]

Glossary

abolish To formally put an end to.

abridging Limiting or reducing.

advice and consent The right of the U.S. Senate, granted in Article II of the Constitution, to review treaties and major presidential appointments. Two-thirds vote of senators is required for treaties and a simple majority for appointments.

alien A foreign-born resident.

Alien and Sedition Acts Laws passed during President John Adams' administration that made it a crime for editors, writers, or speakers to criticize the government and its Federalist policies.

allegiance (1) Loyalty to a government, ruler, or nation. (2) Loyalty to a person, social group, or cause.

amendment A change in or addition to a legal document.

American Revolution The war fought by the American colonists to gain their independence from Great Britain. It took place from 1775 to 1783.

Amnesty International An international nongovernmental organization that advocates the protection of human rights.

Anti-Federalists People who were against ratification of the Constitution because they thought it gave too much power to the federal government and did not protect the political rights of the people.

appeal The bringing of a court case from a lower court to a higher court in an attempt to have the lower court's decision reversed or for other reasons.

appellate court A judicial body that hears appeals from a lower court.

appellate jurisdiction The legal authority of a court to hear appeals from a lower court.

aristocrats People of the highest class of society who held inherited titles. They were often part of the ruling class in government.

Article I The part of the Constitution that describes the legislative branch of the government and its powers.

Article II The part of the Constitution that describes the executive branch of the government and its powers.

Article III The part of the Constitution that describes the judicial branch of the government and its powers.

Article IV The part of the Constitution that deals with the relationship between the states and the federal government and states' relationships with each other.

Article V The part of the Constitution that describes the process for amending the Constitution.

Article VI The part of the Constitution that deals with debts and contracts that were entered into before adoption of the Constitution; the supremacy of the Constitution; and the requirement of an oath of office for executive, legislative, and judicial officials. It prohibits the institution of a religious test for officeholders.

Article VII The part of the Constitution that describes the requirement for ratification of the Constitution.

Articles of Confederation The first Constitution of the United States, created to form a perpetual union and a firm league of friendship among the thirteen original states. It was adopted by the Second Continental Congress on November 10, 1777, and sent to the states for ratification. It came into force on March 1, 1781, and served as the nation's constitution until 1789, when the U.S. Constitution replaced it. The Articles provided for a weak central government.

assembly, right of The right or legal claims that allow a person to meet with others to discuss one's beliefs, ideas, or feelings.

association An organized group of people joined together for a common purpose.

Association of Southeast Asian Nations (ASEAN) "The Association represents the collective will of the ten member nations to work together to secure peace, freedom, and prosperity for their peoples." (ASEAN Declaration 1967)

autocratic government Government in which a single ruler or group has unlimited power.

avarice An excessive desire for money; greed.

bail Money or other security given to obtain a person's release from custody, which is forfeited if the person subsequently fails to appear before the court for trial.

bailiff (1) An officer who carries out legal orders, makes arrests, keeps order in court, or serves as a messenger and doorkeeper. (2) (chiefly British) A local official who has some judicial powers.

balance of power The division of governmental powers among different persons or institutions in such a way that no one individual or group can dominate or control the exercise of power by others.

basic rights Fundamental rights such as life, liberty, and property.

Battle of Saratoga (1777) An important battle of the Revolutionary War that lasted from June to October 1777, when the British surrendered in Saratoga, New York. The American victory prevented the British from splitting the colonies in two, increased American morale, and encouraged the French to sign a treaty with the Americans.

bill A proposed law given to the legislature for approval.

bill of attainder An act of the legislature that inflicts punishment on an individual or group without a judicial trial.

Bill of Rights The first ten amendments to the Constitution. It lists basic rights of the people that the federal government may not interfere with and must protect.

Boston Massacre (1770) On March 5, 1770, a mob of colonists harassed British soldiers guarding the tax collector's office in Boston. The soldiers opened fire, killing five Bostonians.

Boston Tea Party (1773) An act of rebellion against British authority, and in particular in response to the Tea Act, in which a band of colonists boarded ships in Boston Harbor and destroyed thousands of dollars worth of tea by throwing it overboard.

boycott To refuse to buy from or deal with a store or company as an act of protest.

Brown v. Board of Education of Topeka (1954) The U.S. Supreme Court case in which the Court declared that "separate but equal" educational facilities are inherently unequal and therefore a violation of the equal protection of the laws guaranteed by the Fourteenth Amendment.

cabinet The advisors to the president who are the heads of the departments of the executive branch.

charter A written document from a government or ruler that grants certain rights to an individual, group, organization, or to people in general. In colonial times, a charter granted land to a person or a company along with the right to start a colony on that land.

chattel Personal property that can be moved from place to place.

checks and balances The distribution and balancing of power among different branches of government so that no one branch is able to dominate the others.

chief justice The head of a court. The Chief Justice of the United States is the highest ranking judicial official in the nation and is the head of the U.S. Supreme Court.

citizen A person who is a legal member of a nation, country, or other self-governing community.

civic (1) Related to citizens or citizenship. (2) Related to the public affairs of a city or country.

civic life The public life of citizens; that which is concerned with a citizen's own interests and the common affairs and interests of his or her community and nation.

civic participation Taking part in formal political processes and community activities outside of government.

civic virtue The dedication of citizens to the common welfare of their community or country, even at the cost of their individual interests.

civil Related to citizens, particularly the relationship between citizens and government.

civil disobedience The refusal to obey laws one regards as unjust.

civil rights Fundamental rights belonging to every member of a society.

Civil Rights Act of 1964 This law ended segregation in public places, including restaurants, movie theaters, and hotels. The law also said that employers could not unfairly discriminate against people because of their race, national origin, religion, or gender.

civil rights movement A social movement in the United States during the 1950s and 1960s, in which people organized to demand equal rights for African Americans and other minorities. People worked together to change unfair laws. They gave speeches, marched in the streets, and participated in boycotts.

Civil War The war between the Northern and Southern states. It took place from 1861 to 1865.

Civil War Amendments The Thirteenth, Fourteenth, and Fifteenth Amendments to the U.S. Constitution ratified after the Civil War. The Thirteenth Amendment abolished slavery. The Fourteenth Amendment granted full citizenship to African Americans. The Fifteenth Amendment guaranteed the right to vote to men regardless of their "race, color, or previous condition of servitude."

commander in chief Highest leader of the military forces. According to the Constitution, the president is the commaner in chief of the nation's armed forces.

commerce The buying and selling of goods, particularly on a large scale.

committees of correspondence Committees that began as voluntary associations and were eventually established by most of the colonial governments. Their mission was to make sure that each colony knew about events and opinions in the other colonies. They helped to unite the people against the British.

common good The good of the community as a whole.

common law The body of unwritten law developed in England from judicial decisions based on custom and earlier judicial decisions, which constitutes the basis of the English legal system and became part of American law.

compromise A way to settle differences by each side giving up some of its claims or demands and agreeing to a common solution.

confederation A form of political organization in which the sovereign states combine for certain specified purposes such as defense. Member states can leave a confederation at any time. The United States was a confederation from 1776 to 1789.

Congress The national legislature of the United States. Congress has two parts, also called houses: the Senate and the House of Representatives.

consent To agree and accept something, approve of something, or allow something to take place.

consent of the governed The expressed agreement by the people to obey the laws and the government they create.

constable A public official with limited police and judicial powers.

constitution A set of customs, traditions, rules, and laws that sets forth the way a government is organized and operated.

Constitution, United States The supreme law of the United States that provides the framework for the government. The Constitution outlines the nation's institutions of government and the most important rights of the people. The document was created in 1787 during the Philadelphia Convention. The government created by the Constitution took effect on March 4, 1789.

Constitutional Convention *See* Philadelphia Convention.

constitutional government A government in which the powers of the ruler or rulers are limited by a constitution.

constitutional principle An essential idea contained in the Constitution. For example, the idea that no branch of government should have a monopoly on power.

contract A binding agreement between two or more persons.

covenant A binding agreement made by two or more persons or parties. The original idea of a covenant was an agreement made in the sight of God. The Mayflower Compact was such a covenant.

cruel and unusual punishment A criminal sanction or penalty that is not in accord with the moral standards of a humane and compassionate society. Such punishments are prohibited by the Eighth Amendment.

currency Any form of money used in a nation.

custom (1) An accepted practice or way of behaving that is followed by tradition. (2) A tax on goods entering a country.

Daughters of Liberty An organization formed by women prior to the American Revolution. They got together to protest treatment of the colonies by their British rulers. They helped make the boycott of British trade effective by making their own materials instead of using British imports.

Dawes Act (1887) An act of Congress that granted American citizenship and small parcels of land to American Indians who would give up allegiance to their tribe, their historical traditions, and ways of life. The law was devastating to Native American cultural traditions and forced many Native Americans into farming.

Declaration of Independence A proclamation that listed the basic principles of democratic government, stated the colonists' grievances against the king, and gave reasons why the colonists were free from British rule. It was signed by the members of Congress on July 4, 1776.

Declaratory Act (1766) A British law that reaffirmed the right of Parliament to pass laws for the colonies in "all cases whatsoever." The purpose of the law was to remind the colonists that the authority of the king and Parliament was superior to colonial governments.

delegate (1) (noun) A person chosen to act for or represent others. (2) (verb) To entrust someone to represent your interests.

democracy A form of government in which political power is exercised by all citizens, either directly or through their elected representatives.

dictator A head of government who has unlimited power.

dictatorial government A political system in which the ruler or rulers has unlimited power and which denies peoples' fundamental rights.

diplomacy The practice of carrying on formal relationships with governments of other countries.

direct democracy A type of government in which the people themselves meet and make the laws that they decide are needed.

discrimination Unfair treatment of people based on such things as their race, religion, or gender.

district court The court of original jurisdiction for most federal cases. This is the only federal court that holds trials in which juries and witnesses are used. Each state has at least one district court.

diverse (1) Of different kinds, types, or forms. (2) People of many different races, cultures, and ethnic groups.

domestic tranquility As used in the Preamble, this phrase means peaceful conditions within our country.

due process of law A requirement, stated in the Fifth and Fourteenth Amendments, that treatment by state and federal governments that involves life, liberty, or property of individuals be reasonable, fair, and follow known rules and procedures.

duty A tax on goods that are either imported or exported.

economic rights Rights essential to citizens that allow them to earn a living, to acquire and transfer property, and to produce, buy, and sell goods and services in open and free markets.

Eighth Amendment An amendment to the Constitution that bans excessive bail or fines and cruel and unusual punishment.

elector (1) One of the 538 members of the Electoral College chosen by the political parties in a state. (2) Any qualified voter.

Electoral College The group of presidential electors who cast the official votes for president and vice president after a presidential election. Each state has a number of electors equal to the total of its members in the Senate and House of Representatives.

English Bill of Rights An act passed by Parliament in 1689 that limited the power of the monarch. This document established Parliament as the most powerful branch of the English government.

enumerated powers Those rights and responsibilities of the U.S. government specifically provided for and listed in the Constitution.

equal protection clause Section 1 of the Fourteenth Amendment, which has been used to prevent states from treating individuals unfairly because of their race, national origin, citizenship status, or gender. It prohibits laws that unreasonably and unfairly favor some groups over others; it states that laws may not arbitrarily discriminate against persons.

equal protection of the law *See* equal protection clause.

equal representation The idea that each state should have the same number of representatives in Congress. The number of representatives in the Senate is based on equal representation.

establishment clause The part of the First Amendment that says the government cannot declare an official religion.

ex post facto law A law that makes an act a crime that was not a crime when the act was committed, that increases the penalty for a crime after it was committed, or that changes the rules of evidence to make conviction easier. Ex post facto laws are forbidden by Article I of the Constitution.

excise A tax on goods produced within a certain country imposed by that country's government.

executive branch The branch of government that carries out the laws made by the legislative branch.

executive power The authority to carry out and enforce the law.

faction (1) A small group within a larger group. (2) According to James Madison, a group that seeks to promote its own special interests at the expense of the common good.

federal courts The courts of the national government that deal with problems between states, with the Constitution, and with laws made by Congress.

federal government Another name for our national government.

federalism or **federal system** A form of government in which power is divided and shared between a central government and state and local governments.

Federalist, The A series of letters to the editor written in 1787–88 by Alexander Hamilton, James Madison, and John Jay, urging the adoption of the Constitution and supporting the need for a strong national government.

Federalists Advocates for ratification of the Constitution and for a strong centralized government; they flourished as a political party in the 1790s under the leadership of Alexander Hamilton. The party disappeared from national politics in 1816.

feudalism A system of social, economic, and political organizations in which a politically weak king or queen shared power with the nobility. The nobility required work and services from the common people in return for allowing them to live on and make use of the noble's land and benefit from the noble's protection.

Fifteenth Amendment An amendment to the Constitution, ratified after the Civil War in 1870, that forbids the denial of voting rights to any person based on race, color, or whether that person was previously a slave.

Fifth Amendment An amendment to the Constitution that states that no person will have their life, liberty, or property taken away by the federal government without due process of law. This amendment protects your right to be treated fairly by the federal government.

First Amendment An amendment to the Constitution that protects freedom of expression and the right of assembly.

First Continental Congress The body of colonial delegates who convened to represent the interests of the colonists and protest British rule. The First Continental Congress met in 1774 and drafted a Declaration of Rights.

Founders The political leaders of the thirteen original colonies. They were key figures in the establishment of the United States of America.

Fourteenth Amendment An amendment to the Constitution that states that no person—including people who are not citizens—will have their life, liberty, or property taken away by state or local governments without due process of law. This amendment protects a citizen's right to be treated fairly by his or her state and local governments. It also defines a citizen as anyone born or naturalized in the United States. It was one of the Civil War amendments.

Fourth Amendment An amendment to the U.S. Constitution that protects citizens from unreasonable searches and seizures

Glossary

and requires that warrants be issued only for "probable cause."

Framers The delegates to the Philadelphia Convention of 1787. They are the group of men who composed the United States Constitution.

free exercise clause The part of the First Amendment that says the government may not stop anyone from holding any religious beliefs they choose and may not unfairly or unreasonably limit anyone's right to practice their religious beliefs.

freedom of assembly The right to meet with others to discuss one's own beliefs, ideas, or feelings.

freedom of belief or conscience The right to freedom from being coerced to believe in something that you do not believe.

freedom of expression The right to make known one's attitudes, emotions, thoughts, feelings, etc., as protected by the First Amendment.

freedom of the press The right to read and write whatever you wish, as well as the right to publish your ideas without government interference.

freedom of religion The right to hold whatever religious beliefs you wish and the right to practice your beliefs without unfair or unreasonable interference from the government.

French Constitution of 1791 A constitution adopted during the French Revolution that established a constitutional monarchy in France. Power was concentrated in the legislative assembly and the power of the king was limited.

fugitive slave clause Article IV, Section 2, Clause 3 of the Constitution, which stated that slaves who escaped must be returned to their owners. It was later abolished by the Thirteenth Amendment.

general welfare What is best for most of the people.

general welfare clause Article I, Section 8, Clause 1 of the Constitution that authorizes Congress to provide for the common defense of the country and for the common good, described as the "general Welfare."

George III King of Great Britain during the American Revolution.

government The people and institutions with authority to make and enforce laws and manage disputes about laws.

grandfather clause A law that stated that a citizen could vote only if his grandfather had been allowed to vote. The law made it impossible for African Americans to vote because their grandfathers had not been allowed to vote.

Great Compromise This was a plan accepted at the Philadelphia Convention that called for Congress to have two houses. In the Senate, representation of the states would be equal, with each state having two senators. The House of Representatives would use proportional representation of the states, and therefore, the number of representatives from each state would be determined by its population. Also called the Connecticut Compromise.

habeas corpus *See* writ of habeas corpus.

285

Hazelwood School District v. Kuhlmeier (1988)
A Supreme Court ruling that students' First Amendment rights were not violated when their principal deleted two articles from the school's newspaper. The Court distinguished between speech that occurs in a public forum and speech that occurs "in school-sponsored expressive activities … related to legitimate pedagogical [teaching] concerns."

hearing A meeting in which citizens give their views to public officials.

higher law As used in describing a legal system, this term refers to the superiority of one set of laws over another. For example, the Constitution is a higher law than any federal or state law. In the natural rights philosophy, it means that natural law and divine law are superior to laws made by human beings.

House of Representatives One part or house of Congress. Often referred to simply as "the House." Each state may send a number of representatives based on its population.

human rights Basic rights and freedoms said to belong to all people everywhere.

humanitarian To have compassion and show concern for the pain and suffering of others.

I Have a Dream speech A speech delivered by Martin Luther King Jr. at the Lincoln Memorial in Washington, D.C., on August 28, 1963, during a civil rights march. King spoke against segregation and the unequal treatment of African Americans. Also known as the "March on Washington" speech.

ideal A standard of perfection that serves as a model for imitation.

impeach To bring to trial a public official accused of committing a crime or engaging in misconduct while in office.

impost A tax or customs duty.

In re Gault (1967) A Supreme Court ruling that the due process rights of Gerald Gault, a minor accused of making rude telephone calls, had been violated.

inalienable rights Fundamental rights that every person has that cannot be taken away by government. This phrase was used in the Virginia Declaration of Rights and the Declaration of Independence. Sometimes spelled unalienable rights.

indentured servant A person who voluntarily sold his or her labor for a set period of time in return for the cost of coming to America. The most important source of labor in the colonies in the seventeenth century and for a large part of the eighteenth century.

independence Self-rule; not ruled by another country.

Indian Citizenship Act (1924) An act of Congress that recognized all American Indians as citizens of the United States and granted them the right to vote in federal elections.

individual rights Specific rights that belong to each person, such as those listed in the Bill of Rights, rather than general rights.

international law Rules, usually the result of treaties, that regulate how countries behave toward one another.

International Red Cross and Red Crescent Two international humanitarian organizations that provide assistance to victims of war and natural disasters.

There are 181 Red Cross and Red Crescent societies throughout the world. Red Cross societies operate out of countries with majority Christian populations; Red Crescent societies operate out of countries with majority Muslim populations.

International Telecommunications Union An agency of the United Nations dedicated to improving and coordinating international efforts related to telecommunications. Also known as the ITU.

Jim Crow laws Laws common in the South from 1877 until the 1950s that required African Americans to use separate schools and other public facilities and that prevented them from exercising the right to vote.

judicial branch The branch of government that interprets and applies the laws and settles disputes.

judicial review The power of the courts to declare laws and actions of the local, state, or national government invalid if they contradict the Constitution.

Judiciary Act of 1789 A law passed by the first Congress to establish the federal court system. The act determined the organization and jurisdiction of the courts.

jurisdiction The power or authority to hear cases and make decisions.

justice (1) Fair treatment according to law. (2) A member of the Supreme Court.

law A rule established by government or other source of authority to regulate people's conduct or activities. In the United States, a bill that is passed by the legislature and is signed by the executive, or which is passed over his or her veto, becomes a law.

law of nature In natural rights philosophy, the law of nature would prevail in the absence of man-made law and contains standards of justice that apply to all people.

legal permanent resident A person who is not a citizen, but who legally lives in the United States. Legal permanent residents enjoy most of the rights of citizens. They have the same right to due process of law as citizens, they must pay taxes, and they may serve in the military.

legislative branch The branch of government that makes the laws.

legislative supremacy A system of government in which the legislative branch has ultimate power.

legislature A group of officials in government who have the authority to make and change laws.

Letter from Birmingham City Jail A letter written to fellow clergymen by Martin Luther King Jr. in Birmingham, Alabama, on April 16, 1963, after his arrest for violating a state court order against participating in protests. In his letter, King explains the reasons for his involvement in the civil rights movement and for his belief in nonviolent methods of protest.

liberty, right to The right to be free. Some examples of liberties are the rights to believe what you wish, to read what you want, to speak freely, and to travel wherever you want to go.

life, right to The right to live without fear of being injured or killed by others or by government.

limited government In natural rights philosophy, a system restricted to protecting natural rights that does not interfere with other aspects of life.

limits Restrictions or boundaries on governmental power.

literacy test A test that requires people to prove that they are able to read and write. Until 1964, these tests were used in various states throughout the country to keep minorities from voting.

lobby To represent a group in trying to influence legislatures.

Loyalists Colonists who opposed American independence and remained loyal to Great Britain during the American Revolution.

magistrate A lower-level judicial officer, usually elected in urban areas, who handles traffic violations, minor criminal offenses, and civil suits involving small amounts of money.

Magna Carta This document, also known as the Great Charter, was agreed to by King John of England in 1215 at the demand of his barons. The Magna Carta granted certain civil rights and liberties to English nobles, such as the right to a jury of one's peers and the guarantee against loss of life, liberty, or property, except in accordance with law. In doing so, it also limited the power of the monarch. The document is a landmark in the history of limited constitutional government.

majority rule A principle of democracy that asserts that the greater number of citizens in any political unit should select officials and determine policies.

***Marbury v. Madison* (1803)** A landmark case in which the Supreme Court, for the first time in American history, struck down an act of Congress as unconstitutional, establishing the Court's power of constitutional judicial review.

Massachusetts Body of Liberties (1641) The first American document to describe the rights of individuals.

Massachusetts constitution A state Constitution ratified by Massachusetts voters in 1780. It is the oldest written constitution still in use in the world today.

Mayflower Compact An agreement to form a political body signed in 1620 by all adult males aboard the Mayflower before the ship landed in Plymouth, Massachusetts. The signers agreed to submit to "just and equal Laws" put into effect under the compact.

misdemeanor A minor criminal offense that is less serious than a felony, a major offense. The punishment for a misdemeanor is a fine or imprisonment for up to one year.

monarchy A form of government in which political power is held by a single ruler such as a king or queen.

monitor To keep watch over something.

National Association for the Advancement of Colored People An interracial interest group founded in 1909 to advocate the rights of African Americans, primarily through legal and political action. Also called the NAACP.

national government The organization having central political authority in a nation. The representative unit of political organization.

nation-state The modern nation or country as the typical unit of political organization in the world.

natural law A higher, unchanging set of rules that govern human relations believed by the Founders to have come from "Nature and Nature's God" (from the Declaration of Independence).

natural rights A doctrine that human beings have basic rights, such as those to life, liberty, and property in a state of nature and that people create governments to protect those rights.

naturalized citizens People who are born elsewhere but pass a citizenship test on the Constitution and the history of the United States and swear an oath of loyalty to their new country.

necessary and proper clause Article I, Section 8, Clause 18 of the Constitution that gives Congress the power to make all laws that are "necessary and proper" to carry out the powers specifically delegated to it by the Constitution. It is also known as the elastic clause.

New Jersey Plan The plan presented at the Philadelphia Convention that called for a one-house national legislature with each state having equal representation. The New Jersey Plan followed the framework of the Articles of Confederation and favored a weak national government.

Nineteenth Amendment Added to the Constitution in 1920, it gave women the right to vote.

Ninth Amendment This amendment states, in effect, that the Bill of Rights is only a partial listing of the rights of the people.

nongovernmental organization An organization independent of direct governmental control that exists to perform humanitarian or educational services or to affect public policy. Also called an NGO.

Northwest Ordinance (1787) An important law passed by Congress under the Articles of Confederation. The law prohibited slavery in the Northwest Territory and provided for settling the western lands and the admission and organization of new states.

null and void Of no legal or binding force; invalid.

opinion of the Court A written explanation of the Supreme Court's decision in a particular case and its reasoning behind the decision.

ordinance A municipal statute or regulation.

Organization of American States A regional organization composed of North, South, and Central American nations. It was formed in 1948 to promote economic, political, military, and cultural cooperation among its members.

original jurisdiction The legal authority of a court to be the first to hear a case.

override To pass a bill after it has been vetoed. Congress may override the president's veto by a two-thirds vote of both houses.

Parliament The British legislature, which consists of two houses: the House of Lords, representing the nobility, most of whose appointments are no longer hereditary, and the House of Commons, representing the people.

participation Taking part in or sharing in the activities of a group, organization, or system.

Patriots Those Americans who supported the war for independence against Great Britain.

peer A person of equal standing or rank.

persecute To harass or cause suffering to a person or group because of such things as their beliefs or principles.

petition, right to The legal claim that allows a person to ask his or her government to correct things that he or she thinks are wrong or to do things he or she believes are needed.

Petition of Rights (1628) A statute that limited the English monarch's power to tax people without the consent of Parliament and guaranteed certain rights to English subjects.

Philadelphia Convention The meeting held in Philadelphia from May to September 1787 at which the Constitution was written. Also called the Constitutional Convention.

plantation A large farm usually located in the Southern states.

Plessy v. Ferguson **(1896)** The case in which the Supreme Court ruled that "separate but equal" public facilities for blacks and whites were permissible under the Constitution.

political action Any organized attempt to influence the political process, from lobbying legislators to seeking the election or defeat of particular candidates.

political parties Any organization that seeks to achieve political power by electing members to public office so that their political philosophies can be reflected in public policies.

political philosophy A set of ideas about government and politics.

political rights All rights of a citizen in a free society that are clearly expressed and guaranteed by the Constitution and implied by natural laws.

politics A process by which people with different opinions and interests reach decisions without the use of violence.

poll tax A tax that voters in many states were required to pay in order to exercise their right to vote. These barriers were used until 1964 to prevent African Americans from voting.

popular sovereignty The natural rights concept that ultimate political authority rests with the people.

population The number of people living in an area.

Preamble The introduction to the Constitution. It states that the people establish the government and lists the purposes of the government.

press (1) Newspapers, magazines, television, and other news media. (2) The reporters and people who produce them.

principle A general statement of moral or political belief.

privacy, right to The right or legal claim that allows a person to be free from intrusion by government officials into areas of one's life that are of no concern to government.

private domain Areas of a person's life that are not subject to governmental interference.

procedure The methods or steps taken to accomplish something.

Proclamation of 1763 A British law that banned settlement in certain western lands to reduce tensions between the colonists and Native Americans. The law was unpopular among American frontiersmen and traders.

property, right to The right or legal claim that allows a person to own things and to transfer them to others. Your labor or work is also your property.

proportional representation The electoral system in which the number of representatives for a state is based on the number of people who live in that state. Proportional representation is used to determine the number of each state's representatives serving in the House of Representatives.

Quartering Act (1765) Also known as the Mutiny Act, this British law authorized colonial governors to requisition certain buildings for the housing, or "quartering," of British troops.

Quebec Campaign (1775–76) A military expedition that was an attempt by the Americans to protect the American North and persuade the Canadians to join their rebellion against Britain. American forces invaded Canada and captured Montreal in late 1774. The British forced the Americans to retreat in the spring of 1776.

ratification Formal approval of the Constitution by the ratifying conventions held in each state.

ratify To confirm and approve.

ratifying conventions Meetings held in the states to approve the Constitution.

Red Cross *See* International Red Cross and Red Crescent.

redress of grievances Correction of complaints. The First Amendment protects the right to petition the government to obtain a remedy for a claimed wrong.

regenerate To revive, renew, or give new life to.

register To enroll one's name officially as a requirement for voting.

representative A person elected to act and speak for others.

representative democracy A system of government in which the people elect officials to make and administer laws for their country.

representative government A system for ruling in which elected representatives are chosen by the people to act on their behalf.

republic A nation that has a government in which power is held by the people who elect representatives to manage the government for them for the sake of the common good.

republican government A system for ruling in which power is held by the people who are eligible to elect representatives to run the government for the common good. The term does not refer to a political party.

Republican Party The first political organization formed in opposition to the Federalist Party by the supporters of Thomas Jefferson. It evolved into the Democratic Party in 1828 and has no connection to the present-day Republican Party.

republicanism A form of government in which the supreme political power resides in the people who are qualified to vote; governance is carried out by representatives who are responsible to the people. Republicanism requires the citizenry and public officials to be devoted to the common good.

rights of Englishmen Basic legal claims established over time, that all subjects of the English monarch were understood to have. They included the right not to be kept in prison without a trial and the right to trial by jury.

rule of law The principle that both those who govern and those who are governed must obey the law and are subject to the same laws. This principle is contrasted to the "rule of men," in which those in power make up the rules as they please.

Second Amendment Part of the Bill of Rights added to the Constitution in 1791. The Amendment says "A well-regulated militia, being necessary to the security of a free State, the right of the people to keep and bear Arms, shall not be infringed."

Second Continental Congress The body of delegates representing the colonies that met in 1775 shortly after the start of the Revolutionary War. They organized the Continental Army, called

on the colonies to send troops, selected George Washington to lead the army, and appointed a committee to draft the Declaration of Independence.

segregation The separation or isolation of a race, class, or ethnic group from the rest of society.

self-evident Easy for anyone to see; obvious.

self-incrimination, right against The Fifth Amendment guarantees that one cannot be forced to give testimony that could subject oneself to prosecution.

self-interest One's personal concern.

self-sufficient Able to provide for most of one's own needs.

Senate One of the two houses of Congress. Each state is represented by two members in the Senate.

separate but equal The argument, once upheld by the Supreme Court but later reversed, that different public facilities for blacks and whites were constitutional if the facilities were of equal quality.

separation of church and state A basic principle of American government that no one religion should be favored by government over other religions. Nor should government interfere with one's right to practice or not practice religious beliefs. This metaphor was used in 1802 by President Thomas Jefferson to explain his understanding of the protection of religious freedom afforded by the Constitution.

separation of powers The division of powers among the different branches of government. In the United States, powers are divided among the legislative, executive, and judicial branches.

serf In feudal times, peasants were also known as serfs. They farmed the land and were not free to leave the area in which they worked.

Shays' Rebellion An armed revolt by Massachusetts farmers in 1786–87 who sought relief from debts and foreclosures of mortgages. Led by Daniel Shays, the group prevented judges from hearing mortgage foreclosure cases and attempted to capture an arsenal.

"the shot heard 'round the world" A line in a poem by Ralph Waldo Emerson describing the effect of the outbreak of the American Revolution in April 1775. The American Revolution and its principles became extremely influential around the world. It was the first of many rebellions by countries against their colonial rulers.

sit-in Nonviolent demonstration in which persons protesting certain conditions sit down in an appropriate place and refuse to move until their demands are considered or met.

Sixth Amendment An Amendment that guarantees the rights to a "fair and speedy" trial by jury in criminal cases, to be informed of the nature of the charges in the case, to call witnesses, and to have the assistance of a lawyer.

slave A person whose human rights are denied and who is forced to work for another person without compensation.

slave trade The commercial practice of forcibly taking people from their homes in Africa and selling them into slavery in the new world.

social action Attempts by groups or individuals to change society using a variety of means.

social contract An agreement among the people to set up a government and obey its laws. The theory was developed by the natural rights philosopher John Locke to explain the origin of legitimate government.

Sons of Liberty An organization created in 1765 in every colony to express opposition to the Stamp Act. A popular goal of the organization was to force stamp distributors throughout the colonies to resign.

sovereign A person or group having the highest authority or power in a country or state.

speech, freedom of The right to express your beliefs, ideas, or feelings.

Stamp Act (1765) A British law that required the payment of a tax through the purchase of stamps for documents such as newspapers, magazines, and legal and commercial papers of all kinds.

state of nature The basis of natural rights philosophy; a state of nature is the condition of people living in a situation without man-made government, rules, or laws.

subject Someone who owes allegiance to a government or ruler.

suffrage The right to vote.

Sugar Act of 1764 A British law designed to stop smuggling of goods into and out of the colonies. The law gave the British navy greater power to search colonial ships.

supremacy clause Article VI, Section 2 of the Constitution, which states that the Constitution, laws passed by Congress, and treaties of the United States "shall be the supreme Law of the Land" and binding on the states.

tariff A tax on imported or exported goods or a list or system that describes such taxes.

Tea Act (1773) The British law that granted the East India Company a monopoly on the importation of tea into the colonies, thus eliminating the profits of colonial importers and shopkeepers.

Tenth Amendment This Amendment holds that the "powers not delegated to the United States by the Constitution, nor prohibited by it to the States, are reserved to the States respectively, or the people." The Tenth Amendment embodies the principle of federalism, which reserves for the states the residue of powers not granted to the federal government or withheld from the states, and the principle of popular sovereignty, which reserves other rights to the people.

Thirteenth Amendment This Amendment abolished slavery. It was adopted after the Civil War in 1865.

three-fifths clause Article I, Section 2, Clause 3 of the U.S. Constitution, later eliminated by the Fourteenth Amendment. The clause provided that each slave should be counted as three-fifths of a person in determining the number of representatives a state might send to the House of Representatives. It also determined the amount of direct taxes Congress may levy on a state.

***Tinker v. Des Moines School District* (1969)** A Supreme Court case in which the Court ruled that schools cannot limit a student's right to freedom of expression unless the student's exercise of that right disrupts the educational process.

tract An area of land or water.

treason Betrayal of one's country, especially by giving aid to an enemy in wartime or by plotting to overthrow the government. Treason is carefully defined in the Constitution to ensure that government cannot abuse its powers against dissenters.

Treaty of Paris The agreement signed on September 3, 1783, between Great Britain and the United States that ended the Revolutionary War. With the treaty, Great Britain recognized the independence of the United States. Also called the Peace of Paris.

Twenty-fifth Amendment The Amendment that describes who becomes president if the president dies, is removed from office, resigns, or can no longer perform presidential duties. It also describes how the office of vice president is to be filled if a vacancy occurs.

Twenty-fourth Amendment The Amendment adopted in 1964 that forbids the levying of a poll tax or any other tax on eligible voters in elections for federal officials, including the president, vice president, and members of Congress.

Twenty-second Amendment The Amendment that prohibits any person from being elected president more than twice.

Twenty-sixth Amendment The Amendment adopted in 1971 that says a state cannot deny someone the right to vote if they have reached the age of 18 and are otherwise eligible to vote. Although eighteen-year-olds had already been accorded the vote in national elections by the Voting Rights Act of 1970, the Twenty-sixth Amendment assured them the vote in all elections.

tyranny A government in which a single ruler possesses and abuses absolute power.

unalienable rights *See* inalienable rights.

unconstitutional Not allowed by the Constitution; illegal; contradicts the Constitution.

unitary government A centralized form of government in which states or local governments exercise only those powers delegated to them by the central or national government.

United Nations An international organization created in 1945 to maintain peace through the collective security of its members.

United States Supreme Court The highest court in the United States. See Article III, Section 1 of the Constitution.

Universal Postal Union An agency of the United Nations dedicated to improving postal services throughout the world. Also called the UPU.

vassal In feudal times, a person granted the use of land by a feudal lord, in return for which he rendered military or other service.

veto The right of a branch of government to reject a bill that has been passed in an effort to delay or prevent its enactment. Under the U.S. Constitution, it is the power of the president to refuse to sign a bill passed by Congress, thereby preventing it from becoming a law. The president's veto may be overridden by a two-thirds vote of both the Senate and House of Representatives.

Virginia Declaration of Rights The first state declaration of rights, which served as a model for other state declarations of rights and the Bill of Rights and influenced the Declaration of Independence. It was adopted on June 12, 1776.

Virginia Plan The plan presented at the Philadelphia Convention that provided for a national government composed of three branches. It proposed a Congress of two houses, both of which would be based on proportional representation. The Virginia Plan favored a strong national government.

Voting Rights Act (1965) The act further protected the right to vote for all U.S. citizens. It forced the states to obey the Constitution. It made it clear that the right to vote could not be denied because of a person's color or race.

writ of habeas corpus A court order directing that a prisoner be brought to court before a judge to determine if the detention of the person is lawful. From the Latin term meaning, "you shall/should have the body."

writs of assistance Documents giving a governmental authority the power to search and seize property without restrictions.

Yorktown Surrender The final military act that ended the Revolutionary War. In October 1781, American and French forces blocked a British escape from the Yorktown Peninsula in Virginia. On October 17–19, 1781, the British forces under Lord Cornwallis surrendered at Yorktown to the American army under George Washington.

Index

A

Adams, Abigail 11, **78**

Adams, John
Alien and Sedition Acts and, 169
American Revolution and, **78**
Declaration of Independence and, 64
as Founder, 11
Jefferson and, 169
Philadelphia Convention and, 101
as president, 169–71
as vice president, 158

Adams, Samuel 78, 150

advice and consent (def.) 131

African Americans
American Revolution and, **69**
Brown v. Board of Education and, 216–16, **220**
civil rights movement and, (def.) 207, 217
discrimination against, 214–19, 217, **220**
equal protection clause and, (def.) 214, 215
Federalists, Anti-Federalists and, **156**
Jim Crow laws and, (def.) 215
Plessy v. Ferguson and, 215, **220**
voting rights of, 10, 205, **212**

Alien and Sedition Acts (def.) 170, **172**

amendments *See* Bill of Rights; Civil War Amendments; Constitution, amending;
individual constitutional amendments by number

American Indians
American Revolution and, **69**
in colonies, 10, **12**, 57–58
commerce with, 118, 236
Dawes Act and, 208
Eastern Woodland tribes, 5
Indian Citizenship Act of 1924, 208
Iroquois League, 5
Philadelphia Convention and, 101
Proclamation of 1763 and, 58
three-fifths clause and, 119
voting rights and, 10, 203–204, **212**

American Revolution
Articles of Confederation and, 90
Battle of Saratoga and, 74
Boston Massacre and, 61
British government of colonies and, 11, 16, 29, 55, 68, 81
colonists' resistance, 60–61, **62**
colonists' rights and, 11, 29, 55–56, **59**–60
Continental Congress and, 61, 64, **69**, 73, **78**
debt resulting from, 167
Declaration of Independence and, 63–64, 67, **70**
diplomacy and, 76
government (state) after, 11, 29, 79, 81
ideals and ideas of, 16, 29
influence on other nations of, 72, 76

LEGEND | Page numbers in bold indicate activities or exercises.

declarations of rights in, 84

influence of Locke on, 14

Maryland, **86**

Rhode Island, 204

See also Massachusetts, constitution of; Virginia, Declaration of Rights

Continental Congress

First, (def.) 61

Second, (def.) 61, **69**, 73, **78**, 88

See also Articles of Confederation

Cornwallis, Lord (Charles) 77

Crèvecoeur, Jean de 8–9

D

Daughters of Liberty (def.) 60, 61–**62**

See also Sons of Liberty

Dawes Act 208

Declaration of Independence 61, 63–65, **70**, 73, 80

Constitution and, 148

Hancock, John and, 80

influence of Locke on, 14, 16–18, 84

influence on other countries of, 231, 237–**40**

declarations of rights 84–85

See also Vermont bill of rights; Virginia, Declaration of Rights; Women's Declaration of Rights

Declaratory Act (1776) (def.) 59

Delaware 56, 102, **107**

democracy

constitutional, 187, 227, **248**

direct, (def.) 25, **30**

representative, (def.) 25, **30**, 189, 203

See also republican government

diplomacy 71, (def.) 76, **78**, 234

due process of law 90, 180, 221, (def.) 222, 223, 227

due process clause, 221, **228**

duties *See* taxes (taxation)

E

economic rights 243, (def.) 244, **248**

Eighth Amendment 226

Eisenhower, Dwight 217

election of 1800 170–71, **172**

Electoral College (def.) 133, **136**, 158, 170–71

England *See* Great Britain

English Bill of Rights (def.) 53, **54**

enumerated powers of Congress (def.) 123, 124–25, **127–28**, 165, 167

See also general powers of Congress

equal protection clause 186, 213, (def.) 214, 215, 229, 219–**20**.

See also Fourteenth Amendment

equal representation (def.) 106, **107**, 109, **110**–11

establishment clause 196, (def.) 197, 200, **201–202**

executive branch 42, **86**

Articles of Confederation and, 89

checks and balances and, 39, 42, 126, **136**

in colonial governments, 57

Constitution and, 180–81

equal protection and, 212, 216–17, **220**

judicial review and, 175, 177

in Massachusetts, 82

New Jersey Plan and, 109, **112**

organization of, 158–59, **162**

powers (and limits) of, 41, 57, 80, 89, 122–**27**, **128**, 130–31, **134**, 151

selection of head of, 57, 82, 132, **162**

in state governments, 81–**83**, **86**

Virginia Plan and, 108

See also president

ex post facto law (def.) 125, **128**, 143, 152

F

factions (def.) 24, 81, 91, 164

federal courts 157, (def.) 159–60

See also judicial branch; Supreme Court (U.S.)

federalism 108, 139–40, (def.) 141, **146**, 242

delegation of powers under, 141–42, **146**

supremacy clause and, 145

federal system *See* federalism

Federalist Party (def.) 165, 169–**72**

Federalist, The (def.) 149, **156**

Federalists (def.) 149

Bill of Rights and, 160–61

Constitution and, 150–**56**, 160–61

Federalist Party, 165, 171

See also Anti-Federalists

feudalism (def.) 48, 49, **54**

Fifteenth Amendment 205

Fifth Amendment (def.) 222, **226**

First Amendment (def.) 188,–89, **193**, 196–98, 202

Fortas, Abe 191

Founders (def.) 11, **12**

abuse of power and, **40**–41

Articles of Confederation and, 87–89

beliefs and ideas of, 14, 16–18, 25, 28–29, 46, 65, 80–81, 237

Constitution and, 158

Declaration of Independence and, 65, 72

freedom of expression and, 188

historical influences on, 21–25, **30**, 237

state governments and, 80–81, 82

Fourteenth Amendment (def.) 205, 213–16, **220**, 222–23, **225**

Fourth Amendment (def.) 181

Framers (def.) 98

Constitution and, 138, 140–41, 145–50, **156**, **181**

executive branch and, 130–33, **136**, 158

federal system and, 140–41, **146**

intention of, 182

judicial branch and, 135–**36**

judicial review and, (def.) 174, 175

legislative branch and, 121–22

North–South conflict and, 114–**17**, 119–**20**

Philadelphia Convention and, 96, 98, 101, **104**, 106, 114

political parties and, 164, 171, **172**

France 4, 7, 48, 58, 76, **78**, 101, 140, 168–69, 237

Franklin, Benjamin

abuse of power and, **40**

American Revolution and, 68–69, **78**

Declaration of Independence and, 64

diplomatic mission to France, 76, **78**

as Founder, 11

Philadelphia Convention and, 99, 259

free exercise clause (def.) 196, 198, **202**

See also establishment clause

freedom of assembly 152, 161, (def.) 188, **193**, 244

See also First Amendment

freedom of belief or conscience 11, 198, **202**, 244

See also First Amendment; freedom of religion

freedom of expression (def.) 188–90, **191–94**, 243–44

See also First Amendment

freedom of the press 84–**85**, 161, 169–70, 188–89, 190

See also First Amendment

freedom of religion 151, 161, 195–200, **201–202**, 219, 243

See also establishment clause; First Amendment

fugitive slave clause 113, (def.) 119

G

Gault, Gerald *See* In re Gault

general powers of Congress 124–25, **127–28**, 151

See also enumerated powers of Congress

general welfare clause 123, (def.) 124, **151**

LEGEND | Page numbers in bold indicate activities or exercises.

jurisdiction (def.) 135, 214

K

King, Martin Luther, Jr. 218–20, 246

Knox, Henry 78, 158

L

Lee, Richard Henry 88, 150

legal permanent resident (def.) 242, **248**

legislative branch (def.) 42, 43, 57, 81, **83**
   in colonial governments, **57**, 59, 80–81, 123
   Constitution and, 42–43, 80, 82, 122–**27**, **128**, 236, 265–68
   due process and, 222, **228**
   in Great Britain, 48, 52–53
   judicial review and, 174–75
   New Jersey Plan and, 109–**10**
   in state governments, 80–**83**, **86**, 122–23
   Virginia Plan and, 108, **110**
   See also Congress

legislative supremacy (def.) 81, 82

Lexington and Concord 61, 72

limits 18, (def.) 32, 33–**34**, **38**, 40–41
   Anti-Federalists v. Federalists and, 151–**54**
   Articles of Confederation and, 89–91

   on British government, 48, 50–**51**, 52–53, 58–**59**, **68**
   colonists and, 58–**59**, 81, 204
   on Congress, 122–25, **128**, 177
   due process and, 222
   on executive branch (and president), 42, 130–31, **134**, **136**
   on federal and state governments, 142–**44**, 145
   freedom of belief and, 198, **202**, 244
   on freedom of expression, 188–**92**, **192–93**, **194**, 243–44
   on freedom of religion, 196–**99**, 200–**201**, **202**, 219
   on government, 32–**34**, **38**, 41–**44**, 151–52
   higher law and, 33–**34**, 35–**37**, **38**
   interpretation of Constitution and, 165–66, 168, 181–**84**
   judicial review and, 177
   on opportunity, 10
   on responsibility of citizens, 28, 244–46
   on rights, 28, 244
   rule of law and, (def.) 50, 57
   social contract and, 18–**19**
   on voting rights, 82, 204–209, **212**
   See also constitutional government; Congress, limits on powers of

literacy test (def.) 206

Livingston, Robert 64

Locke, John 14–**15**, 16–**20**, 84, 237
   See also natural rights; social contract

LEGEND | Page numbers in bold indicate activities or exercises.

LEGEND | Page numbers in bold indicate activities or exercises.

Q

Quartering Act (1765) 59

Quebec Campaign (def.) 74

R

Randolph, Edmund Jennings 150, 159

ratify (def.) 148

ratifying convention 149, **155**

redress of grievances 86, (def.) 188

register (def.) 209

representative (def.) 22, (def.) 23, 24–**26**, **30**, **107**, **110**, **112**

representative government 25, **30**, 47, 52, 57, 59, **176**, 189, **254**

   See also republican government

republic (def.) 22, 24, **152**

republican government 21, (def.) 22–23, **30**
   advantages of, 23, **30**
   civic virtue and, 28–29
   Constitution and, 103, 150, **152**, **154**, 182
   disadvantages of, 24, **30**
   Federalists and Anti-Federalists and, **152**
   Founders and, 23, 25, 237
   ideals and values of, 28–**30**

Washington, George and, 98

Virginia Declaration of Rights and, 84

See also democracy, representative; Roman Republic

Republican Party (def.) 165, 168–**72**

responsibility (responsibilities) 50, **151**
   civic, 158, (def.) 244, 251, 253
   civil disobedience and, 245–**46**
   of Congress, 145–**46**, 180
   and constitutional government, 34
   of executive branch, 130, 158
   under feudal system, 48–49
   of government, 32–33, 141, 145–**46**, **151**, 230
   of government and due process, 222–23, 227
   of judges, 57
   of nations, 233–34
   to participate, 251, 253
   personal, (def.) 244, 250
   of representatives, 23
   of State Department, **240**
   See also citizens, rights and responsibilities of

Revere, Paul 72, **78**

Revolutionary War *See* American Revolution

Rhode Island 101, 204

right of assembly **152**, 161, (def.) 188, **193**, 244

LEGEND | Page numbers in bold indicate activities or exercises.

religious instruction and, 200–**201**

shared power and, 142

Virginia Plan and, 108

voting rights and, 204–207

without representation, 48, 52–53, 57, 59, 68, 85–**86**

See also tariffs

Tea Act (1773)

Tenth Amendment (def.) 161–**62**,

Thirteenth Amendment (def.) 205, 214, **220**

Thoreau, Henry David 246

three-fifths clause (def.) 119

Tinker v. Des Moines School District 191, **193**

trade

American colonies and, 58–59, 61, **62**, 68

Articles of Confederation and, 88, 91–92, 109, 122, 151

ban on British, 61

Declaration of Independence and, 68

Federalists and, 151

government and, 58–59, 61, **62**, 68, 88, 91–92, 109, 115, 119, 122, 125, 142–43, 151, 168–69, 234

Hamilton and, 167–68

international, 232–33

New Jersey Plan and, 109

North–South conflict and, 114–15, 119

Shays' Rebellion and, 92

slave, 119, 125

treaty with British and, 168–69

See also tariffs

treason (def.) 77, 135

treaty (def.) 77, 90, 91, **144**, 168–69, 174, 234–35

during war between France and Great Britain, 168–69

to create United Nations, 234

Treaty of Paris (def.) 77, 90–91

Twenty-fifth Amendment 136

Twenty-fourth Amendment (def.) 207

Twenty-second Amendment (def.) 132

Twenty-sixth Amendment (def.) 209

Two Treatises of Government 14

U

unalienable rights *See* inalienable, (unalienable) rights

unitary government (def.) 140, 145, **146**

United Nations (def.) 234, 234–35, 240

V

Valley Forge 75

Vermont bill of rights 85

veto (def.) 82, 123, 126, 130, 131, 132

Virginia
    American Revolution and, 77, 174
    colonies' first elected legislature in, 57
    debts to the British and, 174
    Declaration of Rights, 84, **86**
    home of Jefferson, Madison, and
        Washington, 64, 98
    in Mayflower Compact, 20
    population of colonial, **107**

Virginia Plan (def.) 108, 108–**110**, **112**

von Steuben, Friedrich 75, **78**

voting rights *See* suffrage

Voting Rights Act (1965) (def.) 207, 209

W

Warren, Mercy Otis 11, **78**, 150

Washington, George
    American Revolution and, 61, 74–75, 78
    civic virtue and, **30**, 98, 132, 158
    as first president, 132, 158–59, 164–65,
        168–69
    as Founder, 11
    Philadelphia Convention and, 98–99, 101,
        104, 132

Washington, Martha 75, **78**

William the Conqueror 48, **54**

women
    in colonies, 6, 10–11, **12**, 61
    discrimination against, 10–11, 101, 203,
        204, 207, 219
    equal protection and, 219
    Philadelphia Convention and, 98, 101
    suffrage for, 10, 203, 204, 207, **212**
    See also Daughters of Liberty

Women's Declaration of Rights 207

writ of habeas corpus (def.) 125, **128**, 143,
    152, 268

writs of assistance (def.) 58, **60**

Y

Yorktown Surrender 77

LEGEND | Page numbers in bold indicate activities or exercises.

PHOTO CREDITS

Many of the images listed below were licensed using Creative Commons licenses. These are listed with credits such as the following: CC BY-SA 3.0. Detailed information about this and other Creative Commons licenses can be found at www.creativecommons.org.

Cover

The Continentals by Frank Blackwell Mayer, Prints & Photographs Division, Library of Congress, PGA-Mayer-Continentals (C size) [P&P].

Front Matter

P. vi, Warren Burger, Supreme Court Historical Society; x, Rotunda for the Charters of Freedom, National Archives and Records Administration.

UNIT 1

P. 1, *Writing the Declaration of Independence, 1776*, by Jean Leon Gerome Ferris, Virginia Historical Society/Prints & Photographs Division, Library of Congress, cph.3g09904/Wikimedia Commons.

Lesson 1

P. 3, *Clearing Land* by Allyn Cox, 1973–74, Architect of the Capitol/Flickr; 4, Detail from *The Wiley Family* by William Williams, 1771, Wikimedia Commons; 5, Red Jacket, Seneca war chief, Wikimedia Commons; 6, *The Residence of David Twining* by Edward Hicks, 1845–48, Abby Aldrich Rockefeller Folk Art Collection/Wikimedia Commons; 7, Detail from *The Rebels of '76: Or the First Announcement of the Great Declaration*, Prints & Photographs Division, Library of Congress, LC-DIG-pga-03091; 8–10, Richard Stein, Center for Civic Education; 11, *John Adams* by John Trumbull, c. 1792–93, White House/Wikimedia Commons.

Lesson 2

P. 13, Detail from *The Florida Case before the Electoral Commission* by Cornelia Adèle Strong, U.S. Senate Collection; 14, *J. Locke* by H. Garnier, Prints and Photographs Division, Library of Congress, LC-USZ62-59655; 15, Richard Stein, Center for Civic Education; 16, Title page from *Two Treatises of Government* by John Locke, Library of Congress; 17, Statue of John Locke, 1867–70, Andreas Praefcke/Wikimedia Commons/CC BY 3.0; 18–19, Richard Stein, Center for Civic Education.

Lesson 3

P. 21, *Cicero Denounces Catiline* by Cesare Maccari, 1889, Wikimedia Commons; 22, *Appius Claudius the Blind* by Cesare Maccari, 1882–88, Wikimedia Commons; 23, President Barack Obama speaks to a joint session of Congress regarding health care reform, September 9, 2009, Lawrence Jackson/White House/Wikimedia Commons; 24, *James Madison* by Gilbert Stuart, c. 1821, National Gallery of Art/Wikimedia Commons; 25–27, Richard Stein, Center for Civic Education; 28, Campaign poster for William McKinley, Prints & Photographs Division, Library of Congress, LC-USZC4-1329; 29, Supreme Court following façade restoration, Architect of the Capitol, USCapitol/Flickr.

Lesson 4

P. 31, Rotunda for the Charters of Freedom, National Archives and Records Administration; 32, First page of the U.S. Constitution, National Archives and Records Administration; 33 (top), Richard Stein, Center for Civic Education; 33 (bottom), *Temple of Liberty*, detail from 1876 campaign broadside, Photographs Division, Library of Congress, LC-USZ62-91368; 34, *Guardian of Law* by James Earle Fraser, U.S. Supreme Court, Daderot/Wikimedia Commons; 35–37, Richard Stein, Center for Civic Education.

Lesson 5

P. 39, *Henry VIII* by Hans Holbein, 1540, Galleria Nazionale d'Arte Antica/Wikimedia Commons; 40, Richard Stein, Center for Civic Education; 40, *Alexander Hamilton* by John Trumbull, 1806, Washington University Law School/Wikimedia Commons; 40, *Benjamin Franklin* by Joseph-Siffrein Duplessis, c. 1785, National Portrait Gallery, Washington/Wikimedia Commons; 40, *George Mason* by Albert Rosenthal, 1888, University of Chicago Library/American Memory, Library of Congress; 41, Detail from *Vercingetorix Throws Down His Arms at the Feet of Julius Caesar* by Lionel Royer, 1899, Museum Crozatier/Wikimedia Commons; 42, Richard Stein, Center for Civic Education; 43, The 114th Congress, July 22, 2015, Office of House Photography/Speaker John Boehner/Flickr/Wikimedia Commons.

UNIT 2

P. 45, *Evacuation of New York by the British, November 25, 1783*, Prints & Photographs Division, Library of Congress, LC-USZC4-1306.

Lesson 6

P. 47, *House of Lords* by Thomas Rowlandson and Augustus Charles Pugin, after John Bluck, Joseph Constantine Stadler, Thomas Sutherland, J. Hill, and Harraden, from *Microcosm of London*, 1809, Wikimedia Commons; 48, *The Famous Zenger Trial* by Alfred Fredricks, from *Wall Street in History* by Martha J. Lamb, 1883, New York Public Library/Archive.org; 49–50, Richard Stein, Center for Civic Education; 50, *King John Signs the Magna Carta* by Joseph Martin Kronheim, from *Pictures of English History*, 1868, Wikimedia Commons; 51–52, Richard Stein, Center for Civic Education; 53, *Portrait of King Charles I in His Robes of State* after Anthony van Dyck, 1636, Wikimedia Commons.

Lesson 7

P. 55, *The Bloody Massacre Perpetrated in King Street Boston on March 5th 1770 by a Party of the 29th Regt.* by Paul Revere, Wikimedia Commons/Prints & Photographs Division, Library of Congress, LC-DIG-ppmsca-01657; 56, Charter deed from Charles II to James, the Duke of York, for Delaware, March 22, 1682, Delaware Public Archives; 56, *"Give Me Liberty, or Give Me Death!"* by Nathaniel Currier and James Merritt Ives, c. 1876, Prints & Photographs Division, Library of Congress, LC-USZC2-2452/Wikimedia Commons; 57–59, Richard Stein, Center for Civic Education; 60, *The Bostonian's Paying the Excise-man, or Tarring & Feathering*, attributed to Philip Dawe, 1774, John Carter Brown Library, Brown University, Providence, Rhode Island/Wikimedia Commons; 61, Detail from *The First Continental Congress, 1774*, by Allyn Cox, 1973–74, Architect of the Capitol/Flickr.

Lesson 8

P. 63, *The Rebels of '76*, c. 1860, Prints & Photographs Division, Library of Congress, LC-DIG-pga-03091; 64, *Writing the Declaration of Independence, 1776*, by J.L.G. Ferris, c. 1932, Prints and Photographs, Library of Congress, LC-USZC4-9904; 65, First page of the Declaration of Independence, National Archives and Records Administration; 66, *The Declaration of Independence, 1776*, by Allyn Cox, 1973–74, Architect of the Capitol/Flickr; 67, Richard Stein, Center for Civic Education; 68, *Portrait of King George III* by Thomas Gainsborough, 1781, Royal Collection, Buckingham Palace, London/Wikimedia Commons; 69, *The Alternative of Williams-Burg* by Philip Dawe, 1775, Prints & Photographs Division, Library of Congress, LC-USZC4-5280.

Lesson 9

P. 71, *"Evacuation Day" and Washington's Triumphal Entry in New York City, Nov. 25th, 1783*, by Edmund P. Restein and Ludwig Restein, Prints & Photographs Division, Library of Congress, LC-DIG-pga-02468; 72, *The Shot Heard 'Round the World* by Domenick D'Andrea, The National Guard/Flickr; 73, Richard Stein, Center for Civic Education; 74, *Washington Crossing the Delaware by Emanuel Leutze*, 1851, Metropolitan Museum of Art, www.metmuseum.org/Wikimedia Commons; 75 (left), *Surrender of General Burgoyne* by John Trumbull, 1821, Architect of the Capitol/Wikimedia Commons; 75 (right), *Martha Dandridge Custis Washington (Mrs. George Washington)* by Eliphalet Frazer Andrews, 1878, White House/Wikimedia Commons; 76, *Benjamin Franklin's Reception at the Court of France, 1778*, by Anton Hohenstein, c. 1860, Prints & Photographs Division, Library of Congress, pga.01591/Wikimedia Commons; 77 (left), Richard Stein, Center for Civic Education; 77 (right), *Surrender of Lord Cornwallis* by John Trumbull, 1820, Architect of the Capitol/Flickr/Wikimedia Commons.

Lesson 10

P. 79, Old State House, Hartford, Connecticut, Daderot/Wikimedia Commons; 80, *Portrait of John Hancock* by John Singleton Copley, 1765, Museum of Fine Arts, Boston/Wikimedia Commons; 81, *The Concord Stage* by E. Percy Moran, Prints and Photographs Division, Library of Congress, LC-USZC4-623; 82–83, Richard Stein, Center for Civic Education; 84 (foreground), *George Mason* by Albert Rosenthal, 1888, Library of Congress/Wikimedia Commons; (background), Virginia Declaration of Rights by George Mason and Thomas Ludwell Lee, 1776, George Mason Papers, Manuscript Division, Library of Congress (33.00.00), Digital ID# us0033tt_1; 85, Detail from *The First Federal Congress, 1789*, by Allyn Cox, 1973–74, Architect of the Capitol/Flickr.

Lesson 11

P. 87, Detail from the Articles of Confederation, National Archives and Records Administration; 88, First page of the Articles of Confederation, National Archives and Records Administration; 89 (left), Map of the colonies, Center for Civic Education; 89 (right), Richard Stein, Center for Civic Education; 90, *Tom Edmundson as Schoolmaster*, from *Southern Life in Southern Literature*, 1917, Archive.org/Mpaa/Wikimedia Commons; 91–93, Richard Stein, Center for Civic Education.

UNIT 3

P. 95, *Signing of the Constitution* by Howard Chandler Christy, 1940, Architect of the Capitol/Flickr.

Lesson 12

P. 97, *Washington at Constitutional Convention of 1787, Signing of U.S. Constitution* by Junius Brutus Stearns, 1856, Virginia Museum of Fine Arts/Wikimedia Commons; 98, *James Madison* by John Vanderlyn, 1816, White House Historical Association (White House Collection); 99, *Signing of the Constitution* by Howard Chandler Christy, 1940, Architect of the Capitol/Flickr; 100–102, Richard Stein, Center for Civic Education; 103, First page of the Constitution, National Archives and Records Administration.

Lesson 13

P. 105, U.S. President Barack Obama Delivers the 2011 State of the Union Address to a joint session of Congress, Lawrence Jackson, Executive Office of the President of the United States/Wikimedia Commons; 106, Guy Moore using a tractor to bail hay in a field,

June 18, 2014, at Larriland Farm, Md, SrA Dennis Sloan, USAF, U.S. Department of Defense Current Photos/Flickr; 107, *Population of American Colonies, 1790*, by Mapping Specialists/Center for Civic Education; 108–109, Richard Stein, Center for Civic Education; 110 (top), U.S. Capitol, Master Sgt. Ken Hammond, Department of Defense; 110 (bottom), *The Connecticut Compromise* by Bradley Stevens, 2006, U.S. Senate, Cat. no. 35.00003.000; 111, Senate Chamber: Photo of the 111th U.S. Senate, United States Senate/Architect of the Capitol, USCapitol/Flickr.

Lesson 14

P. 113, *A Cotton Plantation on the Mississippi* by Nathaniel Currier and James Merritt Ives, 1884, Prints & Photographs Division, Library of Congress, LC-DIG-pga-00675; 114, *Sharecroppers*, EverGreene Painting Studios, 1993–94; 115, Richard Stein, Center for Civic Education; 116, *A Slave-coffle Passing the Capitol* (colorized), c. 1876–81, Prints and Photographs Division, Library of Congress, LC-USZ62-2574/Center for Civic Education; 117–18, Richard Stein, Center for Civic Education.

Lesson 15

P. 121, United States Capitol in daylight, Kevin McCoy, Wikimedia Commons/CC BY-SA 2.0; 122–23, Richard Stein, Center for Civic Education; 124, President Woodrow Wilson asking Congress to declare war on Germany, causing the United States to enter World War I, April 2, 1917, Prints & Photographs Division, Library of Congress, LC-USZC4-10297/Wikimedia Commons; 125, Launch of the Space Shuttle Discovery, July 26, 2005, National Aeronautics and Space Administration/Wikimedia Commons; 126 (top), Richard Stein, Center for Civic Education; 126 (bottom), U.S. Supreme Court: View from West Terrace, Architect of the Capitol, USCapitol/Flickr; 127, Richard Stein, Center for Civic Education.

Lesson 16

P. 129, President George W. Bush is sworn in for his second term as the 43rd President of the United States by U.S. Supreme Court Chief Justice William Rehnquist in Washington, D.C., on January 20, 2005, U.S. Air Force photo by Tech. Sgt. Kevin J. Gruenwald, Department of Defense/Wikimedia Commons; 130, Meeting with President Eisenhower, President Kennedy, and military aides, Camp David, MD, April 22, 1961, National Archives and Records Administration, ARC Identifier 194198/Wikimedia Commons; 131, President Barack Obama signs the New START (treaty) in the Oval Office, Feb. 2, 2011, Chuck Kennedy, White House/Wikimedia Commons; 132, Richard Stein, Center for Civic Education; 133, *Washington's Inauguration, 1789*, by Allyn Cox, Architect of the Capitol, USCapitol/Flickr; 134, Richard Stein, Center for Civic Education; 135, The U.S. Supreme Court, October 8, 2010, Steve Petteway, Collection of the Supreme Court of the United States/The Oyez Project/Wikimedia Commons.

UNIT 4

P. 136, The western side of the United States Capitol, Noclip/Wikimedia Commons.

Lesson 17

P. 139, *Montana State Capitol Building*, by Geo. R. Mann, 1896, Prints & Photographs Division, Library of Congress, LC-DIG-pga-03345/Wikimedia Commons; 140, The Swiss Bundeshaus (Parliament) in Bern, Wikimedia Commons/Harshil Shah/Flickr/CC BY-ND 2.0; 141, Richard Stein, Center for Civic Education; 142, President Franklin D. Roosevelt signing the declaration of war against Japan, in the wake of the attack on Pearl Harbor, December 8, 1941, Abbie Rowe/National Archives and Records Administration/Wikimedia

Commons; 143, Two container ships pass in San Francisco Bay, National Oceanic and Atmospheric Administration/Wikimedia Commons; 144, Robert Kauffman, FEMA; 145 (left), Richard Stein, Center for Civic Education; 145 (right), Teacher teaching students in an early childhood setting [image edited to remove date], woodleywonderworks/Flickr/CC BY 2.0/Wikimedia Commons.

Lesson 18

P. 147, *Vue de Salem* by Balthasar Friedrich Leizelt, c. 1770s, Prints & Photographs Division, Library of Congress/cph.3g04292/Wikimedia Commons; 148, *The Albany Congress, 1754*, by Allyn Cox, Architect of the Capitol, USCapitol/Flickr; 149, Title page of first edition of *The Federalist*, 1788, Rare Books and Special Collections Division, Library of Congress; 150, Bill of Rights, Library of Congress, American Memory, Printed Ephemera Collection, Portfolio 244, Folder 44; 151 and 153–55, Richard Stein, Center for Civic Education.

Lesson 19

P. 157, *Washington's Inauguration at Philadelphia* by J.L.G. Ferris, Prints & Photographs Division, Library of Congress, LC-USZC4-12011; 158, *Portrait of George Washington* by Gilbert Stuart, 1795, Metropolitan Museum of Art/Wikimedia Commons; 159, *A View of the Federal Hall of the City of New York, As Appeared in the Year 1797; with the Adjacent Buildings Thereto* by George Holland, Prints & Photographs Division, Library of Congress, LC-USZCN4-180; 160, Richard Stein, Center for Civic Education; 161, *The First Federal Congress, 1789*, by Allyn Cox, 1973–74, Architect of the Capitol, USCapitol/Flickr.

Lesson 20

P. 163, Richard Stein, Center for Civic Education; 164, Congressional Pugilists, 1798, Prints and Photographs Division, Library of Congress, LC-DIG-ppmsca-31832; 165, *Thomas Jefferson* by Charles Willson Peale, c. 1790, U.S. Diplomacy Center/Wikimedia Commons; 166, *Alexander Hamilton* by John Trumbull, 1792, Metropolitan Museum of Art/Wikimedia Commons; 167, First Bank of the United States, Prints and Photographs Division, Library of Congress, HABS, PA, 51-PHILA, 235-6; 168, *Portrait of John Jay* by Gilbert Stuart, 1794, National Gallery of Art/Wikimedia Commons; 169, Richard Stein, Center for Civic Education; 170, Tally of electoral votes for the 1800 presidential election, February 11, 1801, Records of the United States Senate, National Archives; 171, Paul Ryan with Mitt Romney in Norfolk, Virginia, August 11, 2012, James Currie/Flickr/Wikimedia Commons/CC BY-SA 2.0).

Lesson 21

P. 173, U.S. Supreme Court building, Washington, D.C., Prints & Photographs Division, Library of Congress, LC-DIG-highsm-14781; 174, Minnesota Governor Mark Dayton (right) signing a law with Secretary of State Mark Ritchie (left), July 20, 2011, Mark Dayton/Flickr/CC BY 2.0/Wikimedia Commons; 175–76, Richard Stein, Center for Civic Education; 177, *John Marshall* by Henry Inman, 1832, Library of Virginia, Virginia Memory/Wikimedia Commons.

Lesson 22

P. 179, West façade of the Supreme Court building, 1993, Franz Jantzen, Supreme Court of the United States; 180, Chief Justice John G. Roberts, Jr. and Justice Elena Kagan in the justices' conference room prior to Justice Kagan's investiture ceremony, October 1, 2010, Steve Petteway, Collection of the Supreme Court of the United States/Wikimedia Commons; 181, Richard Stein, Center for Civic Education, 182 (left), A U.S. Air Force B-2 Spirit "Stealth" bomber, U.S. Air Force/Wikimedia Commons; 182 (right), Student walking through the streets of Berkeley, Andrew Ratto/Flickr/CC BY 2.0/Wikimedia Commons; 183, *Stand Your Ground* by Don Troiani, The National Guard/Flickr.

UNIT 5

P. 185, *Embarkation of the Pilgrims* by Robert W. Weir, 1843, Architect of the Capitol/Flickr/Wikimedia Commons.

Lesson 23

P. 187, *The Death of Socrates* by Jacques-Louis David, 1787, Metropolitan Museum of Art, New York/Wikimedia Commons; 188, Friday, Day 14 of Occupy Wall Street, September 30, 2011, David Shankbone, Wikimedia Commons/CC BY 3.0; 189, Detail from *Save Freedom of Speech* by Norman Rockwell, c. 1941–45, National Archives and Records Administration/ARC Identifier: 513711; 190, Richard Stein, Center for Civic Education; 191, Mary Beth Tinker, Andrew Imanaka, Flickr/CC BY 2.0; 192–93, Richard Stein, Center for Civic Education.

Lesson 24

P. 195, Detail from *The Creation of Adam* by Michelangelo Buonarroti, c. 1511, Wikimedia Commons; 196, *Desembarco de los Puritanos en America [Landing of the Puritans in America]* by Antonio Gisbert Perez, 1883, Palacio del Senado de Espana, Madrid/Wikimedia Commons; 197, Lt. Jose Bautista Rojas offers the sacraments during a Catholic Mass aboard the Nimitz-class aircraft carrier *USS John C. Stennis*, U.S. Navy/Wikimedia Commons; 198, Handling serpents at the Pentecostal Church of God, Lejunior, Harlan County, Kentucky, September 15, 1946, Russell Lee, National Archives and Records Administration, ARC Identifier: 541335/Wikimedia Commons; 200, San Francisco, California, Flag of allegiance pledge at Raphael Weill Public School, Dorothea Lange/War Relocation Authority/Department of the Interior/National Archives and Records Administration/ARC Identifier: 536053; 201, Richard Stein, Center for Civic Education.

Lesson 25

P. 203, Voting rights march, Wikimedia Commons; 204, Detail from *Giddap!* by Gordon Grant, from *Puck*, v. 75, no. 1932, March 14, 1914, Prints & Photographs Division, Library of Congress, LC-USZC2-1184; 205 (top) Detail from *Lincoln's Second Inaugural, 1865*, by Allyn Cox, 1973–74, Architect of the Capitol, USCapitol/Flickr; 205 (bottom) , Richard Stein, Center for Civic Education; 206, *Democracy's Turnstile*, published originally in *PM*, October 12, 1942, courtesy of Mandeville Special Collections Library, University of California, San Diego, copyright holder unknown; 207, Elizabeth Cady Stanton (left) and Susan B. Anthony (right), Prints & Photographs Division, Library of Congress, LC-USZ61-791; 208, President Calvin Coolidge with Native Americans, February 18, 1925, Prints & Photographs Division, Library of Congress/ LC-USZ62-111409; 209, Da Nang, Vietnam—A young Marine private waits on the beach during the Marine landing, August 3, 1965, National Archives and Records Administration, Records of the U.S. Marine Corps, 127-N-A185146; 210, A large group of African American children gather around a sign encouraging people to register to vote, c. 1960s, The Kheel Center for Labor-Management Documentation and Archives/Cornell University/Flickr/CC BY 2.0/ Wikimedia Commons; 211, Absentee Voting Night, October 3, 2012, U.S. Embassy photo by Vince Alongi, Flickr.

Lesson 26

P. 213, Civil Rights Movement Co-Founder Dr. Ralph David Abernathy and his wife Mrs. Juanita Abernathy follow with Dr. and Mrs. Martin Luther King as the Abernathy children march on the front line, leading the SELMA TO MONTGOMERY MARCH in 1965, Wikimedia Commons; 214, *Scene in the House on the*

317

Passage of the Proposition to Amend the Constitution, January 31, 1865, Harper's Weekly/Prints and Photographs Division, Library of Congress/LC-USZ62-12759; 215, Negro Expulsion from Railway Car, Philadelphia, 1856, Prints & Photographs Division, Library of Congress, LC-USZ62-45698; 216, Thurgood Marshall, June 13, 1967, National Archives and Records Administration, ARC Identifier: 2803441/Wikimedia Commons; 217, Civil rights march on Washington, D.C., Warren K. Leffler, August 28, 1963, Prints & Photographs Division, Library of Congress, LC-DIG-ppmsca-03130; 218, Rosa Parks, Judith Sedwick, Black Women Oral History Project, Schlesinger Library on the History of Women in America, Flickr; 219, President Lyndon B. Johnson signs the 1964 Civil Rights Act as Martin Luther King, Jr., and others, look on, July 2, 1964, Cecil Stoughton, White House Press Office/Lyndon Baines Johnson Library and Museum/Wikimedia Commons.

Lesson 27
P. 221, Police officer taking fingerprints, United States Immigration and Customs Enforcement/Wikimedia Commons; 222–25, Richard Stein, Center for Civic Education; 226, FEMA Administrator Craig Fugate testifies about addressing the needs of children in disasters before the Senate Committee on Homeland Security and Government Affairs, Ad Hoc Subcommittee on Disaster Recovery, FEMA/Wikimedia Commons.

UNIT 6
P. 229, Visions of America, LLC/EyeWire Images.

Lesson 28
P. 231, United States President Barack Obama chairs a United Nations Security Council meeting at U.N. Headquarters in New York, N.Y., Sept. 24, 2009, Peter Souza, White House/Wikimedia Commons; 232, Map of Africa with nation-states, Center for Civic Education; 233 (top), President Bush and Russian President Boris Yeltsin sign the Start II Treaty at a Ceremony in Vladimir Hall, The Kremlin in Moscow, Russia, January 3, 1993, Susan Biddle/National Archives and Records Administration, ARC Identifier: 186462/Wikimedia Commons; 233 (bottom), United States President Barack Obama presents a gift to King Bhumibol Adulyadej of Thailand during their meeting at Siriraj Hospital in Bangkok on 18 November 2012, Pete Souza, White House/Wikimedia Commons; 234, Department of Defense photo by Petty Officer 3rd Class Rebecca J. Moat, U.S. Navy; 235 (top), UN photo, United Nations; 235 (bottom), UK Secretary of State for International Development, Andrew Mitchell, looks on as Dr Faraza, a Red Cross physiotherapist treats Faisan, aged 8, at a hospital in Kabul, October 31, 2011 [cropped], Kanishka Afshari/FCO/DFID/Wikimedia Commons/CC BY 2.0; 236, U.S. Ambassador to Japan Caroline Kennedy pays a courtesy call on Japanese Prime Minister Shinzo Abe, November 20, 2013, State Department photo by William Ng/Flickr; 237, Tech. Sgt. Brian Davidson, U.S. Air Force; 238–39, Richard Stein, Center for Civic Education.

Lesson 29
P. 241, USAF photo by T.C. Perkins Jr., released, U.S. Air Force/Flickr; 242 (left), Photo Courtesy of the Indian Health Service/ U.S. Department of Health and Human Services; 242 (right), America Gains a Famous Citizen, Al Aumuller/New York World-Telegram and the Sun Newspaper Photograph Collection, Prints & Photographs Division, Library of Congress, LC-DIG-ppmsca-05649; 243, Richard Stein, Center for Civic Education; 245, Howard University volunteers participating in the International Coastal Cleanup Day found an exhaust system along the banks of the Anacostia River in Washington, D.C., Photo by Gwen Bausmith, U.S. EPA/USEPA Environmental-Protection-Agency/Flickr; 246 (left), Henry David Thoreau, Prints & Photographs Division, Library of Congress, LC-USZ61-361; 246 (right), I Want You for U.S. Army: Nearest Recruiting Station by James Montgomery Flagg, Prints & Photographs Division, Library of Congress, LC-USZC4-3859; 247, Richard Stein, Center for Civic Education.

Lesson 30
P. 249, Don Norman from FEMA's Individual Assistance program, addresses a community meeting at the Buttonwoods Community Center on assistance available to individuals and businesses affected by the recent flooding, April 15, 2010, Michael Rieger, FEMA/Wikimedia Commons; 250, Working America canvassers Ebony Taylor and Dave Ninehouser, Bernard Pollack/Molly Theobald/AFL-CIO/Flickr/Wikimedia Commons/CC BY 2.0; 251, Richard Stein, Center for Civic Education; 252, Board of Public Works Meeting, Annapolis, Maryland, Jay Baker, Maryland GovPics/Flickr/CC BY 2.0; 254, Richard Stein, Center for Civic Education; 253, Vince Serna, along with his daughter Kassandra (left) and family friend Skylar, paint a parking strip at New Hogan Lake during National Public Lands Day, Sept. 29, 2012, U.S. Army Corps of Engineers Sacramento District, Flickr; 255, Richard Stein, Center for Civic Education; 256, A mentor shows students some of the work she does on the computer, ENERGY.GOV/Flickr; 257, Center for Civic Education; 258, Jocelyn Augustino/FEMA; 259, Richard Stein, Center for Civic Education.

Reference
P. 261, The School of Athens by Raphael, 1511, The Vatican/Wikimedia Commons.